MAKING A
GARDEN

A Frances Tenenbaum Book

HOUGHTON MIFFLIN COMPANY

Boston ▪ New York ▪ 1998

MAKING A GARDEN

RELIABLE TECHNIQUES, OUTSTANDING PLANTS, AND HONEST ADVICE

by Rita Buchanan

illustrations by Steve Buchanan

Library of Congress Cataloging-in-Publication Data

Buchanan, Rita.
   Making a garden : reliable techniques, outstanding plants, and
honest advice / by Rita Buchanan ; illustrations by Steve Buchanan.
      p. cm.
   "A Frances Tenenbaum book."
   Includes index.
   ISBN 0-395-89753-X
   1. Gardening.   I. Title.
SB453.B8685   1998
   635 — dc21   98-28215
                                                                      CIP

Printed in the United States of America.

WCT 10 9 8 7 6 5 4 3 2 1

Book design by Deborah Fillion

Introduction

Gardening Techniques

Garden Design

Special Plants to Grow

Perennials, ornamental grasses,
shrubs, and dwarf conifers add
year-round color to a terraced,
south-facing slope.

HOW TO SUCCEED WITH PLANTS

This book has a mission. It's designed to inspire you to go dig up part of your yard and plant a garden there. When that place is full, dig another spot and transform it, too. Keep this up until you're totally surrounded with fragrant flowers, tasty herbs, tender vegetables and juicy fruits, colorful foliage, distinctive shrubs and trees. You'll never look back.

Instead, you'll always be looking forward. That's something about gardening—you never run out of enthusiasm and ideas. You'll "discover" a corner of your yard that you'd overlooked before and spend weekends working to develop something special there. You'll fall in love with a group of plants, such as roses, herbs, or berries, and want to learn everything about them.

As you keep acquiring new plants and looking for places to put them, you'll also contine finding ways to expand, diversify, and refine what you've already done. There's no such thing as an ex-gardener. Once you start down this path, gardening becomes a lifelong passion.

Gardening leads in many directions, but they all revolve around growing plants, so mastering the basic skills of talking about, choosing, planting, and caring for plants is the best place to begin.

PLANT NAMES

You don't have to know a plant's full proper name in order to grow it well and enjoy living with it. I've visited beautiful gardens where the owners identified their plants with names like "the fern I got from Martha," "the iris I bought on sale last year," and "the myrtle that was here when we came."

Common names

To participate in the larger world of gardening, though, you have to speak the language. Learning common names is a good start, but it's insufficient. Sometimes the same common name has been given to different plants, which leads to mixups. And while some plants don't have any common names at all, others have a string of aliases.

Latin names

Latin or scientific names (which are usually printed in italics) are unpopular because people think they're hard to pronounce and remember. Don't worry about that; you rarely need to say Latin names aloud. But you do have to learn to recognize them as you read, because almost all plant reference books and most nursery catalogs are organized alphabetically by Latin name.

The system of scientific names was designed both to identify each separate kind of plant and to group related plants together. The first word in a Latin name identifies the group, or genus. For example, all hollies belong to the genus *Ilex*. All irises belong to *Iris* (often the Latin name for a genus is used as a common name for that group of plants).

Adding the second word to a Latin name identifies a particular species or kind of plant within that genus. For example, *Iris virginiana* is a wild iris native to Virginia and adjacent states. It has blue flowers in late spring and is commonly called blue flag. But a few other irises are also called blue flag, so you need to use their Latin names to distinguish among them.

Cultivar names

A cultivar is a kind of plant that has been selected for some particular feature, assigned its own name, and propagated (usually by cuttings or division) in a way that preserves its unique quality. There are excellent cultivars of many garden plants, and people talk about them by pairing the cultivar name (which is usually in English) with the common name. If you visit a nursery to buy a popular cultivar, such as 'Blue Princess' holly or 'Blue Star' juniper, you can ask for it this way; they won't expect you to know the plant's Latin name.

CHOOSING PLANTS TO GROW

American interest in gardening has mushroomed in recent decades, and the nursery business has responded with an uncountable assortment of plants. There are tens of thousands to choose from, if you include every variation of popular flowers like daffodils and daylilies. How wonderful! And yet, it's overwhelming. You only need a dozen or so kinds to start a garden, and your property might hold just a few hundred plants altogether. How will you decide which ones to grow?

You'll see two different approaches in this book. One is to focus on plants with a particular feature or use, such as herbs for cooking or flowers to cut for arrangements. The other is to look for plants suited to particular growing conditions, such as ground covers for a dry sunny site or vines to plant at the base of a tree. Both approaches are helpful, and they can compliment each other, as many plants fill dual roles. For example, you could plant creeping thyme as a ground cover on that sunny site and harvest it for cooking, as well.

As you're collecting ideas for plants you want to grow, learn all you can by reading about them in books, magazines, and nursery catalogs. Better yet, tour public and private gardens in your area whenever you get the chance. When you stand beside it in a garden, a plant often seems different from its photo. You'll react to its overall size and habit, its health and grooming, its fragrance. Take a notebook, so you can record your impressions. Meet the gardener and ask questions about plants that interest you. Go back repeatedly to see which plants impress you at different times of year.

Buying locally

When you're shopping for plants, compare all the nurseries and garden centers within reasonable driving distance of your home, *not* on the prices they charge, but on the appearance and vigor of their plants and the knowledge and friendliness of the staff. Higher prices are a bargain if you get better plants and service. The staff at a good nursery (which may be large or small) can help you select plants, tell you how to care for them, and answer questions about your previous purchases; they may also be willing and able to custom-order special or uncommon plants for you from a wholesaler. You rarely find help like that at cut-rate, mass-market garden shop or chain stores.

Shopping by mail

This is the easiest way to get interesting and unusual plants and seeds. Order catalogs from suppliers that advertise in your favorite gardening magazines or refer to *Gardening by Mail,* by Barbara Barton, 5th ed. (Boston: Houghton Mifflin, 1997). The catalogs themselves are a valuable resource, full of helpful information and tempting photos.

Although mail-order plants are typically sold in small sizes, to save shipping costs, the prices are low, also. Quality varies, so it's a good idea to place a minimum order the first time you deal with a nursery and see if you like what you get. Many plants arrive in fine condition. Others look skimpy or discouraged at first but quickly recover and develop into fine specimens in your garden. A few may get damaged in shipment (notify the nursery immediately, and they'll usually work out a settlement) or die later (some nurseries have a generous guarantee, but others point out that circumstances in your garden are beyond their control). In general, I've had positive experiences with mail-order nurseries and am delighted with the plants I've obtained that way, but I

recommend it mostly as a way to get something special. If you can buy a plant locally, there's no reason to order it by mail.

MATCH THE PLANT TO THE SITE

To survive in your garden, a plant has to be adapted to the climate and growing conditions there. Some plants adjust to a range of situations, while others have specific needs and don't tolerate anything else.

Winter cold

The USDA hardiness zone system divides the country into 11 zones based on average winter low temperatures, and rates plants according to the coldest zone in which they're likely to survive outdoors without special protection. Most of the plants in this book are assigned to Zones 4, 5, 6, or 7; any plant that's hardy in a colder zone (lower number) is hardy in milder zones (higher numbers) also. Winter survival depends on a plant's age and health, soil moisture, and day-to-day weather conditions as well as exposure to cold, but the hardiness zone rating is a starting point for deciding whether or not a plant is suited for your garden. If you don't know what zone you live in, ask another gardener or the staff at a local nursery.

Summer heat

There isn't a widely accepted system for rating heat-tolerance yet, although this is an important consideration. Except where noted, the plants in this book can tolerate summer daytime highs in the 80s and 90s, but not the 100s.

Sun/shade

Most garden plants require direct sun for at least several hours a day throughout the growing season. With insufficient sun, they don't grow as fast, aren't as shapely, and don't flower well. Some plants that do prefer or tolerate shady sites are suggested on pp. 52–54, 60–63, 79, 91, 100.

Sun, heat, and water have overlapping effects. Plants can tolerate extra

Creeping moneywort and billowing

heat if they're shaded from the blazing midday sun and growing in moist soil. Plants that would shrivel and scorch on a sunny dry site might survive on a shady dry site. Plants that are normally associated with shade, such as ferns, can often tolerate direct sun if the soil is moist and temperatures aren't hot.

Watering

How often and how much you'll need to water your garden depends on where you live, what plants you're growing, and the depth and makeup of your soil. The basic guideline is to water plants enough to prevent wilt-

lady's-mantle bear yellow flowers in early summer and thrive in the moist, humid setting beside this pond.

ing. Once they're established in the ground, most of the perennials, shrubs, vines, and trees named in this book will need watering only during severe dry spells in the eastern United States, but they'll need occasional or frequent watering in the arid West. In all areas, be prepared to water annual flowers, vegetables, new plantings, and plants in containers.

BASIC PLANTING AND AFTERCARE

The following steps apply to most situations, whether you're planting annuals, perennials, ground covers, shrubs, or combinations.

Prepare the soil

For a single plant, outline an area at least as wide as you expect it to grow. If you're preparing a bed for several plants, outline the entire area. Clear the site by removing weeds and other existing vegetation, roots and all (see pp. 21 to 25).

Dig or till the soil across the entire area, working 6 to 8 inches deep. If your soil is too shallow or wet for that, make a raised bed (see pp. 64, 104) instead of planting at ground level. Spread a 1- or 2-inch layer of organic matter (homemade or municipal compost, composted tree leaves, aged manure, peat moss, composted bark, etc.)

on top, then mix that into the soil. It's also helpful to work some high-phosphorus fertilizer, such as bone meal, into the soil before planting. Phosphorus promotes root growth and flowering. Unlike some nutrients, phosphorus scarcely moves through the soil, so you have to work it into the root zone before planting; it does little good to sprinkle it on the surface later. Once the soil is prepared, you can plant right away, or wait for suitable weather.

Planting

It is best to plant on a cool, overcast or cloudy day or to work in the evening. This reduces wilting and stress. First, set the plant(s) on top of the soil, step back, and make sure you're satisfied with the placement.

As you handle each plant, check its top growth. Remove any discolored leaves and cut off any weak or damaged shoots. Then take care of its roots. For plants grown in pots, slide or cut the container away from the rootball. If any roots were coiled around the inside of the pot or crowded at the bottom, tease or pull them loose. For plants that you purchase bare-root, follow the supplier's directions on soaking and trimming the roots. For plants that you're moving or transplanting from another part of the garden, just be careful that their roots don't dry out.

Working with one plant at a time, scoop out a hole big enough to hold its roots without folding or crowding them, set the plant in place, and make sure it's positioned at the right depth. Normally the top of a plant's rootball should be level with or slightly higher than the surrounding soil. Add or remove soil to adjust the height if needed, then refill the hole with soil, packing it gently but firmly.

Water immediately and generously, using enough to settle the soil into place around the roots of each plant.

Follow-up care

Spread a thin (1 to 2 inches is usually deep enough) layer of mulch over the surface of the soil, to moderate soil temperatures, retain moisture, and help control weeds.

If you anticipate sunny weather, provide temporary shade to keep tender-leaved plants from wilting. Use a teepee of leafy twigs, drape an old sheet or a piece of row-cover fabric over a framework of stakes, or prop an inverted box or basket over the plant. Remove any shelter as soon as the plant stops wilting, usually within a week or so.

Continue watering as often as needed to keep the soil from drying out. Even plants that can survive on normal rainfall later may need watering for the first year or so, as they develop their root systems.

In cold climates, as soon as the ground has frozen the first winter after planting, cover the new plant's root area with conifer boughs, pine needles, oak leaves, or any other coarse-textured mulch. This prevents frost heaving, which can lift a newly set plant right out of the ground. Remove the mulch when the ground thaws in spring.

TROUBLESHOOTING AND REMEDIES

It takes experience and close observation to diagnose what's wrong when a plant doesn't grow as you expect, or to identify what's damaging a plant. You'll get better with practice. As an introduction, here are some common problems and possible solutions.

Wrong placement

Many problems stem from putting plants in places where the growing conditions aren't right. This can lead to stunted growth, yellow leaves, failure to flower, wilting, rotting, and/or death. As you become more aware of the soil and exposure in each part of your yard and learn more about what each plant wants, you'll do better at positioning plants where they're likely to thrive.

In the meantime, if you think you've made a mistake but the plant is still alive and you want to give it a second chance, try transplanting it to see if it grows better in a different spot (see p. 72 for advice on transplanting shrubs, and p. 31 for directions on dividing and replanting perennials).

Lack of blooms

Failure to flower often means the plant is simply too young or too small to bloom; be patient. It might need more sun; consider moving it. On shrubs and trees, the buds might have frozen, or you might have pruned them off; wait until next year and see what happens then.

Pest problems

Damaged or missing parts mean something is eating your plants. Dozens of insects and related pests feed on plants. Although chewed leaves and flowers look messy, healthy, established perennials, shrubs, and trees usually recover from insect damage. With those plants, it's your choice whether to ignore or fight the problem. Vegetables, fruits, and houseplants are more vulnerable; if you don't protect these plants, you may lose them. In any case, to control an insect pest you have to identify it first.

Catch one of the culprits, compare it with the photos and illustrations in reference books, or put it in a glass jar along with a sample of the damaged plant and take it to a nursery or garden center and ask for advice. There are safe-to-handle modern pesticides for controlling many kinds of insect pests, but these products work only if used as directed. Thorough control usually requires repeated applications.

Deer, rabbits, woodchucks, gophers, voles, and other mammals can cause much more damage than insects do. If these animals are in your area, you can try deterring them with repellents or scare-away devices, but you may need to use a fence or traps.

Disease problems

Plant diseases are as numerous and common as insect pests. Their names refer to typical symptoms, such as wilts, rots, spots, blights, rusts, and mildews. Diseases can cause serious damage or death, and they're notoriously hard to control. Prevention is more effective than treatment, so follow these guidelines: choose plants that are described as disease-resistant. Leave enough space between plants for air to circulate, especially in humid climates. Apply a shallow, not too thick, layer of mulch. If your soil is soggy, make raised beds. Remove and destroy sick or rotten plants immediately. Keep your garden neat and your tools clean.

TOOLS

Along with collecting and growing plants, acquiring and using tools is part of making a garden. For any garden task, there are different types of tools. Which ones you choose is

Gold daylily leaves, red rose hips, and white boltonia flowers color this border in mid-October.

mostly a matter of personal preference. What's important is getting tools that are sturdy and well built, and that feel good in your hands. As you're shopping, hold the tool and pretend you're really using it to judge its weight, balance, size, and handle. Make sure it "fits" you. A basic collection includes the following types of tools:

Digging tools. A strong-tined fork plus a spade or shovel for preparing beds, digging holes, and digging up plants; a trowel; a rototiller (optional) for loosening soil and adding organic matter. You can use a sharp spade to trim the edges between lawn and beds, or get a special edging tool for that job.

Rakes. One with a straight, heavy, metal head, for leveling soil and distributing mulch; another with soft, springy, plastic or bamboo tines, for raking leaves, grass clippings, and litter off a lawn.

Weeding tools. Use any short- or long-handled model that suits you. Keep the cutting edge sharp.

Gloves. Stretchy disposable rubber gloves that protect your hands without reducing your sense of touch are good for planting and weeding. Sturdy leather or rubberized gloves are better for heavy work or dirty jobs.

Cutting tools. Invest in good hand pruning shears and keep the blades clean and sharp. Get a pruning saw or bow saw for trimming tree limbs and large shrubs. Hedge shears or an electric trimmer are optional, for shearing shrubs. Grass shears or a string trimmer are optional, for clipping where you can't mow.

Watering tools. A watering can (the bigger the better) is handy when you're planting and for watering individual plants afterwards. A hose and sprinkler or some kind of automatic irrigation system are necessary in almost all climates.

Tidiness and transportation. Get something with wheels — a cart, wagon, or wheelbarrow — for carrying plants, trimmings, mulch, soil, etc. Plastic pails, tubs, and trays are indispensable, along with a heavy plastic or fabric tarp.

Composting. You need a homemade or purchased compost bin big enough to hold all your clippings and debris. Get a gas-powered chipper if you're growing many vegetables, annual flowers, or perennials; clearing brush; or have lots of tree leaves every fall. Chipping reduces the volume of debris and makes it compost much better and faster.

Miscellaneous: A yardstick, a 25-foot tape measure, stakes and string, weatherproof labels or markers, a quart- or gallon-size plastic sprayer, old sheets and blankets for protecting tender plants from late and early frosts, supports for floppy perennials, an assortment of pots and containers.

Three years ago, this area was a muddy weed patch. Now ferns and wildflowers shade a stone-lined drainage channel.

STARTING FROM SCRATCH

Facing an empty or overgrown lot, it's easy to squint your eyes and imagine a wonderful garden there. The challenge is making that dream come true. Whether you're a novice gardener on your first plot of ground, or an experienced horticulturist who's just moved to a new home, starting from scratch means you have lots of work to do and lots of choices to make. In this book, I'm assuming that you plan to do most of the work and decision-making yourself, that you appreciate plants and want to learn more about them, and that your budget is limited but your enthusiasm isn't.

The first thing to do

Other writers will tell you to start by drawing a site plan, or getting a soil test, or listing your goals—all good ideas, but they can wait. I say the very first thing to do is get a camera—one of those point-and-shoot models that prints the date on the picture is especially handy—and shoot a roll of "before" pictures. Do this right away, because you'll never get a second chance.

Then, make it a habit to take pictures often. Take pictures of major undertakings and achievements such as cutting down an overgrown hedge, building a fence, or planting a bushel of bulbs—reviewing what you've done will give you confidence to tackle new projects. Take pictures of trees and shrubs when you plant them—in a few years, you'll be amazed to see how much they've grown. Choose key vantage points—looking at your house from the street, the view from a second-story window, etc.—and photograph those same scenes repeatedly, to document how your garden develops over time.

Start keeping a journal

Get a garden journal, a notebook, or just a calendar with space for writing, so you can keep track of what you observe and do. It's helpful and interesting to review this information later. For example, every week or so, record which plants catch your attention as you drive around town—these are candidates for planting in your own yard. As you acquire plants of your own, note when you buy them, where you put them, how they grow, when and how long they bloom. Write when the trees leaf out in spring and turn color in fall, and when the first tomato or peach gets ripe. Record when you apply fertilizer or spray for pests. Keep track of the weather, noting major storms, dry or wet spells, spring and fall frosts. All journal-writers lapse sometimes, but when that happens, just start again. If you don't write it down, you can't look it up.

Scout out local resources

Along with exploring your own property, explore the neighborhood, too. Again, this is especially important if you've just moved to a new region. Visit the local nurseries and garden centers to see what kinds of plants and supplies they stock and how helpful and friendly their staff people are.

Watch the classified ads in the local paper for suppliers of mulch, compost, topsoil, gravel, and other supplies you may want delivered by the truckload. If you're thinking about having some outdoor construction or installation done, watch for contractors active in your neighborhood and monitor their work.

If there's a botanic garden or arboretum nearby, sign up for membership or subscribe to their newsletter, and attend any tours, classes, or programs that they offer. Look for any gardening books or magazines that are written especially for your region.

Garden clubs are variable—some focus on gardening, while others are mostly social groups. Check the ones in your area by attending as a guest to see what kinds of programs and activities they sponsor, then decide if you think membership would be a resource or a waste of time.

Don't pressure yourself

A professional landscape contractor can draw up a design, send out a crew of workers and a truckload of big plants, and install an instant garden, just like that. A home gardener rarely works so fast. Instead, you'll probably explore the site, choose a place to begin, think of something to do there, get your hands dirty, buy some plants and see how they grow, change your mind and move the plants around, dig up a new area, buy more plants, refine your designs, start giving plants away and replacing them with new favorites, and so on. Working this way, it can take years to create a garden, but you'll be having so much fun that you won't worry about how long it's taking.

Explore your situation

Imagine taking a bird's-eye view of your property. How much land do you have? What fraction of it is committed to structures and pavement, such as the house and garage, driveway and walkways, deck, pool and other features; and how much is available for growing plants? Of the potential gardening area, how much is sunny open space or lawn, and how much is shaded by trees or filled with shrubs and brush? Is the site level or sloping? Are there any wet spots or dry spots, exposed rocks, waterways, or other natural features? What surrounds you? Can you see the neighbors? Are there views to enjoy, or eyesores to avoid? All of these factors are things to think about as you develop plans for your yard.

Work with what you have

The existing conditions on your land suggest possibilities for developing it. Consider these situations and solutions:

- In a subdivision of former farmland, the lots are typically square, level, and featureless, with little shade or privacy, but the soil is good (unless the builder scraped off the topsoil and sold it—an egregious but not uncommon practice). You could carve big beds and borders from the inevitable expanse of lawn and take advantage of the full sun and fertile soil to grow exuberant displays and crops of flowers, herbs, vegetables, and fruit.
- A forested site invites a carefree garden of naturalized bulbs and spring wildflowers, ferns, and shade-tolerant shrubs, although you may be limited to plants that are unattractive to deer, rabbits, woodchucks, and other varmints. Instead of struggling with a lawn, build a patio or deck for outdoor living space, then relax and enjoy the view.
- An older house with a neglected, overgrown landscape is a mixed blessing. Clearing brush and weeds is a big job, but underneath the excess growth and debris you're likely to find trees and shrubs with maturity and character, stalwart perennials that can form the basis for a new border, a patch of ground cover that you can divide and spread around, and perhaps some old stonework or structures that could be restored.
- A small city or suburban lot where the landscape consists of conventional evergreen foundation planting, a bland lawn, and a few common trees or shrubs poses a creative challenge—it needs color and variety. You might replace the foundation evergreens with deciduous shrubs and ornamental grasses, surround the front yard with a hedge of shrub roses, or turn the back yard into an herb garden with raised beds and brick paths.

Remove anything you dislike

When you're exploring a new site, single out any features that you find ugly, tacky, irritating, or inconvenient, and resolve to get rid of them right away, so you really can start from scratch and not have to work around something annoying. Get rid of that misshapen tree, that ugly barbecue pit, that leggy hedge, that flimsy arbor—whatever it is, you can hire someone to take it down and cart it away, or do the job yourself.

If your land is infested with weedy perennials, vines, or shrubs, start a control program immediately. It takes awhile to get rid of these pests, and you want to be sure they're totally destroyed before you start new plantings.

Monitor the climate and microclimates

You *can* do something about the weather: you can pay attention to it and garden accordingly. Learning about the climate is especially important if you've just moved into the area. Ask your new neighbors about the average and extreme temperatures; typical monthly accumulations of rain and/or snow; and the frequency of plant-damaging ice, hail, or wind storms. Get a thermometer and rain gauge and start making your own weather observations.

Find the microclimates on your property—a south-facing slope where the soil warms early in spring, the north side of a building where the soil stays cool and damp all summer, a low spot that's white on frosty mornings, a sheltered corner where the wind doesn't blow. These are places where you can—or should—grow different plants than you'd choose for the rest of your property.

Get to know your soil

The soil may be uniform from one side of your property to the other, or there may be a patchwork of different

Marking your observations and ideas on a site plan or map of your property will help you think about how to develop it.

soil types. Either way, characteristics of the soil will determine how much work it is to prepare a bed for planting and will influence your choice of plants. You can tell a lot about your soil by looking at what's growing there now. A lush, vigorous stand of any plants, even weeds, indicates that the soil has the potential to support a garden. Sparse, straggly vegetation means the soil needs improvement.

To learn more, dig some test holes (the size of a wastebasket is big enough) here and there. Is the soil loose or compacted, rocky or not, easy or hard to dig? Can you distinguish the layers of topsoil and subsoil? (Look for a change of color and texture.) How deep is the topsoil? (The deeper,

the better.) Fill the holes with water and check the next day to see if it has all soaked in. (If so, fine; if not, the spot is poorly drained.) Contact your local Cooperative Extension Service for information about having a sample of soil tested for fertility and pH; most states offer this service and provide advice on how to fertilize or amend your soil along with the test results.

Develop one area at a time

When you convert a brushy field, a weed patch, or even a lawn into a garden bed, you're signing up for extra work. Don't risk getting discouraged by tackling more than you can handle. Develop an area small enough that you can thoroughly prepare the soil,

fill it with enough plants to make a good show, and keep it neat and attractive. It's better to be proud of a small garden than frustrated by a big one. When you're confident that one area is under control, you're ready to start the next one.

As you're preparing an area, you'll generate lots of debris — brush, stones, buried trash, compostable clippings, etc. Clean as you go, moving all those scattered piles to a single dumping point, preferably out of sight. Don't let messiness diminish your feeling of accomplishment. Meanwhile, keep giving the rest of your yard a lick and a promise, in anticipation of developing the whole property someday.

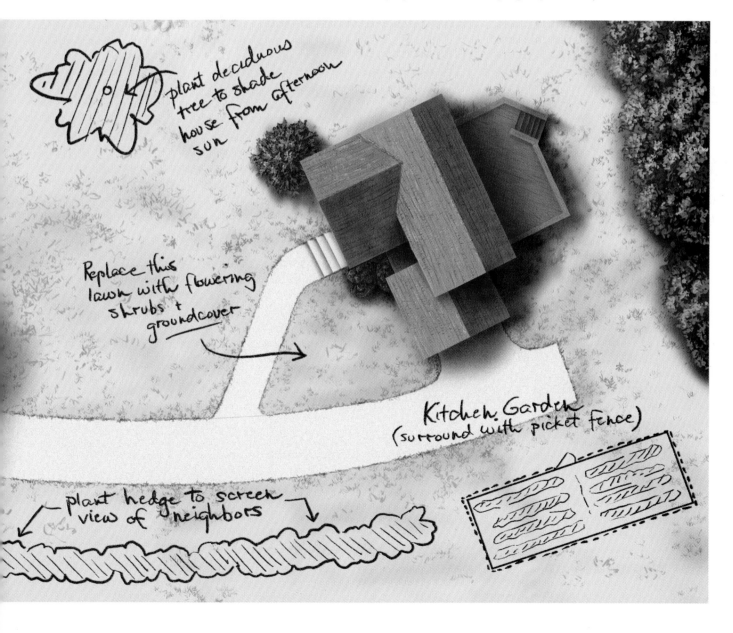

Give perennial divisions and small, young shrubs a head start by growing them in a raised nursery bed for a year or two before moving them into the garden.

Start growing some plants

If gardening is an art form, then plants are the medium. But choosing and arranging the right plants to express your vision takes thoughtful planning—you have to find plants that are suitable for the growing conditions, learn how big they get and what they look like, and decide how many of which ones to use and how to combine and arrange them.

Then, waiting for your permanent plantings to mature takes patience. The annual growth of most garden shrubs and trees is measured in inches, rarely in feet. Some perennials reach their full stature in just a year or two, but most take three or more years to form a truly impressive clump or patch. It typically takes a few years for a ground cover to hide the soil, a hedge to screen a view, or a vine to cover a trellis.

A strategy for success

Knowing how slowly they grow, most gardeners want to start planting perennials, shrubs, and trees right away. That's understandable, but there are good reasons for taking your time. When you're starting from scratch, especially if you haven't done much gardening before or if you've moved to a new site and are unfamiliar with the growing conditions there, I think the best approach is twofold. (1) Make a nursery bed where you can collect, evaluate, and propagate a variety of perennials and shrubs for future use. (2) Use annuals generously and creatively as you prepare areas for permanent planting, learn about your soil and climate, and explore design ideas.

Make a little nursery

This is one of the most useful garden projects you can do. Pick a convenient site that will be easy to monitor, water, and maintain, and start your own nursery. Prepare one or more beds about 4 feet wide and as long as you choose. A raised bed edged with timbers, then filled with your best topsoil amended with plenty of compost, looks neat and provides better-than-average but not unrealistic growing conditions. Growing plants in a bed like this is easier than keeping them in containers, and they grow bigger and faster.

There are many ways to use a nursery bed. For example, collect perennials that you've admired in magazines and books, and test-grow them to see how they perform in your climate, how big they get, when they bloom, and how they look together.

Stockpile impulse purchases, bargains, starts from other gardeners, and other plants that you acquire with no plan for where to put them.

Study up on shrubs, choose some kinds that sound wonderful, and order them from catalogs. Mail-order specialists offer an incredible assortment of shrubs at low prices. The plants you receive will be small, but if you give them a head start by keeping them in the nursery for a few years, they'll be sizable specimens by the time you're ready to put them in their permanent locations.

Save money by propagating your own plants from seeds or divisions, and grow them in the nursery until they are big enough to go in the garden. Group similar plants in rows or blocks; this makes it easier to keep track of them.

Someday when your garden is completely full, you can use the old nursery bed to grow vegetables, strawberries, cutflowers, or specialties that don't fit elsewhere.

Indulge in annuals

No matter what you plan to grow eventually, there are many reasons for using annual flowers, herbs, and vegetables at first.

- They're inexpensive, especially if you raise them from seed. Use the money you save by growing annuals to pay for soil amendments, tools, building projects, hired help, and other start-up costs.
- They give fast results—you'll have a lush garden in just a few months.
- They make great prototypes for trying out design ideas. For example, if you think you might like a hedge, make one with sunflowers. Wondering about the size and shape for a perennial bed or border, what height or size plants to use in it, what flower colors to emphasize? Experiment with annuals, observe the results, refine your ideas, and make permanent plantings next year.
- While growing annuals, you'll be learning about your soil—how easy or hard it is to work, how fast it dries out, how plants respond to it. At the end of the growing season, you can rework the soil in the bed (it's much easier the second time) and make it better.
- Growing annuals for a year or two will give you time to learn more about your climate and microclimates and to watch how the patterns of sun and shade change over the course of the season.
- Meanwhile, you'll discover any weed problems and meet any furry critters who think your garden is a diner.
- Annuals are lots of fun, and you'll never have as much space for them again after your garden starts filling up with other plants.

Fill a bed with annual flowers for fast results as you learn about your climate and growing conditions and plan permanent plantings.

Designing your garden

For many gardeners, thinking about design is the most intimidating aspect of starting from scratch. They're uncertain about how to lay out the basic elements—where the walkways should go, how to outline the lawn, what size and shape to make the beds and borders, where to plant specimen trees and shrubs, whether or not to build a fence, arbor, or other structure, etc.

You'll feel more confident if you tell yourself that you don't have to figure everything out in advance. It never hurts to prepare a master plan, but whatever ideas you have at first are liable to change as you learn more about the site and the growing conditions, observe which plants do well, and discover your own tastes and ambitions as a gardener. That's okay. Let your garden evolve.

This traditional, formal design features geometric shapes and evergreen foliage.

Tie things together

Any site can be developed in different ways: it's your choice. For example, you and your neighbor could buy matching houses on bare lots and proceed to make contrasting landscapes, as shown here, yet both be delighted with your results.

Look at pictures, visit gardens, and analyze your reactions. Do you prefer straight lines or curves? Bold masses or intricate patterns? Do you think plants should be allowed to grow loose and floppy, or should they be pruned and staked into orderly shapes? Would you rather have a garden that feels spacious or crowded, spontaneous or deliberate, calm or exciting?

Whatever your preference, if you choose a style or theme at the start and stick with it as you proceed, your garden will look coherent and integrated. Otherwise, if you just do one project at a time without any overall sense of style, you'll probably end up with a hodgepodge.

Also, choose just one or two kinds of each building material, path surface, mulch, and edge treatment, and use them throughout the garden. Then pick a sturdy, reliable ground cover and use it as "mortar" to bind separate elements together. For example, you can use a ground cover to unite scattered trees into a grove or frame a series of beds.

Think big

Being outdoors changes your sense of scale and proportion. It makes things look small. You notice this when you carry something out from the house. A normal chair, for example, looks like kindergarten furniture outdoors, especially when you view it from a distance.

Even if your lot is considered small, the sky is high and the house itself and any trees around it are large enough that you have to think big to make an effective design. Make the paths wide enough to feel roomy, and the shapes bold enough to look decisive. Grow fewer kinds of plants, and group enough of each kind together to make a visible patch.

Outlining the basic shapes

The most straightforward way to lay out a design is by working directly on the ground. There are many easy ways to do this. For example, if you want to make an island bed in the middle of your lawn, experiment with shapes by laying a hose or rope on the ground, lining up empty nursery pots or cardboard boxes, driving in stakes and connecting them with a string, letting the grass grow long then carv-

ing it with the mower, sprinkling a line of ground limestone, using spray paint to mark the grass, or trompling on fresh snow. After marking a tentative outline, walk around and look at it from all directions. Look from inside the house and across the street. Keep adjusting the shape until it seems just right.

Many people find it hard to look at a shape on the ground and imagine a garden in three dimensions. It's even harder to work from a paper site plan or map. To visualize how plants of different sizes or shapes would look in a particular setting, try sketching on photos (see p. 49).

Positioning plants in a bed

Height, width, habit, texture, leaf size and color, time of bloom, flower color, seasonal interest, rate of growth, care requirements — there are so many things to think about when you're arranging plants in a garden. Along with the plans on pp. 72, 77, 84, and 96, I've given explanations of how and why I chose certain plants and positioned them as shown. Use these as examples to help you think about this aspect of gardening.

Learning to design your own plans takes experience, as you have to know how each plant will perform in your yard. Some will behave just as they're "supposed" to; others will bloom earlier or later or look different than you expected; some will disappoint you or die. A garden never turns out exactly as you designed it, but that's no reason not to try and do your best to arrange plants in a way that's both practical and attractive.

Give each plant enough space

If you're going to go out and buy plants to fill a new bed, it really is a good idea to measure its size and shape, draw it to scale on graph paper, and spend some time figuring how many plants you could fit there.

Setting plants too close together is probably the most common mistake that gardeners make. It's so easy to do, because you're eager to try one of everything, and because plants are small when you set them out. As they grow, though, crowded plants look uncomfortable, their shapes get distorted, they flop over, they're more susceptible to pests and diseases, and they're harder to care for. (If you want to collect lots of plants, *expand* your garden, don't crowd it.)

Think about this as you plan a garden, and monitor yourself as you do the actual planting. Check reference books to learn how wide each plant will spread (usually the estimates in books and catalogs are for perennials 3 years old, or shrubs 5 to 10 years old). Use a yardstick, and keep measuring as you go to be sure you're giving each plant room to grow.

Whether or not you plan a layout on paper before you start putting plants in the ground, you should map what you've done afterward. Sketch out some kind of diagram that identifies which plants are where. Otherwise, you'll forget their names, and you'll lose track of dormant perennials and bulbs when they're hidden underground. Put labels or markers in the garden, too, but keep that map. You'll need it in a year or two, after the labels have faded, disappeared, or migrated, as they inevitably do.

Curved shapes and mixed plantings with lots of colorful flowers give a more casual, contemporary look.

Hand-pull dandelions, plantains,
and other lawn weeds when
the soil is damp and soft, so that
the roots come out and don't just
break off.

CONTROLLING WEEDS

What plants act weedy in your garden? We each have a different answer to that question. If you've gardened in two or more locations, you must have noticed that weeds which were common in one place didn't even grow in the other. Every garden has its own collection of weeds, depending partly on soil and climate and partly on how the land has been used over the years.

What counts as a weed?

Cockleburs, ragweed, crabgrass—almost everyone agrees that these plants are weeds. They're prolific, fast-growing, aggressive, ugly, and useless.

But the list of universally condemned weeds is surprisingly short. For example, you might think a thistle is a terrible weed, but a bird-watcher would point out that thistles provide food and nesting material for goldfinches. Do you kill dandelions, chickweed, and sorrel? Some people relish these weeds as salad greens. What about Queen Anne's lace, chicory, and ox-eye daisy? Are they weeds or wildflowers? Are yarrow and St.-John's-wort weeds or herbs?

People have different opinions and different experiences with particular plants, so there's little agreement on what counts as an weed. Botanists and ecologists can't agree on a definition. In your garden, it's your decision. Any plant you don't want, call it a weed.

When most people think of weeds, the first examples they think of are broadleaf annuals and perennials, but of course there are many weedy grasses, and there are weedy vines, shrubs, and trees, too. Some native plants are weedy, but most of our weeds are "exotic" or "alien" plants that were introduced from abroad, usually from Eurasia or Mexico.

Are weeds bad?

Weeds compete with other plants for space, sun, water, and nutrients. If there are too many weeds in a vegetable garden or farm field, yields are reduced. Too many weeds in a perennial border leads to fewer, smaller flowers. Some weeds are prickly, smelly, or poisonous.

But other weeds are edible, medicinal, or pretty. And often, weeds are the only plants growing on a difficult site. I always smile when I see a weed growing up from a crack in a city sidewalk. There it is, surrounded by pavement but green and alive. Weeds are nature's Band-Aids; they cover the scars we make on this Earth. For that, we should be grateful.

Garden weeds

Back to your garden and your weeds. You need to know how to get rid of plants that you don't want, reduce the time you spend weeding, confine plants that might take over, and avoid introducing new problems.

Sometimes the worst weeds in a garden are cultivated plants, especially herbs and perennials, that are too vigorous for the site. Paying attention to how you manage these plants, to keep them from spreading underground or scattering seeds, is just as important as controlling ordinary weeds.

Where to get more help

Many gardeners can recognize a plant that they consider a weed and decide to pull it out, without being able to name it. If you want to learn the names of your weeds, contact the local office of your state's Cooperative Extension Service, the staff at a local nursery, local biology teachers, a local botanic garden, the state botanical society, or the state wildflower society. Keep asking, and you'll find someone who can help you identify your weeds and give you advice on how to deal with them.

Do you fuss over dandelions, or smile at them?

Clearing ground

Clearing a thicket of blackberries and poison ivy that's grown up along the edge of a woods. Renovating a perennial border that's infested by bindweed. Replacing a straggly hedge that's plugged with weedy tree seedlings. Many gardeners have projects like these on their "To Do" list, but they're the sort of tasks we postpone from season to season. Reclaiming an area that's overrun with plants you don't want is a big job. Fortunately, the results are always worth the effort. Not only do you gain space to expand your garden and the chance to start anew, but you get a wonderful feeling of decisiveness and accomplishment.

Blackberry

Timing

Most weed-killing techniques work best during the growing season. Depending on what weeds you have and what methods you use, it can take as little as a week or as much as several months to finish the job. Be patient, and wait until you're sure that the weeds are totally eradicated before you replant.

Make a clean sweep

It's time-consuming, inconvenient, and often ineffective to do selective clearing, trying to eliminate some plants while preserving others. The job is much easier and you almost always get better results if you clear the whole area down to the ground, removing or killing all the plants that are growing there (except for trees or large shrubs—it's not too much trouble to work around them). If you want to save any small shrubs, perennials, bulbs, ferns, etc. that are growing in the area, move them out of the way by digging them up and storing them in containers or in a holding bed, or replanting them elewhere.

Cut them down

Cutting it down once usually isn't enough to kill an established weed, but it does weaken the plant. And if you continue cutting new shoots whenever they appear, you can conquer tree saplings, most shrubs, and perennials with erect stems, such as milkweed and goldenrod. This may take more than one growing season, but don't give up. Use hand pruners,

Poison ivy

a lawnmower, or a string trimmer, and keep cutting those stems as close to the ground as possible.

Smother them

You can eliminate many perennial weeds, including weedy grasses, by smothering, or covering them with a dense, lightproof barrier that blocks out the sun and air. In most cases, if you cover the weeds soon after they start growing in spring, they'll be dead by fall. You can replant the area then or wait until the next spring.

To smother weeds, first cut or mow the stems close to the ground. Then cover the weedy area with flattened cardboard boxes or sections of newspaper, overlapped like shingles. Top that with a layer of leaves, hay, lawn clippings, wood or bark chips, etc., spread several inches thick. All these materials (even the cardboard) gradually decompose into organic matter, which is good for the soil. If you'd rather end up with bare soil, cover the weedy area with a thick tarp, a sheet of plywood, or an old carpet.

"Solarize" them

This works well on sunny sites in hot climates. Cut the weeds to the ground, water well, cover the area with a sheet of clear plastic, and leave it in place for six to eight weeks in the heat of summer. Enough heat builds up under the plastic to kill most weeds and weed seeds.

Spray them

Applying an appropriate herbicide is a way to destroy persistent, mature, deep-rooted, perennial weeds that aren't intimidated by cutting or smothering. Read the label carefully before buying any herbicide. For

clearing ground, choose a product that is meant to be sprayed on the leaves of actively growing plants, that kills all plants it contacts, and that decomposes promptly afterwards.

Follow the label directions exactly when mixing and applying the product, and note how soon you should expect to see results and how long you should wait before cutting down the sprayed plants and replanting in that area. Weedy shrubs and vines may not be totally killed by a single application. Check the label to see how long you should wait before spraying them again.

Get a goat

Don't laugh! If you live in the country and want to clear a half-acre or more, fencing some goats in the area is a practical solution. Goats, especially angora or mohair goats—the ones with curly white hair—eat most kinds of weedy brush, briars, and vines as well as herbaceous weeds. Angora goats can be raised all around the United States. Ask at a local feed store to see if anyone in your area has angora goats and can help you get started with them.

What about the roots?

When you're trying to get rid of a plant, is it enough to kill back the tops, or should you dig up the roots, too? Except on steep slopes, where disturbing the soil can lead to erosion, I think it's best to dig up as much as possible of a weed's root system and destroy it, since otherwise it might recover and send up more shoots. Also, digging out the old roots is a good way to start preparing the soil for adding new plants.

Sort the debris

Sort carefully when it's time to dispose of whatever you cut down or dig up. Some materials can be composted or recycled, but others should be discarded. For example, put soft, leafy weed stems and tops on the compost pile—they'll decompose harmlessly. However, don't put any roots, runners, seedpods, or fruits into the compost, since any of these could sprout into a new problem.

If you've cut down a lot of shrubs or woody vines, it's worth borrowing or renting a chipper to tranform the brush into chips that you can use for mulch. Or, depending on local regulations, you can burn the brush or bundle it for curbside pickup.

Sort out any poison ivy or poison oak and don't chip or burn them—either process could give you a terrible rash. Put them in the trash, or pile them out of the way.

Weeding is never done

Here's one way to reduce the time you spend weeding: garden in a dry climate, and don't irrigate. Weed seeds need moisture to germinate and grow, so the drier the garden, the fewer the weeds. Or, garden on a shady lot. Weeds need light to grow, so more shade means fewer weeds.

Weeds grow best on a sunny sites in rainy climates. If that's your situation, adopt a strategy of prevention. Weeds can destroy your enthusiasm for gardening. Don't let that happen.

Keep weeds at bay by filling your garden with healthy plants. Cover the soil with mulch. And be vigilant about stopping weeds while they're small, before they become major problems.

Plant ground covers

Any patch of soil that isn't filled with other plants is likely to be invaded by weeds. In most home landscapes, these patches are where the lawn isn't growing well—under a tree, next to a building, in a narrow strip between pavements, on a steep bank with shallow soil. Replace the weak grass with a suitable ground cover (there's one for every situation; see pp. 47 to 55). As soon as the groundcover has filled in, you'll be done with weeding that spot.

Spread mulch

Using mulch to control weeds is one of the few new ideas in gardening. (Traditionally, most gardeners equated mulch with litter and thought bare soil looked neater.) Mulch is a great time-saver. If you spread it around and between the plants in a vegetable garden, flower bed, or border early in the season, you'll hardly have to weed those areas later. Mulch works by shading the soil so that weed seeds don't germinate.

What should you mulch with? The choice is yours. Try whatever you can get—wood or bark chips, pine needles, shredded tree leaves, grass clippings, rotten hay, straw, cottonseed or buckwheat hulls, homemade or purchased compost. These all break down sooner or later and add organic matter to the soil. Spread fine-textured mulches 1 to 2 inches deep, and coarse-textured mulches 2 to 4 inches deep. Add more mulch every spring, or whenever the old layer gets thin.

Although they're hard to spread in the first place and tedious to remove if you ever decide you don't want them anymore, coarse sand, gravel, or crushed rock make good mulches, too, especially for plants from dry climates.

Pull weed seedlings

Most weeds—not just annuals, but weedy perennials, vines, shrubs, and trees, too—get started in your garden as seedlings. When they're just a few inches tall, their roots are just a few inches deep. Hand-pull seedlings, uproot them with a prong-type cultivator, or cut them off with a sharp hoe. Pulling is easiest a day or two after a good rain or watering has softened the soil. You can cultivate or hoe any time.

Red sorrel

Ground ivy

Dandelion

Mulching reduces the number of weeds, but a few seedlings always make it up through the mulch, other seeds land on top of the mulch and germinate there, and weeds will sprout wherever you didn't use mulch. To stay ahead, try to pull all the weed seedlings from the garden every week or two throughout the growing season. This task seems more manageable if you subdivide (mentally or physically) the garden into a series of smaller plots and tackle them one at a time or one a day.

Spot-treat spreading weeds

It's hard to uproot a weed after it's been growing for weeks or months, and pulling may or may not be effective then. If the weed has a simple root system, like dandelion or plantain, you can probably pull most of it out and kill the weed. But many weeds, such as red sorrel, ground ivy,

Bermuda grass, and oxalis, form underground runners. In that case, when you pull up a shoot, part of the root system comes up, but the rest stays below and sends up more shoots. Eventually you'll notice the runners and realize that you're re-pulling the same weed week after week, and probably falling behind in the contest.

At this point, you can dig up that area and remove every bit of weed root you can pick or sift out of the soil, or apply an herbicide. Any garden center has one or more brands of "spot weeders," sold ready-to-use in small squirt bottles. Follow the label directions exactly. Spray on a windless day to avoid drift, and hold a sheet of stiff cardboard behind the weed to protect nearby plants from overspray.

Weeds in the lawn

In ideal conditions, turf grass grows as thick as fur, leaving no space for weeds. Most of us don't have ideal lawns. We have weeds. Can you accept a weedy lawn, or does it bother you?

Growing healthy grass is the first step towards having a weed-free lawn. Ask a local lawn-care specialist how often and how much to fertilize, water, and mow your particular kind of grass, then follow those guidelines.

It's not much trouble to maintain a small lawn of healthy grass by hand-weeding, but if your lawn is large, there are lots of weeds, your schedule is busy, or your expectations are high, you'll probably turn to herbicides.

There are two main products for lawns: pre-emergent herbicide to keep crabgrass and other weed seeds from sprouting, and broadleaf weed killer to eliminate dandelions, etc., from established turf. These products work only if used as directed; read the labels.

Weeding paths and edges

Weeds that are lodged in cracks or along the edges of a patio or walk are hard to extract. If you can't pull them out, you can spray them with a spot weeder, singe them with a propane torch, or simply pour boiling water on the weeds, using enough to scald both leaves and roots.

Bermuda grass

Oxalis

Plantain

Beebalm

Ribbon grass

Avoid future problems

Every gardener knows this scenario. You bring home some new kind of perennial and watch with delight as it settles right into the garden, obviously thriving. You point it out to visitors, tell your friends about it. The next spring, your new plant forms a patch 3 feet wide. What a handsome specimen! You take photos of it. A year later, the patch is 6 feet wide. You give generous starts to anyone who asks. Finally, the plant dominates your garden. You moan, "Why didn't anybody warn me?"

Invasive perennials

This is a warning: under favorable conditions, many perennials spread surprisingly fast (see lists on p. 28). Catalogs and books sometimes label these plants as invasive; gardeners often call them thugs. Should you avoid them? I don't think so. Some of my favorite perennials are invasive, and I wouldn't be without them. But if you decide to include any of the plants on the list in a flowerbed, I'd advise you to watch it closely,

be suspicious, and intervene early if you need to regain control.

How to confine spreaders

Let's say you're planning a hummingbird garden, and want to include a clump of bee balm, or you have a moon garden that features silver and white plants, and want to add some ribbon grass. These are good perennials, but they do spread fast. One way to confine them is illustrated above.

Take a 5-gallon or larger plastic nursery pot (you can get these free or cheap at any nursery), and use a utility knife to cut off the bottom. Bury the bottomless pot rim-deep in the ground. If your soil is well prepared, you can insert the pot like a cooky cutter; otherwise, you'll have to dig a hole and "plant" the pot. Then plant the invasive perennial inside. Every year or two, in the spring, lift and divide the plant, refill the pot with fresh soil, and replant with a single division.

When to let them run

Perennials, herbs, grasses, and ferns that spread to form a patch can make excellent ground covers, especially for difficult sites—dry shade, sloping banks, rocky ground, low areas with

poor drainage, roadside verges, and island beds surrounded by pavement. A tough, vigorous, invasive perennial is the ideal candidate for these situations.

Also, fast spreaders give encouraging results when you're starting a new garden on a wide-open site. If you have a big lot, you *need* big patches of plants to fit the scale and make an impact. Don't be afraid to use invasive perennials—just realize what you're doing.

You'll have to watch the boundary between an invasive plant and your lawn. Invasive plants can grow right across most kinds of buried strip edges or mowing strips. A more effective way to keep plants out of the lawn (and vice versa—bermuda grass is a terrible weed when it crosses into flower beds) is by cutting a shallow trench with a sharp edging tool. You will have to recut the edge two or three times during the growing season.

Plants that self-seed

Here's another familiar scenario. Someone gives you a tray of seedlings, naming an herb you haven't grown before. The seedlings look cute, and you find a place for them. That summer you watch them grow, enjoy their aroma, and feel like you've made a new friend. Winter passes, spring comes, and you're busy cleaning up the garden. Gradually it dawns on you that you're pulling up a lot of seedlings that all look the same. What are they? Oh, that new herb! It's everywhere now!

Many herbs, as well as many popular garden flowers and wildflowers (see the lists on p. 28), produce seeds that often germinate and grow with no help from the gardener. In fact, these volunteer seedlings are typically more vigorous than plants started indoors or in a greenhouse. Golden feverfew and sweet violet, shown below, are typical overachievers.

Self-seeding is a mixed blessing. It means that once you acquire a plant, you'll always have it, as it pops up here and there year after year. But the drawback is that if a plant self-seeds at all, it's liable to make hundreds of seedlings, not just a few. After awhile, you may decide that it's really quite a weed.

Seed management strategies

Seed germination depends on light, moisture, and temperature, and most seeds have fairly specific requirements.

A plant that self-sows in my garden might not volunteer in yours, but don't count on it. If you want to keep a plant from self-seeding, ruthlessly cut off all its flowers as soon as the petals fade.

Put flowerstalks of potentially invasive plants in the trash, not the compost pile. Even if they're immature when you cut them off the plant, many seeds can ripen afterwards. Unless your compost gets quite hot and you turn it several times, these seeds may remain viable. Then, by spreading that compost, you'll be moving plants through your garden much faster than they would have gone on their own. The moral is clear: keep weedy seeds out of the compost. (Also, keep diseased plants out of the compost, since disease spores are even more pernicious than weed seeds.)

If you don't have time to remove the flowerstalks from potentially invasive plants, seeds will ripen and scatter. In many cases, these seeds can germinate just as well

Golden feverfew

if they land on top of mulch as they would on bare soil. But if you bury them by mulching the garden in fall or early spring—after the seeds have dropped but before they germinate, you can reduce the number of volunteers significantly.

Watch what you spread on the garden

Most mulch materials are weed-free, but hay is risky. Farmers sometimes cut overgrown pastures or fields and sell the product as "mulch hay". This stuff can introduce many coarse grasses and pasture weeds into your garden. Avoid it by pulling a bale apart to see what's inside before you buy a batch of hay. Don't buy hay that's laden with seedheads. Even if the hay is moldy or rotted, the seeds might still be viable.

Sweet violets

Pay attention to these plants

The plants listed here are often grown in gardens. They're typically attractive and carefree, but under some circumstances, they can turn weedy.

PERENNIALS THAT MAY SPREAD

Whether or not a particular plant is invasive depends a lot on soil type and moisture level, and climate. That said, here are some perennials, herbs, grasses, and ferns that tend to spread faster than average, mostly via underground runners but also by seed in some cases. Plants marked with an asterisk make good ground covers, useful for difficult sites or confined areas.

Taller perennials and herbs

These are potentially invasive plants that typically grow more than 1 foot tall and can reach 2 to 6 feet:

Some **yarrows** (especially *Achillea millefolium* and *A. ptarmica*), some **artemisias** (especially *Artemisia ludoviciana*), some **asters** (*Aster*), some **bellflowers** (especially *Campanula poscharskyana* and *C. rapunculoides*), **perennial cornflower** (*Centaurea montana*), **crown vetch** (*Coronilla varia*), **hardy ageratum** or mist flower (*Eupatorium coelestinum*), most **loosestrifes** (especially *Lysimachia clethroides* and *L. punctata*), **plume poppy** (*Macleaya cordata*), **purple loosestrifes** (*Lythrum*), most **mints** (*Mentha*), most **bee balms** (*Monarda*), **showy evening primrose** and **sundrops** (*Oenothera*), **obedient plant** (*Physostegia virginiana*), **Japanese bamboo** (*Polygonum cuspidatum*), **matilija poppy** (*Romneya coulteri*), **soapwort** (*Saponaria officinalis*), most **goldenrods** (*Solidago*), most **comfreys** (*Symphytum*), **tansy** (*Tanacetum vulgare*).

Shorter perennials and herbs

These are potentially invasive plants that typically stay under 1 foot tall:

Goutweed (*Aegopodium podagraria*), **bugleweed** (*Ajuga reptans*), **snowdrop anemone** (*Anemone sylvestris*), **snow-in-summer** (*Cerastium tomentosum*), **lily-of-the-valley** (*Convallaria majalis*), **mock strawberry** (*Duchnesia indica*), **cypress spurge** (*Euphorbia cyparissias*), **sweet woodruff** (*Galium odoratum*) and other bedstraws, **yellow archangel** (*Lamiastrum galeobdolon*), **moneywort** (*Lysimachia nummularia*), **mazus** (*Mazus reptans*), **creeping phlox** (*Phlox stolonifera*), some **sedums** (*Sedum*), **American germander** (*Teucrium canadense*), **foamflower** (*Tiarella cordifolia*).

FERNS, GRASSES, GRASSY PLANTS

These are potentially invasive plants with attractive foliage but inconspicuous or absent flowers:

Various **running bamboos** such as *Arundinaria viridistriata* and *Sasa veitchii*, **hay-scented fern** (*Dennstaedtia punctilobula*), **blue lyme grass** (*Elymus glauca*), **manna grass** (*Glyceria maxima* 'Variegata'), **creeping lilyturf** (*Liriope spicata*), **sword fern** (*Nephrolepis exaltata*), **ribbon grass** (*Phalaris arundinacea* 'Picta'), **reed grass** (*Phragmites australis*.

HERBS THAT OFTEN SELF-SOW

These herbs may produce dozens or hundreds of volunteer seedlings:

Anise hyssop (*Agastache foeniculum*), **garlic chives** (*Allium tuberosum*), **dill** (*Anethum graveolens*),

Queen Anne's lace

Artemisia and sundrops

Bee balm, mint, and hay-scented fern

Yellow loosestrife

Variegated goutweed

sweet Annie (*Artemisia annua*), borage (*Borago officinalis*), fennel (*Foeniculum vulgare*), horehound (*Marrubium vulgare*), lemon balm (*Melissa officinalis*), catmints (*Nepeta*), perilla (*Perilla frutescens*), most thymes (especially *Thymus pulegioides*).

FLOWERS THAT OFTEN SELF-SOW

These annuals, biennials, and perennials often self-sow, sometimes in abundance. Plants marked with an asterisk grow well and look appropriate in natural settings or meadow gardens.

Most columbines (*Aquilegia*), English daisy (*Bellis perennis*), bachelor's buttons (*Centaurea cyanus*), most coreopsis (*Coreopsis*), oxeye daisy (*Chrysanthemum leucanthemum*), feverfew (*Chrysanthemum parthenium*), spider flower (*Cleome hassleriana*), larkspur (*Consolida ambigua*), Queen Anne's lace (*Daucus carota*), sweet William (*Dianthus barbatus*), foxglove (*Digitalis purpurea*), Indian blanket (*Gaillardia pulchella*), dame's rocket (*Hesperis matronalis*), morning glory (*Ipomea purpurea*), sweet alyssum (*Lobularia maritima*), honesty (*Lunaria biennis*), lupines (*Lupinus*), forget-me-not (*Myosotis sylvatica*), flowering tobacco (*Nicotiana*), Scotch thistle (*Onopordum acanthium*), annual poppies (*Papaver*), moss rose (*Portulaca grandiflora*), black-eyed Susans

(*Rudbeckia*), clary sage (*Salvia sclarea*) and other salvias, nasturtium (*Tropaeolum majus*), mulleins (*Verbascum*), most verbenas (*Verbena*), most veronicas (*Veronica*), violas and pansies (*Viola*), violets (especially *Viola odorata*).

DON'T BUY INTO TROUBLE

When weedy vines, shrubs, or trees naturalize and spread through an area, it's a major undertaking to remove them. Watch out for these plants if you're looking at real estate and hope

Bush honeysuckle

to create a garden at your new home. Single plants or small patches aren't a problem, but don't buy property that's overrun with these weeds unless you're prepared to spend a lot of time and money clearing ground. Hire a botanist or horticulturist if you need help identifying the plants or assessing the situation.

Vines to avoid

Akebia (*Akebia quinata*), porcelain berry (*Ampelopsis brevipedunculata*), Chinese bittersweet (*Celastrus orbiculatus*), English ivy (*Hedera helix*), Japanese honeysuckle (*Lonicera japonica*), Virginia creeper (*Parthenocissus quinquefolia*), kudzu (*Pueraria lobata*), poison ivy (*Rhus radicans*), wisterias (*Wisteria*), wild grapes (*Vitis.*)

Shrubs and trees to avoid

Tree of heaven (*Ailanthus altissima*), common barberry (*Berberis vulgaris*), Scotch broom (*Cytisus scoparius*), Russian olive and autumn olive (*Elaeagnus angustifolia* and *E. umbellata*), winged euonymus (*Euonymus alata*), privets (*Ligustrum*), bush honeysuckles (*Lonicera*), golden bamboo (*Phyllostachys aurea*), common buckthorn (*Rhamnus cathartica*), multiflora rose (*Rosa multiflora*) and other aggressive roses, blackberry and other brambles (*Rubus*), buffaloberry (*Shepherdia canadensis*), tamarisk (*Tamarix*).

Division is an easy way to propagate catmint, bearded iris, ornamental grasses, and other perennials. You can buy a single plant, and divide it a year or two later to make a showy patch.

DIVIDING PERENNIALS

Most gardening tasks, such as watering, weeding, and spreading mulch, are basic jobs that have to be done no matter what kind of plants you grow. Other jobs do relate to the plants. For example, if you grow grapes or apples, you'll need to spend time pruning. If you grow perennials, you'll need to do some dividing.

Dividing is a task that's associated almost exclusively with perennials because it relates to the way they grow. Most perennial plants spread wider each year by forming clusters or patches of many shoots, each with their own roots. Dividing means pulling or cutting apart these rooted shoots and replanting them as separate new plants.

Why divide?

Division is a versatile, practical skill, and there are many reasons why you should give it a try.

It's an easy, thrifty, and virtually foolproof way of making more plants. Making divisions is a good way to expand your own garden or help a friend start a new one. You can usually get at least three, and sometimes as many as ten or more divisions from a single clump, and some perennials increase fast enough to be divided every year or two.

Division is a reliable way to propagate cultivars of perennials, which usually don't come true from seed, and preserves what's special about them.

After several years in one spot, some perennials tend to decline, as they get overcrowded and exhaust the soil. Dividing these plants and putting them in fresh soil rejuvenates them so they grow and bloom more abundantly again.

Some perennials spread too far too fast, and go where you don't want them. Dividing and replanting them every year or two helps keep them under control.

Why not divide?

Despite its advantages, division isn't recommended for all perennials, nor for all gardeners. It can be heavy, tiring, dirty work, especially if the plants have formed large clumps. Don't strain yourself. Find a helper. Any eager new gardener will be glad to assist with the work if you share some of the plants.

Some perennials, such as false indigos (*Baptisia*), baby's breath (*Gypsophila paniculata*), sea lavender (*Limonium latifolium*), perennial flax (*Linum perenne*), lupines (*Lupinus*), and sweet cicely (*Myrrhis odorata*), aren't made to be divided, either because their shoots are squeezed so close together that you can hardly split them apart, or because they have big or deep roots that don't recover well from damage or disturbance. It's also hard to divide perennials that form a spreading mat and are woody at the base, such as basket-of-gold (*Aurinia saxatilis*), most pinks (*Dianthus*), and evergreen candytuft (*Iberis sempervirens*). These hard-to-divide perennials are usually propagated from seeds or cuttings.

Other perennials *can* be divided if you want to make more plants, but they don't *have* to be divided. Peonies, hostas, daylilies, and many kinds of perennial wildflowers, such as goatsbeard (*Aruncus dioicus*), butterflyweed (*Asclepias tuberosa*), bugbane (*Cimicifuga racemosa*), and false indigo (*Baptisia australis*), can thrive for decades without division, spreading slowly into magnificent clumps.

Many plants are perennials

Along with the familiar examples named above, many other plants can also be counted as perennials. For example, all ferns and most ornamental grasses are perennials. Virtually all plants that form bulbs, corms, tubers, etc., are perennials. Many houseplants are perennials from the tropics.

Perennials can be hardy or tender, deciduous or evergreen. In any case, if a plant lives from year to year and tends to spread or widen itself by sending up new shoots around the base of the old ones, you probably can, and perhaps you should, divide it from time to time.

Newly divided grass, hostas, and lungworts will soon spread to fill this bed.

Dividing and replanting

Spring is a wonderful season to work in the garden, and a good time for dividing most perennials, but before you rush out and start tearing things apart, take a moment to plan what you're going to do and how you're going to do it.

To divide or not to divide

If you're wondering whether or not to divide any of the plants in your garden, first make sure it's a perennial that can be divided, not one of the exceptions. Then go ahead and divide it under these conditions:

• You want to propagate it.
• You want to relocate it. You may as well divide it at the same time, and plant a few divisions rather than one intact clump. They'll recover faster and look better in the future.
• The plant is too big or has spread too far, and you want to scale it down.
• The plant is producing lots of foliage but not many flowers. Dividing may renew it (unless there's some other problem; e.g., it might need more sun).

If you don't have any reason to divide a plant now, just relax and wait. You can always divide it next year.

When to do the job

If you didn't have anything else to do and could schedule your life around your garden, you would divide a perennial:

• When it wasn't flowering or getting ready to flower.
• When its new leaves are just coming out, or its old leaves are mature.
• Usually in spring or early fall where winters are cold, or from fall to spring where winters are mild.
• On a cloudy day when the forecast calls for rain.
• At least six weeks before the onset of winter cold or summer heat.

But if you have to fit gardening around work, family, and other re-

sponsibilities, regardless of the weather, don't worry too much about breaking these rules. An ill-timed division may cause a minor setback, but most popular perennials are tough plants that soon recover.

Useful tools and equipment

Along with a fork or spade for digging up the plants you want to divide, and a trowel for replanting the divisions, you'll need various cutting tools—pruning shears, a butcher knife, a pruning saw, a machete, or even an ax. It's easier to clean up afterwards if you spread a tarp on the ground to catch soil and debris, or you might prefer to use a wheelbarrow or garden cart as a portable work bench. Designate a trash bin for the old or broken plant parts that you'll take to the compost pile, and get some boxes, flats, pots, or bags to hold the divisions that you want to replant. (In mid-job, if you don't have separate containers for the discards and the good parts, it's surprisingly easy to get them all mixed up.) On sunny days, use another tarp or covering to shade the divisions and keep them from drying out before you can replant them.

Doing the dividing

Which way to divide a plant depends on how it grows. Some plants fall to pieces when you lift them out of the ground, others you can pull or tease apart by hand, and some have to be cut with a tool. We've shown four examples on the following pages to illustrate common situations. Many perennials can be treated like one or another of these examples, but remember that these are just examples, not neat categories.

Plants are so variable that you always have to take them one at a time and decide how to handle each one. When in doubt, use a hose to wash all the soil away from the crown—the zone where the shoots and roots come together—and look for the buds that will produce new shoots. They're sometimes green, but more often white or red. Each division you make must have at least one of these buds. Actually, this opportunity to examine a plant and see how its parts fit together is one of my favorite things about dividing. I always say you don't really know a plant until you can describe its roots. After all, the half that's underground is just as important as the half you see on top.

A cloudy day in spring is a good time to divide perennials.

Replanting the divisions

If you want to replant a division in the same place where the mother plant was growing, rework the soil first. Fill the hole with compost, loosen the surrounding soil with a fork, then mix it all together and level it out. If you're putting the divisions in a new bed, just prepare the soil as you usually would.

If you have some divisions that are too small or too valuable to put out in the open, plant them in containers, or in a nursery bed where you can watch them closely, watering as needed and sheltering them from extreme heat and cold.

Normally you should replant a division at the same depth as it was growing before. Sometimes it's okay to plant divisions a little deeper, to keep them from tipping over or to bury a section of rhizome so it will bear roots. When planting a division, don't cram its roots into a tight hole. Make the hole big enough that you can spread them out and put soil between and around them. Be sure to cover all the roots as you fill the hole and pat the soil into place. Thoroughly water each plant, or the whole bed, as soon as possible.

Plants divided when their new leaves are just starting to grow settle in quickly with no special care. Later in the season, leafy divisions are liable to wilt on sunny or windy days. It's a good precaution to protect them for a week or so after planting with an inverted basket or box, a teepee of leafy twigs, a sheet of lightweight fabric or some other temporary shelter.

If you can't replant now

If you don't have the time or place to plant them right away, wrap the divisions in damp newspaper, then with plastic, and put them in a cool dark place. You can store them for a week or more in spring, and at least a few days in summer or fall.

Dividing bulbs

Perennials such as daffodils that grow from bulbs, corms, tubers, or other underground storage organs are almost all very easy to divide. You don't often have to divide them, and sometimes they don't flower as well for a year or two after being divided, but you can divide them easily if you need or want to. Along with daffodils (*Narcissus*), other bulbs that recover quickly and multiply fast enough to make dividing a good idea are crocus, meadow saffron (*Colchicum*), snowdrop (*Galanthus*), grape hyacinth (*Muscari*), bluebell (*Endymion*), squill (*Scilla*), species tulips (*Tulipa*), ornamental onions (*Allium*), and Asiatic hybrid lilies (*Lilium*). Use the guidelines for daffodils as an example for how to divide those other bulbs.

When to divide daffodils

Wait a few weeks after flowering, until the leaves start turning from green to yellow. You can divide any- time from now until the leaves die down altogether, but the sooner the better, because following the leaves down into the soil is the easiest way to find the bulbs. Without the leaves as a marker, you're likely to miss or stab the bulbs. Also, the leaves make a good handle for lifting the bulbs, and for dropping them down into new holes as you replant.

How to divide daffodils

Dig all the way around the edge of the clump to loosen the soil, sticking your fork or spade as deep as possible. Then slide the tool underneath and try to lift up the whole clump. Be careful—the bulbs are probably deeper than you expect them to be— and you don't want to stab them. When you get it out, grab the clump by its leaves and shake it. Extra soil will fall off and the bulbs will come loose. Simply pick, pluck, or snap them apart. Leave the roots and leaves attached to the bulbs—it's okay if they break off accidentally, but don't pull them off.

Sort through the bulbs you've di- vided. Discard any that got cut or bruised by the spade. Daffodils are rarely affected by pests or diseases, but if you find any bulbs that look un- healthy in any way, put them in the trash, not the compost. Take count: If you now have more bulbs than you need, you might want to grade them by size, and replant the best, biggest ones first.

Replanting the bulbs

Go ahead and replant the daffodils right away, if possible, or within a few days. Unlike the dormant bulbs you buy, in the fall, these plants are still growing, so they belong in the soil. Plant them individually, spacing them several inches apart. Bury them as deep as they were before. Hold them by the leaves as you drop them into the holes, then pile soil around the leaves and pat it down. You don't have to water the daffodils now, but rain or watering won't hurt them. The leaves will con- tinue turning yellow and then disap- pear after a month or so.

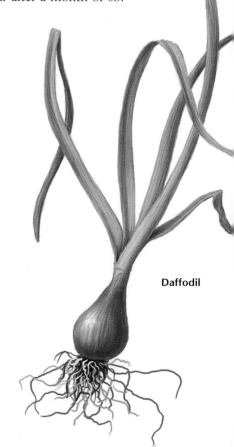

Daffodil

Primrose

Dividing clumps of rosettes

Primroses are an example of the type of perennials whose stems are very short, often completely underground, and whose leaves are arranged in distinct rosettes, tufts, or fans. Each year's new rosettes form right next to the old ones, and the plant soon makes a dense clump, which you can pry, pull, or tease apart.

Along with primroses (*Primula*), other perennials of this type are bergenias, daylilies, gerbera daisies, hardy geraniums, lamb's ears (*Stachys byzantina*), lobelias, lungworts (*Pulmonaria*), violets, clump-forming ferns such as Japanese painted fern (*Athyrium goeringianum* 'Pictum'), and several common houseplants such as African violets (*Saintpaulia*) and peace lilies (*Spathiphyllum*). Use the guidelines for primroses as an example for how to divide these other plants.

When to divide primroses

Most primroses bloom in the spring, and the best time to divide them is right after they bloom, every two or three years. You can also divide them in late summer or fall, as long as the leaves are still green, but don't wait too late if your winters are cold, as late-planted divisions are vulnerable to frost-heaving.

How to divide primroses

Dig all the way around the clump, a few inches beyond the edge of the leaves, and lift it out of the ground. You may want to shake or wash away some of the soil to make it easier to see how to proceed. Starting at one side of the clump, choose a rosette and pinch it firmly at the place where its leaves and roots come together. Right at that place, the rosette is more or less firmly connected to the rest of the plant by a short underground stem. Usually you can snap it off like you'd pluck a grape, but you may have to use pruning shears or a knife to sever the connection. Then pry or pull the rosette away from the clump.

Sometimes a clump is so dense that you can't detach a rosette by hand. In that case, a great big screwdriver is a handy tool. Use it like a pry bar to loosen the soil around the roots and force the rosettes apart. Don't try using one of your kitchen knives for this job, because it would surely bend or break.

For dividing perennials like daylilies and hostas, which form much larger clumps than primroses, the traditional advice is to stab a clump with two garden forks arranged back to back, then split it by pushing apart the fork handles. This works best if you ask a friend to bring a fork and do the job together. If you're working alone, an easier way to divide these big plants is to leave the clump in the ground, slice it into wedges with a sharp spade, and lift out one division at a time.

When dividing a dense clump, you can hardly avoid breaking a few of the individual rosettes. Don't worry—there are usually more good divisions than you have space for. Sort out the best ones for replanting, and remove any flowerstalks or withered or broken leaves.

Replanting the divisions

Replant the divisions promptly in freshly prepared soil. Firm the soil over the roots, but don't bury the leaf bases. Water well right after planting. Use temporary or portable shelters to shade the new divisions for a week or so, if the weather is sunny, to prevent unnecessary wilting.

Yarrow

Dividing mats and patches

Yarrows spread in a way that is typical of many popular perennials. They have slender horizontal stems called rhizomes, located right under the surface of the soil. The rhizomes reach out in all directions, often branching as they go and overlapping each other to form tangled mats. New shoots sprout up from all parts of the mat, forming a dense patch with lots of foliage and dozens of flowerstalks.

Other perennials that spread like yarrows (*Achillea*) include several types of anemones and artemisias, asters, phloxes, bee balms (*Monarda*), loosestrifes (*Lysimachia*), sundrops and evening primroses (*Oenothera*), mountain bluet (*Centaurea montana*), sweet woodruff (*Galium odoratum*), and various spreading ferns and grasses. Some of these plants make good ground covers, but in a flowerbed, perennials that spread like yarrow usually should be divided every few years to limit their size and

to renew their appearance. The guidelines for yarrow will help you divide this and other mat-formers.

When to divide yarrows

Where winters are cold, divide yarrows anytime during the growing season, except during the peak of flowering. Where winters are mild, divide them anytime from fall to spring. Before dividing, cut any flowerstalks or shabby old foliage down close to the ground, so you can see what you're doing.

How to divide yarrows

There are various ways to do this job. To renew a plant that you're going to replant in the same place, study the patch, choose the best part, dig around it, lift it out, and set it aside. Tear out the rest of the patch, amend the soil, and replant the division you saved.

To start a few new plants without disturbing the mother patch, use a sharp spade to cut blocks or wedges about 3 to 6 inches square from around the edge of the patch. Lift

them out and refill the holes with fresh soil.

To divide an entire patch into several new plants, cut it all into squares, like cutting a pan of brownies, and lift them out one at a time. Or, lift the patch as a whole, set it on the ground or on a tarp, and then cut it and take the squares apart. Fewer of the squares turn to crumbs if you lift the whole patch first.

If you lift the yarrow patch out of the ground, whole or in parts, and shake it with your fork, it will separate into more pieces than you can count. Don't do this unless you want to have hundreds of plants to use as a ground cover or plan to start a yarrow nursery. Being small, the divisions will need extra TLC, but they all have the potential to grow.

Replanting the divisions

Dig a shallow hole, set the division in place, firm the soil around it, and water. Big divisions rarely need further care. Small divisions are liable to dry out and wilt, so watch them and water as needed.

Dividing tough clumps

Hybrid astilbes (*Astilbe × arendsii*) are an example of the type of perennial that forms very dense clumps of foliage and flowerstalks, with equally dense clumps of roots below. In fact, their crown—the area where the shoots and roots come together—is so tight and tough that you'll probably need a sharp tool and a strong arm to split it into three or four wedge-like divisions.

Fortunately, not too many kinds of perennials tend to produce these super-tough crowns. Expect to find them in old clumps of goatsbeard (*Aruncus dioicus*), lady's mantle (*Alchemilla mollis*), Joe-Pye weeds (*Eupatorium*), false sunflower (*Heliopsis helianthoides*), lilyturf (*Liriope muscari*), and most sages or salvias (*Salvia*). Toughest of all are the clump-forming ornamental grasses such as Japanese silver grass (*Miscanthus sinensis*). As always, each plant is unique, but the guidelines for dividing astilbes will give you a basis for dividing these other plants.

When to divide astilbes

Where winters are cold, it's best to divide astilbes in spring. Early fall is okay, too, if you divide at least six weeks before hard frost. Where winters are mild, divide astilbes in spring or fall. Divide every three to five years.

How to divide astilbes

Pull away any mulch, identify the area where the shoots come out of the ground, and dig a circle at least three times that wide around the edge of the clump. Pry underneath with your fork or spade and lift the whole clump up and out. Hose off some of the soil for a better look at the job ahead.

Draw imaginary lines that divide the clump into a few more or less equal sections. Cut along those lines, working from the top down. An old pruning saw, too dull for cutting limbs anymore, is a good tool for this job. A stout knife or machete works, too, and so does a spade if you sharpen the blade.

Whatever you use, try to aim your cut so you go between the major shoots or buds and slice as few as possible. You'll probably encounter some woody, gnarled knots in the crown. It's virtually impossible to cut around these knots, and okay to cut right through them. They heal. You'll end up with some big, angular divisions, and very little debris.

Replanting the divisions

Because these divisions are relatively large and intact, they almost always grow well and need little attention. The main concern is keeping the top of the crown level with the soil. A heavy division is likely to sink when planted in soft, recently worked soil, so set it a little high at first, expecting it to settle over the next few weeks. On the other hand, where winters are cold, divisions are liable to frost-heave if planted too late in the fall. Because of their smooth sides, they can pop like a cork and lift out of the ground. Prevent this by making divisions early enough that they'll have time to anchor themselves with strong new roots. For added insurance, apply a winter mulch such as evergreen boughs after the ground freezes.

Astilbe

Other perennials that you can divide

The following plants can all be propagated by division, using the methods shown on the previous pages or other simple techniques, as described below.

Ajuga (*Ajuga reptans*): Divide every few years in spring, early summer, or fall. Fork up the whole patch, shake or pull it apart, and replant individual rosettes.

Lady's mantle (*Alchemilla mollis*): Divide every three to five years in early spring before the leaves expand, or in mid- to late summer after cutting back the flowerstalks and shabby foliage. You'll probably have to cut the clump, like dividing astilbes.

Artemisias (*Artemisia*): 'Silver King', 'Valerie Finnis', and other artemisias with shallow runners can spread quite fast. Every few years, lift the whole patch in spring or fall and divide like yarrow.

Asters (*Aster*): Every one to three years, lift the whole clump in early spring. Pull off healthy new shoots from around the perimeter and plant them singly or in small groups. Discard weak shoots or woody material from the center of the clump.

Bergenia (*Bergenia*): Every three to five years, or when the patch gets crowded, divide like primroses in spring or fall.

Boltonia (*Boltonia asteroides*): Every few years or when the patch gets too large, divide like yarrow in spring.

Chrysanthemum (*Chrysanthemum × morifolium*): Divide every year or two in late spring. Look for new shoots that form on the end of short runners radiating from the old stalks. Stick a fork underneath to loosen the soil, then work with your fingers to separate the shoots and lift them up. Break them off with a few inches of runner attached, and bury the runner when you replant the divisions.

Lily-of-the-valley (*Convallaria majalis*): Divide almost anytime when it isn't in bloom. Lift a patch, pull apart the runners, and replant them separately or in small clumps.

Coreopsis, thread leaf (*Coreopsis verticillata* 'Moonbeam' and 'Zagreb'; also *C. rosea*): Whenever patches get too dense or too large, divide like yarrow in spring or fall.

Ferns: Some ferns grow slowly and infrequently need division. Others spread or multiply quickly. Either way, it's best to divide ferns in spring just as the new fronds start to unfurl. Most species of *Athyrium, Dryopteris, Osmunda*, and *Polystichum* form separate rosettes that you can pull or cut apart. Ferns that spread by runners and form continuous patches can be cut into chunks, like yarrow.

Blanketflower (*Gaillardia × grandiflora*): Every few years, or when the center of the clump dies out, divide like yarrow in spring.

Geraniums, hardy (*Geranium*): Divide like primroses every few years in spring or fall. Replant the divisions deeper than they were before, covering the rhizomes.

Grasses, ornamental: Most ornamental grasses look and grow best if you divide them every few years in early spring, just as they show signs of new growth. Don't wait too many years before dividing large grasses, as the roots become quite massive and tough. Divide clump-forming grasses by digging up the clump and cutting, chopping, or sawing it into a few smaller chunks, like dividing astilbes. Divide spreading grasses as you would yarrow.

Daylilies (*Hemerocallis*): Divide every three to five years, or wait longer if you choose. Dig in spring or fall and cut, pry, or pull apart into smaller chunks, each with one or more fans of leaves. Big old clumps may be too heavy to lift. Use a spade to cut them apart in the ground, then lift one section at a time.

Coral bells (*Heuchera*): Divide like primroses, every few years in fall or spring. Replant the shoots a little deeper then they were before, covering the rhizomes with soil.

Hostas (*Hosta*): Hostas can go indefinitely without division, or you can divide them every few years to make more plants. Dig clumps when the new leaves appear in spring, and cut them apart like astilbes. To take just one division from an established clump, slice down into it with a sharp shovel, like cutting a slice of pie.

Coreopsis 'Zagreb'

Hardy geranium and ferns

Flame grass

Bearded iris

Iris, bearded (*Iris germanica*): Divide every few years, in early summer. Dig clump, shake away soil, and cut leaves back by half. Note how the fans of leaves grow from the tips of the rhizomes. Break or cut apart the fans, leaving a few inches of rhizome attached to each one. Replant with the rhizome at soil level, and don't cover with mulch.

Other rhizomatous irises, including Siberian iris and many other species, can go several years without division, and may not bloom well for a year or two after you do divide them. But if you want more plants, or if the clump has gotten bare in the center, you can divide most iris in summer or fall. If the clump is too big to dig, cut it apart and move one section at a time.

Bee balms, monardas (*Monarda*): Every few years or when the patch gets too large, divide like yarrow in early spring.

Sundrops, showy evening primrose (*Oenothera fruticosa, O. speciosa*): Divide like yarrow in spring or fall, to limit the spread of the patch. You can make a few big divisions or many small ones.

Peony, herbaceous (*Paeonia lactiflora*): Peonies can go many years without division, but if want to propagate a big clump, dig it up in early fall. The roots will surprise you—they're huge. Wash off the soil and cut the roots into chunks with three to five buds apiece. When replanting, cover the buds with no more than an inch of soil and mulch.

Phlox (*Phlox*): Most kinds of phlox can be divided in spring or fall by cutting the patch into chunks, like yarrow. The low, spreading phloxes can go for decades without division, but the tall, clumping types should be divided every few years.

Coneflowers and **purple coneflowers** (*Rudbeckia, Echinacea*): Divide in spring every few years, or whenever the clump gets too big. Pull, pry, or cut apart the clumps into thirds, quarters, or as many divisions as you want to replant.

Sedums (*Sedum*): Sedum 'Autumn Joy' and other cultivars that form upright clumps can be divided like astilbes, every few years in early spring. Low, spreading sedums can be divided anytime simply by breaking them apart. Every piece will grow.

Lamb's-ears (*Stachys byzantina*): Divide every few years, in spring or fall. Pull them apart like primroses.

Coneflower

Japanese primrose and lamb's ears

About four weeks after the seeds were sown, these China pinks are ready to be transplanted into recycled plastic six-packs.

RAISING SEEDLINGS INDOORS

Raising plants from seeds is one of the easiest and most satisfying ways to fill a garden. You can choose from thousands of different kinds of seeds, and the cost is just a fraction of what you'd pay for started plants.

Although some seeds do better if sown directly in the garden, many garden plants can be started indoors and grown under fluorescent lights. Starting seeds indoors gives you a head start on the season, so you can begin picking vegetables and flowers much earlier than if you waited to sow them outdoors. You get better results with rare or tiny seeds indoors, where you can protect them from pests and severe weather. Best of all, watching seedlings grow indoors buoys your spirits during those slow weeks of late winter and early spring when the garden is still dormant.

Raising seedlings doesn't require much equipment or space. You can do it in the corner of a spare bedroom or in the basement, with inexpensive or recycled supplies. Plan to spend an hour or so now and then on the tasks of sowing and transplanting, depending on how many seedlings you grow. It takes just a few minutes a day to water and check the seedlings. That's the fun part—you'll be delighted at how cute the little plants are and how fast they grow.

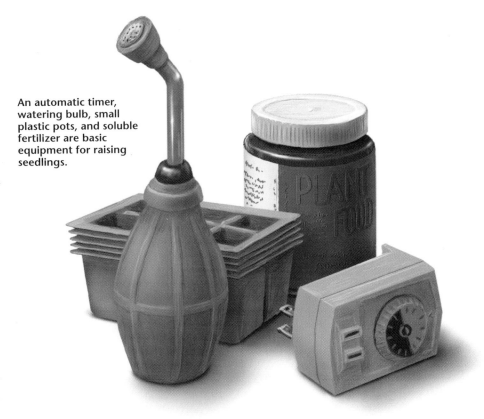

An automatic timer, watering bulb, small plastic pots, and soluble fertilizer are basic equipment for raising seedlings.

Unparalleled selection

One of the best reasons for raising your own seedlings is that it gives you more choice of varieties, particularly among vegetables, annual herbs, annual flowers, everlastings, and wildflowers. The seed racks in local garden centers and hardware stores usually offer a good assortment of the most popular vegetables and annual flower seeds, but for the widest possible selection of interesting, desirable plants, refer to mail-order seed catalogs.

Imagine selecting snapdragons or petunias in exactly the color you want, planting a garden of unusual everlasting flowers, experimenting with a dozen kinds of basil, or choosing from hundreds of different kinds of tomatoes, including heirloom varieties with unsurpassed flavor. Seed catalogs offer all that and more. Compare this diversity with the uninspired selection of transplants at most local garden centers in spring, and you'll understand why avid gardeners raise their own seedlings.

Plan ahead

If you mail-order seeds in January or February, before the companies are overwhelmed with orders, your seeds will arrive in a week or so, and you'll be ready to start sowing. But if you don't order until March or April, it can take up to four weeks before your seeds come, and by then it will be late for starting them indoors. In that case, it would be better to buy seeds locally, so you could sow them right away.

To decide when to sow seeds indoors, you need to know the average date of the last spring frost in your area. If you don't know this, ask any gardener in your neighborhood when "it's safe to plant tomatoes"—that's the last frost date. Then use a calendar, and count backwards. For example, you can sow tomatoes indoors about six weeks before the last frost date. That's enough time for the seeds to germinate and the seedlings to grow 4 to 6 inches tall.

Other plants need more or fewer weeks, depending on how soon they sprout and how fast they grow. Seed catalogs and packets usually give this information, telling how many weeks before last frost you should plant the seeds indoors.

Some transplants can be planted outdoors before the last frost, because they tolerate chilly weather. These plants are labeled as half-hardy annuals or hardy perennials, and the recommended sowing dates take their hardiness into account.

Equipment and supplies

You can buy all the equipment and supplies needed for seed-starting at local garden centers, hardware stores, or discount stores, or mail-order them from seed catalogs. If you had to start from scratch, it would cost about $50 to buy everything listed here, but you probably have some of it on hand already. When not in use, the equipment fits easily into a closet, and you can re-use it year after year.

Pots, flats, and labels

You can buy a variety of special seed-starting pots, or simply recycle small plastic nursery pots or bedding-plant six-packs that you've saved. Wash them in hot soapy water with a dash of bleach added, and they're good as new.

Handling or carrying lots of individual pots is inconvenient, and water that drains out the holes makes puddles, so it's best to group the containers in some kind of tray or flat. Plastic nursery flats are ideal, and you can recycle them many times (wash them well each time). If you don't have any on hand, you can buy new ones. Also, buy at least one of those clear plastic domes that fits over a flat and turns it into a mini-greenhouse.

You can buy packets of plastic or wooden labels at garden centers or from mail-order seed catalogs, or use wooden tongue depressors, popsicle sticks, or strips cut from stiff plastic containers. Write on the labels with pencil or a waterproof marker so the information won't wash away.

Soil and fertilizer

In late winter and early spring, any garden center will have bags of soil mix that's specially designed for starting seeds. It's made from finely ground peat moss and vermiculite, with no "real" soil included. There are several brands, all quite similar. This packaged seed-starting mix gives good results. It is sterile—not contaminated with weed seeds or disease spores, as

garden soil might be. Its granular, lumpfree texture makes it easy to handle when sowing or transplanting. Pre-moisten this soil before you use it. Put some into a plastic pail or tub, add hot tap water and stir well, then wait a few hours for the soil particles to absorb the water. When the soil feels uniformly damp, like a squeezed-out sponge, it's ready to use.

As your seedlings grow, you'll need to fertilize them with a dilute solution of regular houseplant fertilizer or a liquid organic fertilizer. A rubber watering bulb that makes a gentle spray is ideal for watering or fertilizing tiny seeds or seedlings without flooding them.

Lights and timer

Seedlings need plenty of bright light to grow well; if they don't get enough, they become weak, thin and pale. Windowsills generally aren't good places to grow seedlings, as the sunlight can be limited by cloudy days, long nights, or shade from nearby trees or buildings. Instead, the best way to provide enough light for healthy seedlings is to grow them under fluorescent lights. Get a simple shop-light fixture with two 48-inch tubes, available at any discount store, hardware store, or building-supply center. One fixture will accommodate dozens of seedlings. You don't need

special grow-light bulbs; ordinary tubes are okay for seedlings. These fixtures have very short cords, so while you're at the store, get a heavy-duty extension cord that can take a 3-prong plug.

You'll need to support the lights somehow, and to adjust their position as the seedlings grow, keeping the tubes about 3 to 4 inches above the top leaves. Some gardeners hook chains from the ceiling to support lights over a table or bench; other simply balance the ends of the fixture on bricks or blocks of wood. Seed catalogs feature manufactured light stands that look very nice, or you can make your own, as shown at right.

A 24-hour timer that turns the lights on and off automatically is a worthwhile convenience. Seedlings grow fastest with about 18 hours of light daily, so you might set the lights to turn on at 6 A.M. and off at midnight.

Thermometer, heat pad, fan

As for temperatures, most seedlings do fine if the air temperature is between 60 and 70°F in the daytime, and a little cooler at night. Fluorescent lights don't give off much heat, so the temperature underneath them is about the same as the room temperature. However, it's a good idea to check with a thermometer, especially if the seedlings are in a room away from the main thermostat.

Many seeds germinate best if the soil temperature is about 70°F; it's okay if the air is cooler than that, as long as the soil is warm. You can purchase an electric soil-heating mat from garden centers or catalogs, or use a drugstore heating pad that's approved for moist heat. Check with a thermometer to determine which heat setting to use. Plug the heating mat into the same timer that controls the lights, so they turn on and off together.

Use a small fan to keep air circulating in the vicinity of the seedlings. This promotes sturdy, healthy growth.

A light stand you can build

This inexpensive homemade light stand holds three shop-light fixtures and easily accommodates six nursery flats of seedlings. You can build it in an afternoon with simple hand tools. When not in use, the light stand can be disassembled and stored in a closet.

Materials list

4 upright legs, 1×2 by 72 inches
4 shelf supports, 1×2 by 60 inches
4 stop bars, 1×2 by 6 inches
1 closet pole for top bar, $1\frac{1}{4}$ inch by 60 inches
1 top shelf, $\frac{1}{4}$-inch plywood cut 16 inches wide by 56 inches long
1 bottom shelf, $\frac{1}{4}$-inch plywood cut 24 inches wide by 56 inches long
1 bottom brace, $\frac{1}{4}$-inch plywood cut 6 inches wide by 60 inches long

8 carriage bolts, $\frac{1}{4}$ inch by 2 inches long, for holding shelf supports
2 carriage bolts, $\frac{1}{4}$ inch by 3 inches long, for holding top bar
10 wingnuts, $\frac{1}{4}$ inch
12 flathead woodscrews, #6 by $\frac{1}{2}$ inch long
4 cuphooks
3 48-inch fluorescent shop-light fixtures, with hanging chains and S-hooks

Tools

Saw, file or rasp, drill, $\frac{3}{8}$-inch drill bit, $\frac{1}{4}$-inch drill bit, screwdriver

Assembly

1. Cut boards to size, or have them cut for you at the lumberyard.

2. Measure and mark each upright at 1 inch, 24 inches, and 48 inches from the top. Drill $\frac{3}{8}$-inch holes at the top marks, and $\frac{1}{4}$-inch holes at the lower two marks on each upright.

3. Use the file or rasp to carve shallow curves in tops of the uprights, so they fit against the round closet pole.

4. Measure and mark $\frac{3}{4}$ inch from the ends of the closet pole and the four shelf supports. Drill $\frac{1}{4}$-inch holes at those marks.

5. Fasten the stop bars under the corners of the bottom shelf, to keep the legs from spreading apart. Use two wood screws for each bar. Screw them down through the plywood shelf.

6. Lay two uprights on the floor. Measure and mark at 12 inches and 20 inches from the bottom ends of the braces. Position the bottom brace between the marks, and make sure that its sides line up square with the uprights. Use two wood screws at each end to fasten the brace in place, screwing down through the plywood.

7. Use the 2-inch carriage bolts and wingnuts to fasten the shelf supports to the uprights. Lean everything against a wall or recruit an assistant to help, then use the 3-inch bolts and nuts to fasten the uprights to the closet pole.

8. Set the shelves in place and spread the legs apart. Hang one light fixture from the top bar. Screw the cuphooks into the top shelf supports, and hang the other two light fixtures from those hooks.

9. If you choose, apply a coat of varnish, paint, or oil finish to make the wood smooth and waterproof.

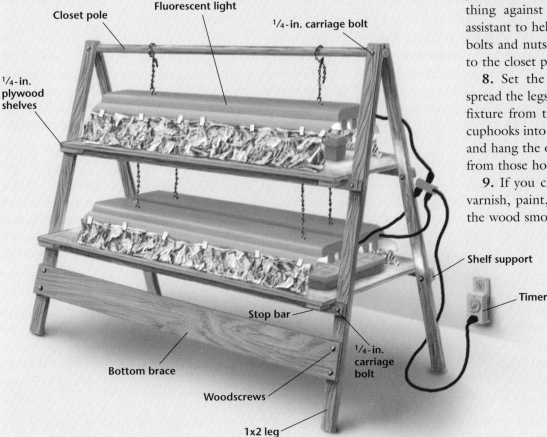

Closet pole
Fluorescent light
$\frac{1}{4}$-in. carriage bolt
$\frac{1}{4}$-in. plywood shelves
Shelf support
Timer
Stop bar
$\frac{1}{4}$-in. carriage bolt
Bottom brace
Woodscrews
1x2 leg

Sowing seeds and caring for seedlings

Basically, there are two methods of raising seedlings in containers. Some people swear by one method or the other and use it all the time, but each system has its pros and cons, so it's worth considering them both. One approach is to sow seeds directly into the individual containers where they will grow until you put them out into the garden. The other method is to sow a quantity of seeds in one container and let them grow there together for a few weeks before transplanting them into separate pots.

In either case, here's a tip: write the plant names on labels in advance so you can insert a label into each pot as soon as you sow the seeds. Otherwise, it's easy to get mixed up.

Sowing in individual pots

Sowing directly into individual pots is good for plants with large seeds that develop quickly, such as melons, sweet peas, and dahlias, and for seedlings with brittle roots, such as okra and hibiscus. It's a good system for children or anyone who might be impatient or have trouble handling delicate seedlings. It saves time by eliminating the task of transplanting and avoids the risk that seedlings might be stunted by waiting in an overcrowded pot until you get around to transplanting them.

Usually it's good to end up with just one plant per pot. You can achieve this by sowing a single seed, or by sowing two or more seeds, waiting until they sprout, then clipping off the weakest-looking seedling(s) with sharp scissors. With a few annuals and herbs—alyssum, calliopsis, flossflower, lobelia, moss rose, phlox, chives, dill, feverfew, parsley, and sweet marjoram—it's okay to sow several seeds in a pot, let them all develop, and transplant them into the garden as a clump. This is an easy way to make bushy specimens, and these particular plants don't seem to suffer from being crowded close together.

To sow seeds directly into separate pots, start by filling the pots level full with moistened soil mix. Gently pat or tap the pots to settle the soil, but don't pack it down hard. Use a pencil to poke a shallow hole in the soil, and put in one or more seeds. Then follow the guidelines below.

Sowing in a starter pot

A big advantage of sowing seeds in one starter pot is that it saves space. This is especially significant when you're sowing tiny seeds that develop slowly. You can sow dozens of dust-fine begonia or moss rose seeds in one 4-inch pot, and leave them there for six weeks or more before they are large enough and crowded enough to transplant. But if sown individually into separate pots, that many seeds would take up a lot of space under your lights.

A starter pot should be shallow. Fill it with no more than $1\frac{1}{2}$ to 2 inches of moist soil mix, and gently pat down the soil to make a smooth surface. You can sow the seeds around the edge of the pot, in rows across the top, in a checkerboard pattern, or at random—but in any case, don't crowd them too close together. Put matchhead-sized seeds at least $\frac{1}{2}$ inch apart, and pinhead- or smaller-sized seeds at least $\frac{1}{4}$ inch apart. To manage this, try folding a sharp crease in the seed packet, then shake the packet so the seeds line up in the crease. Then you can tap them out one at a time. Sometimes tiny round seeds will get away from you and all roll out at once, falling out in a clump. Don't be dismayed. Use a pencil to gently draw them away from the clump and spread them across the surface of the soil. If the seeds are so tiny that you can't really see them, just take aim and hope for the best.

Light or dark?

After you sow the seeds in a pot, the first question is whether or not to cover them with soil. In general, seeds as big as a matchhead or larger germinate best in darkness, so you should cover them. Sprinkle on a layer of soil up to twice as deep as the seeds are wide and pat it down gently. Tiny, dustlike seeds require light to germinate, so you should not cover them at all—just leave them exposed on the surface. Most garden-variety seeds are of intermediate size; some prefer darkness, and some require light. This information is sometimes noted in seed catalogs or on the seed packets.

If seeds need light to germinate, put them under the fluorescent light fixture now. If they don't, you can wait until the first sprouts appear before putting the pots under the lights. But as long as you've covered them with soil, it doesn't hurt to put dark-requiring seeds under the lights, too. That means they'll be exposed to light as soon as they germinate, and that's good for them.

Watering

Whether on not you cover the seeds, the next step is to settle them into place in or on the soil with a gentle watering. You can sprinkle the tops of the containers with a gentle spray from a watering bulb, or set the containers in a shallow tray or flat of tepid water, and let water soak up from the bottom. Watch the surface of the soil, and as soon as it turns dark and glossy, you'll know the water has reached the top. Remove the containers and hold them up to allow any extra water to drain out the bottom.

After this initial watering, if you cover the flats with a tent of clear plastic, a plastic dome lid, or a pane of glass (or set the pots inside one of those clear plastic clamshell salad-bar packages), you probably won't have to water the seeds again until they germinate.

Warm or cool?

Soil temperature affects seed germination. Some, such as peppers and eggplants, sprout fastest at warm (70°F or higher) temperatures, so set them on a soil-heating mat or pad. Cooler soil can delay their germination for several days, and the seedings are weaker when they finally do sprout.

If you sow directly into individual pots, use scissors to thin out extra seedlings.

If you sow in a starter pot, gently separate and transplant the seedlings.

Other plants, such as pansies and dusty miller, sprout best and have the most vigor if the soil is cool (about 55°F). If the soil is too warm, their seedlings tend to be "soft" and more subject to disease. Check the seed packet for more information on specific plants, and do your best to position the seed containers accordingly.

After the seeds sprout

Most garden seeds germinate in less than a month, and many pop up in less than a week. This is an exciting time. Check each pot daily. If you spot any emerging shoots, immediately remove the plastic lid and turn off the heating pad. Extra heat and humidity can weaken tiny seedlings. What they need now is bright light and drier air.

Position the seedlings within a few inches of the fluorescent light tubes. This keeps them compact and healthy. If they are too far from the lights, the stems will stretch and grow weak. As the seedlings continue to grow over the coming weeks, keep adjusting the lights so they are just above the leaves.

Some pots will need watering every few days, others less than once a week—it all depends on the kind of plant, how many there are in the pot, and how big they are. Check each pot daily; if it feels lightweight and the soil surface is pale, it's time to water.

To promote rapid growth, give the seedlings frequent applications of di-lute fertilizer. Mix about ¼ teaspoon of soluble houseplant fertilizer such as 20-20-20 or 15-30-15 or 1 teaspoon of fish emulsion or manure tea per gallon of water, and apply it once a week instead of watering.

Transplanting

If you sowed the seeds individually in separate pots, all you have to do now is wait until they're large enough to move outdoors. If you sowed them in starter pots, they can grow there for a few weeks after germination, but when they start to crowd together, it's time to transplant them.

The tricky part of transplanting is pulling the seedlings apart. For tiny seedlings such as petunias or thyme, begin at one edge of the starter pot and try lifting them out one at a time, using a sharp pencil to prod the roots free. For tomatoes, peppers, zinnias, and other vigorous seedlings, it's easier to slide the whole soil ball out of the pot onto your work surface, then pry apart the separate plants.

Let the root systems determine how you proceed. If a seedling has a large root system, or if the roots are thick or brittle, hold the plant with one hand (hold onto a leaf, not the stem), suspend the roots in the center of an empty pot, and scoop in some soil with your other hand. Fill the pot to the rim and gently tamp in down.

If a seedling has a small or soft root system, fill a pot with loose soil, and make a hole in the middle with a pencil or your finger. Drop the roots into the hole, then push the soil gently into place over and around the roots, and lightly tamp it down.

Hardening-off

Don't move seedlings directly from the light stand to the garden. They need time to adjust from the protected environment indoors to the real world outdoors. Allow several days for the transition, a process called hardening-off. The idea is to expose the seedlings gradually to hotter and colder temperatures, bright sun, drying winds, and overhead watering. At first, set the flats outdoors in a shady, protected area. On subsequent days, move them to places with more sun and wind. Bring them indoors or cover them with an old blanket or sheet at night for the first few days, then leave them outdoors both day and night.

Hardening-off is a critical time for seedlings, because they dry out quickly and may need watering more than once a day. As soon as they are tough enough not to wilt in the sun and wind, go ahead and transplant them. Avoid transplanting in the mid-day sun; a cool overcast day is ideal. Be sure to water them well after transplanting, then stand back to watch them grow.

Sweet woodruff is a
fast-spreading perennial
that makes a carefree,
weedproof ground cover
for rough or rocky sites.

GROWING
GROUND COVERS

The term ground cover has two meanings. It refers to any short, spreading, long-lived plant that covers the ground with a durable, dense carpet of intertwined stems and leaves. Many plants tend to grow this way; various kinds of shrubs, vines, perennials, grasses, ferns, and even moss can be called ground covers. The same term can also describe the overall effect you get when you choose one of these plants and space a number of them close enough together that they converge into a single mass, just as the word hedge describes a planting of shrubs that has converged into a solid row.

Covering ground is a good thing to do, not just because plants look prettier than bare dirt, mud, or dust, but because a covering of foliage protects soil by braking the force of the wind, softening the impact of the rain, and absorbing the heat of the sun. At the same time, a ground cover's underground network of roots and rhizomes opens pathways for water to penetrate into the soil, and protects against erosion by binding soil particles together.

Lawn as a ground cover

A turfgrass lawn is the most common kind of ground cover, familar to all gardeners, so thinking about lawns is a good basis for considering alternatives. Compared to other ground covers, it's true that lawns have a few advantages. Starting a lawn, whether from seed or sod, is faster and costs less than filling the same space with almost any other ground cover. Lawns are so common and so popular that there's a whole industry of lawn-care products and services, with experts ready to answer all your questions and sell you what you need. If you plant a less familiar ground cover, you may have to find your own answers. Turfgrasses are so resilient and flexible that so you can walk, drive, sit, or play on

a lawn without damaging it. Most ground covers don't allow that.

But lawns have several disadvantages, too. In general, turfgrasses don't grow well in the shade. They need regular fertilization, generous watering where summers are dry, and they're susceptible to various pests and diseases. Keeping grass short and neat requires tedious mowing, repeated endlessly. Most turfgrasses go dormant and look drab for months of the year. And finally, even if a lawn is perfectly healthy, soft as velvet, thick as fur, and a gorgeous emerald green, enough is enough. Too much lawn can be boring.

Substituting ground covers for lawn

It's nice to have some lawn, especially where the climate and soil are favorable for grass, but reducing the size of your lawn and planting ground covers instead means you can spend less time mowing and more time doing other projects in the garden, or simply sitting back to admire it all. It's especially helpful to eliminate parts of the lawn that are tricky to mow—on slopes, in tight corners, next to buildings, under low limbs, around trees and obstacles. Using ground covers is even more practical

in situations where grass struggles. With so many kinds of ground covers to choose from, you can find a plant for almost any conditions—sunny or shady, hot or cool, wet or dry. Why keep fussing over bare, brown, or weedy patches? Give up on grass and substitute a ground cover adapted to the site.

Beyond the practical and horticultural advantages, I think the best reason for planting ground covers is the opportunity for adding more color and texture to a garden. Wide expanses of lawn remind me of institutional-grade wall-to-wall carpeting, uninspired and monotonous.

Ground covers, by comparison, are like area rugs. Think of Oriental knotted carpets, Navaho rugs, Greek flokatis, Scandinavian rya rugs, Early American hooked and braided rugs. Just as rugs add variety to the floor of your house, ground covers can make interesting patterns on the "floor" of your garden, with delicate or bold foliage in shades of green, gray, silver, blue, purple, gold, and variegated colors—often with showy flowers, too. This chapter will give you ideas on where to plant ground covers, explain how to grow them, and recommend some of the best plants to use.

Foamflower blooms in spring and has semi-evergreen leaves.

Planning for ground covers

There are places on any property where planting ground covers would simplify maintenance and add beauty. Look for these situations on your lot. Are there areas where grass doesn't grow well, where it's difficult to mow, or where you don't want to bother with it? Are there too many separate specimens, or beds that look like a random collection of stray plants? Are there wide stretches of lawn that look blank and dull? For any of these problems, ground covers offer an answer.

Match the plant to the situation

Analyzing the growing conditions is the first step in choosing a ground cover, because when you're filling an area with one kind of plant, it's really important for that plant to do well. Study a site, noting how much sun it gets, what the soil is like, what kinds of plants are growing there, and how well they're doing. A ground cover planting isn't like a mixed border, where if one species fails, you can pull it out and pop in something else. Replacing a failed ground cover would be an expensive disappointment. Fortunately, there are at least a few kinds of ground covers for almost any situation, as illustrated by the following examples. From a short list of well-adapted candidates, you can make the final selection on the basis of foliage texture, flower color, or other aspects of a plant's appearance.

Replace unwanted grass

It's easy to find alternatives for sites where you want to replace healthy turf grass, because these sites are typically sunny, with average or better soil. Many ground covers thrive in those conditions.

On steep banks or slopes that are slippery and scary to mow, use co-toneasters, junipers, lantanas, fragrant sumac, memorial rose, creeping rosemary, coralberries, and other shrubby ground covers. (For more information on these plants, see pp. 51–55.)

Round the corners of a square lawn with triangular patches of bishop's weed, sweet woodruff, daylilies, moss phlox, or creeping thyme, so you can mow around and around without having to stop and turn. It won't hurt these perennials if the mower occasionally nips them.

Protect tree trunks from the mower, and the mower from rocks, by circling these obstacles with a necklace of bugleweed, sweet violets, mock strawberry, mazus, or dichondra. These plants stay short with no mowing, but they won't be crushed by your footsteps or the mower wheels. Their runners will spread out into the lawn; if that bothers you, add a buried edging to confine them.

For narrow spots like the strip between a house and a driveway, replace lawn with grass lookalikes such as lilyturf or monkey grass, or with colorful sedums or shade-loving ferns.

Reclaim wasted land

Rough or rocky ground is often abandoned to weeds, but with a little effort you can eliminate the weeds and fill the area with a handsome stand of evergreen vines or shrubs instead. Choose akebia, wintercreeper euonymus, or English ivy for shady sites, and honeysuckle, bearberry, junipers or creeping rosemary for sunny sites. These are all vigorous plants that eventually cover a large area with colorful foliage, and their stems trace interesting shapes as they wind over and around rocks. Once established, they need little care from year to year; you won't have to scramble around pruning or tending them. These same plants are good for filling any vacant spots around the perimeter of a property—behind a garage or shed, between the back fence and the service alley, along the edge of a woods or vacant lot.

Unify eclectic plantings

If you're the kind of gardener who pores over catalogs of rare plants and can't resist ordering one each of everything that sounds delightful, your garden may end up like a catalog, too, with a lot of separate entries that don't flow together. The solution to this problem is simple, although carrying it out requires willpower from a one-at-a-time collector. Choose one or two ground covers with low, neat foliage, such as lilyturf, monkey grass, dwarf crested iris, bigroot geranium, small-leaved hostas, or periwinkle, and use them to edge all the beds and borders, to line the paths, and to skirt the trees and shrubs. When this is done, the effect is dramatic. It unites the garden into a single scene, and the individual specimens don't stand apart anymore. Even if you aren't a passionate plant collector, choosing just a few kinds of ground covers and repeating them throughout a garden is a good way to give it character and consistency.

Paint a pretty picture

Some ground covers have such attractive flowers that they serve as showpieces, not backgrounds. Visitors to southern California never forget the roadside plantings of ice plant, with its blindingly brilliant flowers. Daylilies, showy evening primrose, and sundrops also make memorable roadside plantings. On a smaller scale, you can stop neighborhood traffic with a patch of blooming sedums, bugleweed, snow-in-summer, foamflower, moneywort, moss phlox, or creeping thyme. Any of these succulents or perennials can be included in a flowerbed, but using them in quantity as a ground cover is much more dramatic. To extend the display over a longer season, combine two or more ground covers that bloom at different times, and plant generous drifts of each.

Don't overlook the beauty of ground cover foliage, too. Variegated or colorful leaves can be just as showy as flowers, and they last a lot longer. Deciduous ground covers, such as white-striped ribbon grass, the multitude of hostas, or glossy-leaved fragrant sumac, look fresh and vibrant through the growing season, but leave a bare spot in winter. Where year-round appearance is important, choose evergreens, such as European wild ginger, heathers, Asian jasmine, myoporum, or bearberry.

Drawing on a photo is an easy way to visualize a design idea.

Guidelines for choosing plants

Because investing in a ground cover is a big commitment for most gardeners, it's worth reviewing these different points before making your final selection. If you can't answer all the questions yourself, ask for help from local garden clubs, botanic or public gardens, extension agents or master gardeners, nurseries or garden centers.

- Can the plant survive your climate's extremes of winter cold and summer heat? Does it need sun or shade, or tolerate either condition?
- Will it grow well in unamended soil, or does it need extra fertilizer and organic matter? Once established, does it survive on normal rainfall without watering?
- How fast will the planting fill in? Is the plant invasive, likely to spread out of bounds? Should you confine it with an edging?
- How often will the plant need pruning, grooming, or other maintenance? Is it subject to any insect or disease problems in your area?
- Can you find the plant locally, or get a nursery to order it for you? In what size is it sold? What's the recommended spacing? How many will you need? Can you find that many for sale? Is the cost within your budget?

Planting ground covers

The key to planting ground covers is taking the time and trouble to do the job right. That's because a ground cover is intended to be a long-term, low-maintenance part of the landscape. A few extra hours and dollars at planting time is a small price to pay for future years of carefree beauty.

Outline the bed

The first step is to determine the size and shape of the bed and outline it on the ground. One way to envision different options is to take some photographs of the area you're thinking about and have 4- by 6-inch or larger prints made. Draw directly on the photos with a china marker or wax pencil, or lay tracing paper over the photos and draw on that. When you have developed a shape you like, copy it in the garden by outlining the bed with a hose or a series of stakes. Keep the shape simple, with broad curves and no sharp angles, consider it from all sides, and keep adjusting it until it looks just right.

Eliminate weeds

Once established, most ground covers are effective weed barriers, but for the first year or two after planting, weeds can be a big problem in ground-cover beds. It's especially important to control perennial weeds like poison ivy, bindwind, ground ivy, and quack grass. Use one of the methods described on pp. 22–23. Eradicating these weeds takes patience and persistence, and the site will look ugly until the job is done, but if you don't destroy them before you plant a ground cover, you'll never get rid of them later.

Compared to perennials, annual weeds are a minor problem, easily controlled by covering the soil with a layer of mulch and hand-pulling any seedlings that sprout up through it.

Prepare the soil

How to prepare the soil depends on the nature of the site and how far apart the plants will be spaced. On fairly level sites and for plants spaced closer than 3 feet apart, work the whole bed, loosening the soil to a depth of 6 to 8 inches with a spading fork or rototiller, removing any rocks, roots, or debris. On steep slopes or rocky sites or for plants spaced 3 feet or farther apart, you can dig individual holes rather than working the whole bed. Measure a typical root ball, and dig the holes as deep as it is high, and three to five times as wide.

Popular, adaptable English ivy grows well in the dry shade under and around trees and shrubs.

Some ground covers don't need it, but in general, it's a good idea to amend the soil with a small dose of balanced, slow-release fertilizer and a generous portion of organic matter. Work these amendments into the soil; don't just scatter them on top.

Planting under shallow- or sensitive-rooted trees is a special situation; see p. 58 for how to proceed there.

Get healthy plants

A good local garden center or nursery will stock common ground cover plants and can order uncommon ones for you. Often these plants will be grown in containers, and you usually have the option of examining each plant before you buy. Look for bushy top growth with plenty of foliage and no more than a few dam aged or discolored leaves. Ask if it's okay to tip a sample plant out of its pot to check the roots. They should fill the soil and look firm and healthy, neither dry and tough nor rotten and mushy.

Sometimes local nurseries sell rooted cuttings of ground covers such as English ivy, honeysuckle, or pachysandra in flats, and mail-order nurseries sell bare-root rooted cuttings in bundles. (Order a sample bundle before investing in a quantity of plants by mail, especially if you haven't bought from that nursery before.) Rooted cuttings should have one or more stems with several leaves and a well-branched root system as large as the top growth. They usually cost much less than potted plants, but you need to space them closer together, be

more careful when planting them, pay more attention to watering afterwards, and wait longer before the planting looks mature.

Most ground covers are propagated by cutting or division, and when you buy a supply of plants from a single dealer, you'll probably be getting a clone, all propagated from the same origin. If you buy from different suppliers, though, there may be slight but noticeable differences in height, vigor, color, etc. If you suspect that you have two or more batches of plants, alternate them through out the bed like the squares of a checkerboard.

How many plants you need depends on the recommended spacing. Use the general guidelines on pp. 51–55 or ask the nursery for specific advice, measure your plot to determine its area in square feet, then calculate. For plants spaced 6 inches apart, multiply the number of square feet by four. For 8- or 9-inch spacing, multiply the square feet by two. For 1-foot spacing, buy one plant per square foot. For 2-foot spacing, divide the number of square feet by four. For 3-foot spacing, divide the number of square feet by nine.

Planting, mulching, watering

It's usually best to plant ground covers in spring or early summer where winters are cold. Where winters are mild, plant anytime from fall to spring.

As you lift plants out of their pots, check the roots and tease apart any dense tangles. Spread the loosened roots into the planting hole and gen-

tly firm the soil around them. Use a yardstick and check the spacing as you set each plant in place. Arrange the plants in straight or curving rows, and stagger adjacent rows so the spacing is equal in all directions.

Almost all ground covers benefit from a 2-inch mulch of composted bark, pine straw, or whatever else is popular in your area. To spread a layer this thick, you'll need about 1 cubic yard of mulch for each 150 square feet of bed. Some gardeners like to spread the mulch first and rake it out into an even layer, then dig down through it to set in the plants. That's okay *only if* you make sure that the plant roots are placed firmly in the soil, not just tucked into the mulch.

Even if you've chosen a ground cover that's adapted to dry sites or climates, it will probably need to be watered during the first year or so, until its roots are established. Other ground covers may need watering over the long term. Checking the soil is the best way to decide when to water. Use a paint stirrer or similar piece of unfinished, light-colored wood, stick it down through the mulch into the root zone, leave it for an hour or so, and pull it out. If the wood is pale and dry, water immediately. If the wood is dark with moisture, wait a day or two and check again. Depending on your climate and budget, you may want to install an automatic watering system, snake a soaker hose through the bed, or run a sprinkler when needed. Remember to water in cool weather as well as warm, whenever the soil is dry.

Recommended ground covers

The plants recommended here are usually available at local nurseries in the areas where they grow well, or you can get them from mail-order catalogs. Once established on a suitable site, these plants should thrive for years or decades with only occasional grooming, trimming, watering, or other care.

SHRUBS AS GROUND COVERS

The following shrubby ground covers are all low-growing (under 2 feet tall), with arching, creeping, or spreading stems that often root where they touch the ground. Some spread by suckers to form low thickets. These shrubs are usually sold in gallon cans, occasionally in quart cans. Most should be spaced 2 to 4 feet apart. Unless otherwise noted, these shrubs grow best in full sun.

Shrubs for acid soil

Bearberry (*Arctostaphylos uva-ursi*) is evergreen, with glossy round or oval leaves, white flowers, and red fruits like little apples. Zone 3. Several other species and cultivars of *Arctostaphylos* are popular and grow well in West Coast gardens.

Heathers (*Calluna vulgaris* cvs.) and **heaths** (*Erica*) form upright or spreading mounds of needle- or scale-like foliage that is green, gray, or gold in summer, often turning darker or bronzy in winter. A mixed planting of different heaths and heathers can bloom over a very long season. Zone 5; can't take hot summers.

Lowbush blueberry (*Vaccinium angustifolium*) is low and twiggy, with neat leaves that turn crimson in fall and very tasty berries. Zone 3. *V. crassifolium* **'Well's Delight'** bears few berries, but makes a beautiful carpet of evergreen foliage. Zone 7. **Cranberry** (*V. macrocarpon*) makes a low carpet of fine-textured evergreen leaves that turn garnet in winter. Even young plants bear fruit, and although cranberry tolerates wet soil, it does not require it. Zone 5.

Shrubs with showy flowers or fruits

Various **cotoneasters** (*Cotoneaster adpressa*, *C. dammeri*, *C. horizontalis*, *C. salicifolius*) are fast-spreading, low-growing shrubs with stiff stems that branch repeatedly, small deciduous or evergreen leaves, white flowers, and red fruits. Zone 5.

Forsythia **'Gold Tide'** is a new forsythia that grows low and wide, with bright yellow flowers in early spring. *F. viridissima* **'Bronxensis'** doesn't bloom as profusely or as early, but has a nice dense habit and especially neat foliage. Zone 5.

Two kinds of **brooms** (*Genista pilosa* 'Vancouver Gold', Zone 6; and *G. tinctoria* 'Royal Gold', Zone 4) make fast, low ground covers, with green twigs and masses of gold flowers in early summer.

Myoporum (*Myoporum parvifolium*) is prostrate and wide-spreading, with small evergreen leaves and white flowers in summer. Zone 8.

Memorial rose (*Rosa wichuriana*) has long trailing stems with few thorns, glossy semi-evergreen leaves, and clusters of fragrant, single, white flowers in early summer. There are also some new hybrid ground cover roses, such as 'White Meidiland'. Zone 5.

Creeping rosemaries (*Rosmarinus officinalis* 'Prostratus' and 'Irene') trail down slopes or over walls, with gray-green needlelike leaves and millions of tiny blue flowers in early spring. Zone 8.

Coralberries and **snowberries** (*Symphoricarpos*) form thickets of thin stems loaded with clusters of magenta, pink, coral, or white berries in fall and winter. Zone 4.

Shrubs for foliage

Many different **junipers** (*Juniperus*) either hug the ground or form low mounds of green, blue-green, silvery, or maroon foliage. Hardiness varies; ask a local nursery to recommend junipers for your area.

Siberian cypress (*Microbiota decussata*) has graceful, arching, plume-like shoots with soft foliage that is rich green in summer, purple-bronze in winter. Prefers part shade. Zone 3.

Fragrant sumac (*Rhus aromatica* 'Gro-Low') has fragrant, glossy, trifoliate leaves that turn bright red before dropping in fall. Tolerates part shade. Zone 3.

Mixed heathers

Dwarf creeping juniper

Euonymus 'Emerald Gaiety'

Creeping raspberry (*Rubus calycinioides*) makes a neat mat of crinkly, rounded leaves on creeping, thornless stems. Its berries are edible but bland. Tolerates part shade. Zone 6.

Cutleaf stephanandra (*Stephanandra incisa* 'Crispa') has low, arching stems lined with lacy deciduous foliage. Tolerates part shade. Zone 3.

VINES

Most vines, including those listed here, are vigorous climbers that can ensnarl adjacent plants, so be careful where you plant them. Except where noted, the following vines all have semi-evergreen or evergreen foliage. Most grow best in full sun but adapt well to part shade. Space vines purchased in quart or gallon cans 2 to 4 feet apart. Prune young plants hard to encourage them to branch near the base and spread in all directions. Give established plants a hard pruning every few years to restore their vigor and remove dead stems.

Akebia (*Akebia quinata*) has compound leaves with five oval leaflets, small but fragrant flowers in spring, and odd plump fruits in fall. Zone 4.

Wintercreeper (*Euonymus fortunei*) has thick, leathery, green or variegated leaves that turn pink, purple, or bronze in winter. There are many cultivars, some vining and some

bushy, with leaves of different sizes and colors. Zone 5.

English ivy (*Hedera helix*) has lobed leaves that are green or variegated, usually turning purple-bronze in cold weather. There are many cultivars, varying in size, vigor, and hardiness. Zone 6 or 5. **Persian ivy** (*H. colchica*) has large, coarse, lobed or heart-shaped leaves. Zone 6. **Canary Island ivy** (*H. canariensis*) has large leaves that are lobed or heart-shaped, green or variegated. Zone 8. Once established, all ivies are aggressive where winters are mild, but not in colder zones.

Climbing hydrangea (*Hydrangea petiolaris*) is usually trained up a tree or wall, but it can also scramble along the ground or over a rocky bank. The large, heart-shaped leaves are deciduous, but the bare stems are picturesque in winter, with crooked twigs and colorful shredding bark. Zone 5.

Japanese honeysuckle (*Lonicera japonica*) has dark foliage and very fragrant cream-colored flowers. It is quite invasive in the East, but not in the Southwest or West. Zone 5. **Trumpet honeysuckle** (*L. sempervirens*) is less aggressive and has waxy blue-green leaves and bright orange-red or yellow flowers that attract hummingbirds. Zone 4.

Virginia creeper (*Parthenocissus quinquefolia*) is deciduous, with large palmately compound leaves that turn bright red in fall. Zone 3.

Asian jasmine (*Trachelospermum asiaticum*) has slender runners lined with small glossy oval leaves and occasional white flowers. Zone 7. **Confederate jasmine** (*T. jasminoides*) has thicker stems, larger leaves and abundant, fragrant, creamy white flowers. Zone 8.

GRASSES AND GRASSY-LOOKING PLANTS

Like ferns, most ornamental grasses form distinct clumps which can be spaced close together for a more or less continuous cover, or not so close for a mounded, undulating effect. The following grasses and grasslike plants

spread by offsets or runners, thus filling an area and leaving few gaps for weeds. Space these plants 12 to 18 inches apart.

Running bamboo (*Arundinaria viridistriata*) is semi-evergreen, 30 inches tall, with green-and-gold striped leaves. Average soil, part shade. Zone 5.

Lilyturf (*Liriope muscari*) is semi-evergreen, 12 to 18 inches tall. It forms clumps of straplike green or variegated leaves and bears blue-violet or white flowers in summer. Average soil, sun or shade. Zone 6. **Creeping lilyturf** (*L. spicata*) is semi-evergreen, 12 inches tall, with narrow green leaves. It spreads by runners. Average soil, sun or shade. Zone 5.

Monkey grass or **mondo grass** (*Ophiopogon japonicus*) is evergreen, 6 to 12 inches tall, with slender dark green leaves and inconspicuous flowers. Average soil, part or full shade. Zone 7.

Ribbon grass (*Phalaris arundinacea* 'Picta') is deciduous, 2 to 3 feet tall, with bright green-and-white striped leaves. It grows in any soil, sun or shade. Mow it twice a year, in winter and summer, to remove shabby old leaves and promote new growth. Zone 4.

PERENNIALS FOR SHADY SITES

The perennials in this group tolerate full or part shade and can grow under trees or next to buildings. Most need well-drained, moderately fertile garden soil and regular watering during dry spells. None of these shade-lovers tolerate extreme summer heat in the South or Southwest; they go dormant or die out. All do well where summers aren't too hot.

These are mostly short plants, under 1 foot tall, that spread or creep to make a dense, continuous carpet of foliage. Some have inconspicuous flowers, but others make a solid patch of color when in bloom. Unless otherwise noted, plants can be spaced about 8 to 12 inches apart for cover in one or two years.

Variegated lilyturf

Bronze ajuga and hybrid astilbe

Variegated goutweed (*Aegopodium podagraria* 'Variegatum') is deciduous, with compound green-and-white leaves. Invasive, but useful where little else will grow. Zone 3.

Bugleweed or **ajuga** (*Ajuga reptans*) makes low patches of shiny semi-evergreen foliage. It tolerates damp soil and often invades lawns. There are many cultivars, with green, bronze, purple-black, pink-purple, or variegated leaves, topped with spikes of blue flowers in late spring. Zone 3.

European wild ginger (*Asarum euro paeum*) has beautiful, glossy, heart-shaped leaves. Zone 4. **Canadian wild ginger** (*A. canadense*) has larger, fuzzy, deciduous, heart-shaped leaves. Zone 3. Wild gingers spread slowly and don't look like much for the first few years after planting, but eventually make a solid cover.

Dwarf Chinese astilbe (*Astilbe chinensis* 'Pumila') spreads to form a patch, and has finely divided dark green leaves and fluffy pinkish purple flowers in late summer. Regular hybrid astilbes don't spread, but close-set clumps make an impressive ground cover with good foliage all season and stunning blooms. Zone 4.

Bergenias (*Bergenia*) form dense clumps or patches of large shiny evergreen leaves that turn from green to bronze or maroon in winter, and bear spikes of rose, pink, or white flowers in spring. Zone 3.

Green-and-gold (*Chrysogonum virginianum*) bears little yellow daisies off and on from early spring to late fall, over a mat of dark evergreen foliage. Zone 5.

Epimediums (*Epimedium*) are deciduous or semi-evergreen, with lacy compound leaves and small but interesting-looking flowers. Epimediums are expensive and slow-growing, but beautiful and long-lived. Zone 5.

Sweet woodruff (*Galium odoratum*) spreads quickly and can be invasive, but it's very useful under deciduous trees or shrubs. The small whorled leaves are bright green in summer. They dry out, turn tan, and release a pleasant aroma in winter. Starry white flowers open in late spring. Zone 4.

Alumroots (*Heuchera micrantha*, *H. americana*) form clumps of lovely semi-evergreen foliage. There are many new cultivars with purple, green, silvery, and variegated leaves. Remove the long stalks of tiny flowers if you find them distracting. Zone 4.

Hostas (*Hosta*) are very popular perennial ground covers for shady sites, and there are hundreds of cultivars to choose from. Hostas make dense clumps that broaden from year to year, soon filling a bed. The deciduous leaves can be narrow or broad; small or large; green, blue-green, gold, or variegated with white. Spikes of lilac, purple, or white flowers lift

above the foliage in mid- to late summer. Hosta foliage reaches 1 to 3 feet tall; flowerstalks reach 2 to 5 feet. Space large-growing hostas 2 to 3 feet apart. Zone 3.

Yellow archangel (*Lamiastrum galeobdolon*) has semi-evergreen green-and-silver leaves and bears yellow flowers in late spring. 'Herman's Pride' is a popular cultivar. Zone 5.

Spotted dead nettle (*Lamium maculatum*) has pink or white flowers in summer and semi-evergreen leaves on trailing stems. Variegated cultivars with green-and-silver leaves are especially nice. Zone 4.

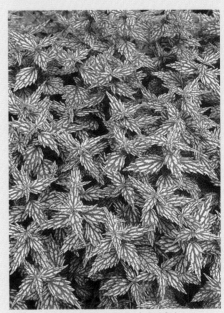

Yellow archangel 'Herman's Pride'

Lungwort

Common **pachysandra** (*Pachysandra terminalis*) has glossy, thick-textured leaves that are rich green in summer, yellow-green in winter. There's also a variegated form, with white-edged leaves. Zone 5.

Lungworts (*Pulmonaria*) flower for weeks in early spring in shades of blue, pink, or white. They form low clumps or patches of large, hairy leaves that are spotted or edged with silver. They may go dormant in summer, but leaf out again in fall and look good into winter. Zone 3.

Foamflower (*Tiarella cordifolia*) has fuzzy evergreen leaves, shaped like small maple leaves, and myriad spikes of tiny white flowers in spring. It sends out long runners and spreads quickly, but isn't really invasive. Zone 3.

Periwinkle or **myrtle** (*Vinca minor*) knits a tangle of trailing stems covered with small glossy evergreen leaves and has blue-violet flowers in spring. There are lovely variegated and white-flowered cultivars. Zone 4. *V. major* has larger leaves and longer runners. Zone 7.

Sweet violet (*Viola odorata*) spreads by runners and by seed, often invading lawns. It makes patches of heart-shaped, dark, evergreen leaves and bears very fragrant purple or white flowers in early spring, sometimes reblooming in fall and weather. Zone 4.

PERENNIALS FOR SUNNY SITES

There are three groups listed below, sorted by height.

Short ground covers

The plants in this group stay very low, under 6 inches tall. Space them 8 to 12 inches apart.

Irish moss (*Arenaria verna*) and **pearlwort** (*Sagina subulata*) are mossy-looking plants with pale green leaves and tiny white flowers. Zone 4.

Dichondra (*Dichondra micrantha*) has rich green, dime-size leaves and inconspicuous flowers. Zone 9.

Blue-star creeper (*Laurentia fluviatilis*) looks almost mossy but is larger and much more vigorous. It has bright green leaves, light blue flowers. Prefers moist soil. Zone 8.

Moneywort (*Lysimachia nummularia*) has flat creeping stems, round green or gold leaves, and bright yellow flowers in early summer. Prefers moist soil. Zone 3.

Mazus (*Mazus reptans*) has hairy leaves and two-lipped lilac or white flowers in summer. Zone 3.

Moss phlox (*Phlox subulata*) has prickly, mossy, evergreen foliage. One of the showiest ground covers, it bears masses of white, pink, rose, or lilac flowers in early spring. Zone 2.

Mother-of-thyme (*Thymus pulegioides*) and other thymes form tangled mats of thin wiry stems, clothed with fragrant evergreen leaves and topped with tiny pink, lilac, or white flowers in summer. Zone 4.

There are several low, creeping forms of **veronicas** (*Veronica*) that form glossy, semi-evergreen leaves studded with clear blue flowers in spring. Try *V. prostrata* 'Heavenly Blue', *V. repens*, or *V.* 'Waterperry'. Zone 5.

Mid-height ground covers

These plants grow 6 to 12 inches tall. Space them 12 to 18 inches apart.

Beach wormwood (*Artemisia stelleriana*) forms a patch of scalloped, silver-gray, semi-evergreen leaves. Zone 4.

Snow-in-summer (*Cerastium tomentosum*) has fuzzy, silver-gray leaves and masses of white flowers in early summer. Zone 3.

Dwarf plumbago (*Ceratostigma plumbaginoides*) has sky blue flowers from late summer until hard frost, and leaves that turn maroon in fall. It dies back in winter. Zone 6.

Most **pinks** (*Dianthus*) form short, grassy semi-evergreen mats of gray-green or blue-green leaves and bear white, pink, or rosy flowers in early summer. Zone 4.

Bigroot geranium (*Geranium macrorrhizum*) and the hybrid *G. x cantabrigiense* both have showy pink or purplish flowers in early summer and slightly hairy, very fragrant, lobed leaves that are medium green in summer, turning reddish purple in cold weather. Cultivars of bloody cranesbill (*G. sanguineum* are also good ground covers, with finely divided leaves and white, pink, or magenta flowers. Zone 5.

'Homestead Purple', 'Sissinghurst', and other hybrids of **rose verbena** (*Verbena canadensis*) form broad mats of fine-cut, semi-evergreen foliage and bear clusters of pink or purple flowers over a very long season. Zone 6.

Bloody cranesbill

Taller ground covers

These reach 1 foot or taller. Space them 1 to 2 feet apart.

Old-fashioned **tawny daylily** (*Hemerocallis fulva*) and sweet-scented yellow **lemon lily** (*H. lilio-asphodelus*) both spread by runners and make patches of long grassy leaves, topped with showy flowers on long stalks. New hybrid daylilies make clumps that don't spread as fast, but if planted fairly close together they make good ground covers with wonderful orange, yellow, red, pink, mauve, or creamy white flowers. Most daylilies grow 2 to 4 feet tall; a few are shorter or taller. Zone 4.

St. John's-worts (*Hypericum calycinum*, *H. patulum*, *H. 'Hidcote'*) are shrubby perennials with graceful arching stems, fresh-looking foliage, and showy yellow flowers. They adapt to sun or shade. Cut old stems to the ground in spring to stimulate new growth. Zone 6.

Showy evening primrose (*Oenothera speciosa*) grows 1 to 2 feet tall, bears large pink flowers in summer, and dies down in winter. Zone 6. **Sundrops** (*O. tetragona*) is similar, with golden yellow flowers. Zone 4.

SUCCULENTS

Succulent ground covers thrive on hot, sunny sites. They're a good choice for slopes or banks that face south or west, or for planting beds adjacent to pavement or buildings that reflect heat. Succulents tolerate dense, dry, infertile soil, but they certainly don't require such harsh conditions. Most succulents actually grow and look best when planted in loose, well-drained soil amended with some organic matter, and they respond well to an occasional deep watering during summer dry spells. Mulch only with sand or gravel, not with leaves, bark, or other organic mulch. Succulent ground covers can be invaded by weedy grasses and other weeds and may need regular hand weeding. These are all short plants, under 6 inches tall. Spacing varies.

Several kinds of **sedums** or **stone-crops** (*Sedum*) form low, spreading patches of thin, rubbery stems lined with plump leaves that may drop off in fall or last all winter, and bear bright, showy yellow, pink, or white flowers that attract butterflies. Some kinds stay neat and compact, like a pad of moss; others are rampant growers that can be weedy. Shop for sedums in fall—that's the best time to judge how vigorous the plants are, and whether or not they're evergreen. These plants are fun to collect and easy to propagate, so local nurseries often have some interesting, unusual finds. Most sedums tolerate dry heat but not humidity. Hardiness varies.

Hens-and-chicks (*Sempervivum tectorum*) forms a densely crowded mat of ball-shaped rosettes, with evergreen, fleshy, triangular leaves that are usually gray-green but can have a gold, red, or purple tinge. The older, larger rosettes send up a stalk of pink flowers in summer, then die, but adjacent rosettes soon expand to fill the gap. Shop around, and you can soon collect several unnamed variants from this and related species. All are charming and carefree, good for filling gaps or cracks in stone walls or walkways. Zone 3.

Ice plants have creeping stems; fleshy fingerlike leaves; and many-petalled round flowers in vivid, even gaudy, shades of pink, purple, red, orange, and yellow. *Carpobrotus edulis*, *Drosanthemum floribundum*, and *Lampranthus* spp. are tender ice plants, popular along the California coast. Zone 9. Two **hardy ice plants**, *Delosperma cooperi* and *D. nubigena*, are prostrate plants with small plump leaves, hardy to Zone 6 or 5 if protected with a light winter mulch. Space ice plants 18 to 24 inches apart.

Hardy prickly pears (*Opuntia humifusa*, *O. polycantha*) form low patches of succulent "pads" that are fleshy and green in summer, wrinkled and purple in winter. The large, waxy, yellow or pink flowers are very showy in early summer, followed by purple fruits in fall. These plants don't spread fast, and it's hard to weed around

Hens-and-chicks

them, but they look unique and fill difficult dry spots where little else will grow. Zone 4.

FERNS

Most ferns form clumps and don't spread fast enough to fill an area unless planted rather close together. The following ferns, however, have creeping rhizomes and spread to form a dense, weed-proof patch. All need part or full shade and average or rich soil with regular watering during summer dry spells. Space small potted plants or divisions 1 to 2 feet apart.

Maidenhair fern (*Adiantum pedatum*) is deciduous, 1 to 2 feet tall, with jet-black stalks and bright green, delicate-looking leaflets. Zone 3. **Southern maidenhair** (*A. capillis-veneris*) is similar but shorter, and semi-evergreen. Zone 8.

Hay-scented fern (*Dennstaedtia punctilobula*) is deciduous, 2 feet tall, with fine-textured fronds that smell good when cut and dried. Zone 3.

Sword fern (*Nephrolepis cordifolia*) is evergreen, 2 to 3 feet tall, with stiff, bright green fronds. Zone 9.

Wood fern (*Thelypteris kunthii*) is deciduous, 2 to 3 feet tall, with medium green, finely divided fronds. It's especially good for Southern gardens. Zone 8.

Removing the lower limbs and thinning the canopies of these existing white pine trees made it possible to grow rhododendrons, azaleas, and other acid-loving evergreen shrubs below, as seen here in late fall.

GARDENING
UNDER A TREE

I f you live in a house that's more than a few decades old, your lot probably features at least one big tree that someone planted years ago. Or perhaps you live in a forested region and have a few wild trees that the builder spared. Either way, a mature tree is a treasure, but it can dominate your whole yard.

Some trees are such perfect specimens that they deserve to dominate the yard. For example, if you have a holly, spruce, beech, or magnolia whose limbs sweep the ground like a long skirt, I'd advise you to count your blessings and leave it alone. Pruning the lower limbs off a tree like this destroys its dignity. But if you have an oak, apple, ash, or any other tree whose lower limbs have already been removed, why not use the space beneath it for a garden?

Certain trees have bad reputations. You may have heard that nothing will grow under beeches, black walnuts, blue gum eucalyptus, hemlocks, lindens, Norway or silver maples, and most spruces. Beware of such generalizations. Granted, some trees are more accommodating than others, but I've seen beautiful gardens under all kinds of trees. In my view, what matters is not the kind of tree, but the *individual* tree, its particular site, and how you respond to the challenges that they present.

What's growing there now

To assess what you might grow beneath a particular tree, start by observing what's already there.

A healthy lawn is a sign that you have lots of options. Anywhere turf grass is thriving, many other kinds of plants would grow just as well.

A sparse lawn, tattered shrub, or even a weedy ground cover shows that *something* can survive under the tree, but suggests that light is limited and the soil is dry, shallow, and infertile. You can improve these conditions,

and also choose plants better adapted to them.

Totally bare ground under a tree usually means that the soil is poor and riddled with tree roots, and that the tree casts dense shade. Even so, there's hope. You can prune the tree to reduce the shade, then plant in raised beds or make a container garden. Many shade-loving plants grow just as well in containers as they do in the ground.

How pruning can help

Sit underneath your tree on a sunny summer day and look up and around. How much sky can you see? The more the better, because anyplace where you can see up to the sky, light can shine down, to the benefit of any plants growing under the tree. It doesn't have to be direct sun. Indirect light is good, too.

Go back out on a rainy summer day and sit under the tree again. How wet do you get? The wetter the better. If rain drips through a tree's canopy, plants underneath have a chance to absorb it. But some trees are like umbrellas; water flows over their canopy and drips off the outer edge (hence the term "drip line"). Under the canopy, the ground stays dry and plants go thirsty.

If your tree blocks the sky and the rain, consider removing its lower limbs and thinning its canopy. The extra light and water would make it much easier to grow smaller plants underneath the tree, in the ground or in pots, and thoughtful pruning can make the tree itself more attractive.

You can prune limbs as thick as your arm and 10 to 15 feet off the ground by reaching up with a pole saw. For limbs thicker or higher than that, call an arborist. Check references to make sure you're hiring someone with an eye for form, not just a firewood-chopper, and try to be home when the job is done, so you can ask

questions and make suggestions. Don't let anyone butcher the tree by "topping" it (cutting the top off).

Check the tree's roots

To see what you'll encounter in planting under a tree, try digging a test hole. Choose a place, insert your spade, and see what you find. Did you hit any tree roots? Try again in a different spot. If you can dig without finding tree roots, give a cheer. Planting will be easy and whatever you plant will have its own root zone.

But if you find many tree roots close to the surface, that's a warning that you must choose tough plants whose roots are aggressive enough to compete with the tree. It's also smart to choose plants that will spread sideways, so you can start them at relatively wide spacing. The fewer planting holes you dig, the less you

Look up to see how much light shines through a tree.

57

Hostas thrive under trees, form dense clumps, and are long-lived and carefree.

will damage the tree's roots. And don't forget the other alternatives for planting under shallow-rooted trees: raised beds and containers.

Use what you've learned about the tree's roots in deciding how to remove any lawn, shrub, or anything else that's growing under the tree now. If you've determined that the tree's reach are out of the shovel's reach, it's okay to strip sod or dig plants out by the roots. But if the tree's roots are close to the surface, minimize your digging and eliminate the vegetation by smothering it (see p. 23).

Favor the underplanting

An established tree has such a head start that whatever you plant beneath it may need extra help getting started. Take these steps to assist new plants:

Build up the soil. If the old soil has worn thin or the tree roots are crowded near the surface, spread a layer of fresh new soil over the area where you want to do some planting. Start by papering the area with newspaper, then spread good topsoil 4 to 12 inches deep around the perimeter of the bed, but not within 12 inches of the tree trunk. Plant the ground cover into the new topsoil. The paper makes a temporary barrier that helps keep tree roots out of the way until the ground cover gets established.

Use mulch. A mulch of shredded leaves, composted bark, or other organic matter helps keep the soil moist and cool, and supplies some nutrients, too. Don't spread it more than a few inches deep, and don't put any mulch right next to the tree trunk, since damp mulch can rot the tree's bark.

Fertilize. A mature tree doesn't need fertilizing, but the plants underneath it probably do. Spray or sprinkle a dilute solution of your favorite soluble fertilizer on their foliage a few times during the growing season.

Irrigate during droughts. When water is limited, a tree takes more than its share and plants underneath it go thirsty. Watering can help them get by. For dry climates or chronically dry sites, though, it's better to plan ahead and choose drought-tolerant plants.

Take a chance

Experts warn that anything you do under a tree that changes the conditions around its roots, or actually wounds its roots, can be harmful. This includes compacting the soil, removing soil, adding soil, adding mulch, starting or ceasing to water, applying fertilizers or herbicides, digging and cultivating, putting in new plants, laying pavement, and whatever else you might do in the course of making a garden.

In fact, if you do anything too drastic, you might even kill the tree. This happens sometimes, although root damage kills a tree so slowly—it may take years to die—that people often fail to draw the connection between the original cause and the final result.

More typically your actions will give the tree just a minor setback. They might even give it a little boost. If you're concerned, spread the work over a few years. Make changes a little at a time, not all at once. Give the tree time to adapt.

But don't be too timid. After all, trees recover from storms, droughts, insect attacks, and other natural disasters. They can usually put up with gardeners, too.

Try replacing the lawn under a tree with shrubs, vines, and ground covers such as winterberry holly and lamb's ears (top) or sweet autumn clematis and periwinkle (above).

Ferns

Ferns are an ideal choice for planting under trees, because that's where many ferns grow naturally. Once established, they typically live for decades and need very little care. Slugs, scale insects, and spider mites may bother them, but deer and other mammals usually leave ferns alone. Diseases are uncommon.

Your local garden center may have only a few kinds of ferns, but several dozen species and cultivars are available by mail. Nurseries don't always say what they're selling, but if you have a choice, I recommend buying container-grown ferns. Ferns that were grown in the ground and then dug up and stuck into pots or sold bare-root usually take longer to get established in your garden. In any case, watch newly planted ferns for at least a year and water them whenever the soil gets dry.

Interrupted fern

Ferns for your site

Here's a checklist of factors to consider when choosing a fern.

- Soil moisture. Most ferns need moist soil. Some that tolerate fairly dry sites are hay-scented fern (*Dennstaedtia punctilobula*),

Brown-eyed Susan

Japanese autumn fern (*Dryopteris erythrosora*), soft shield fern (*Polystichum setiferum*), common polypody (*Polypodium vulgare*), and wood fern (*Thelypteris kunthii*).
- Shade. The amount of shade on the east or north side of a tree is enough for most ferns.
- Size, habit, and vigor. Ferns vary more than you might expect. They can be stay under 6 inches or reach over 6 feet tall, form erect clumps or broad patches, stay in place or spread rampantly. You can use them as specimens, backgrounds, edgings, or ground covers.
- Deciduous or evergreen fronds. Evergreen ferns are attractive all year. Deciduous species may go dormant early on dry sites or in dry summers.

A few favorite ferns

Interrupted fern (*Osmunda claytoniana*) forms a clump of deciduous fronds 3 to 5 feet tall, and tolerates fairly dry, rocky soil. Cinnamon fern (*O. cinnamomea*) looks similar but needs damp, even wet, soil. Both are native to the eastern United States and hardy to Zone 3.

Western sword fern (*Polystichum munitum*), native to West Coast forests, forms large clumps of leathery evergreen fronds 2 to 4 feet long. Zone 7. Christmas fern (*P. acrostichoides*), native to Eastern forests, is similar but smaller, with fronds only 1 to 2 feet long. Zone 3.

Japanese painted fern (*Athyrium niponicum* 'Pictum') forms colorful clumps of deciduous fronds 1 to 2 feet long. Zone 4.

Sword fern

Wildflowers

Many wildflowers that are native to open woodlands or forest edges are good candidates for planting under a tree in your yard. They combine well with ferns and are equally care-free and persistent when established on a suitable site. Almost all woodland wildflowers are perennials, and they tend to spread by runners or by seed to form dense, showy patches. They usually die down to the ground in fall or winter; you can remove the old stalks to be neat or ignore them.

Flowers from spring to fall

Most wildflowers native to deciduous woodland, such as hepaticas, trilliums, and violets, bloom in early spring before the trees leaf out. A garden featuring these species is glorious for a few weeks and quiet thereafter. Fortunately, other wildflowers suitable for planting under trees bloom later in the season. Including some of these late-bloomers will keep your garden colorful for many months.

For example, here are some readily-available species, all hardy at least to Zone 5, with blue or white flowers in summer and/or fall: pearly everlasting (*Anaphalis margaritacea*), goats-beard (*Aruncus dioicus*), white wood aster (*Aster divaricatus*), hardy ageratum and white snakeroot (*Eupatorium coelestinum* and *E. rugosum*), blue lobelia (*Lobelia siphilitica*), and Stoke's aster (*Stokesia laevis*).

Other favorites, shown below, are Solomon's seal (*Polygonatum biflorum*), blooms in spring, 2 to 4 feet tall; wild bleeding heart (*Dicentra eximia*), spring to fall, 1 to 2 feet; bergamot (*Monarda fistulosa*), summer, 3 to 4 feet; and brown-eyed Susan (*Rudbeckia triloba*), fall, 2 to 3 feet. All are hardy to Zone 3, and need part sun and average soil.

Choosing and acquiring plants

In choosing wildflowers to plant under a tree, the most important factors to consider are how sunny or shady it is there, and how dry the soil gets in summer. Without enough sun, wildflowers may grow but not bloom. Without enough water, they may go dormant early, or they may even die. Spend time observing the conditions under your tree, and choose plants whose requirements match the site.

Please don't dig plants from the wild. Many nurseries sell wildflower plants for very reasonable prices. As with ferns, wildflowers that have been growing in 4-inch or larger containers are quick to settle into your garden; bare-root plants usually take more time and care. Check seed catalogs, too. Some wildflowers are easily grown from seeds and bloom in their first or second year.

Solomon's-seal

Bergamot

Bleeding-heart

Japanese painted fern

61

Evergreen shrubs

Grouping a few shrubs under a tree can be an easy way to fill that empty space. Well-sited shrubs are long-term, low-maintenance plants. And while some deciduous shrubs can grow there also, it seems that evergreens have two key advantages for survival under a tree. Being evergreen, their leaves can conduct photosynthesis on warm, bright days from fall to spring, when sunshine reaches farther under the tree but deciduous shrubs are dormant. Extending the growing season in this way helps compensate for being shaded in summer. Also, evergreen leaves are typically more leathery and slower to wilt than deciduous leaves. This helps when a tree and shrub are competing for limited water during dry spells.

Choosing shrubs to grow under a tree

Not all evergreens do well under trees. Some need more light. Most conifers, in particular, get weak and leggy without full sun. Broadleaf evergreens, too, show too much stem and too few leaves when they're not getting enough light, and they flower sparsely if at all. They'll survive for years in a too-dark place, but never thrive. Observe the light levels under your tree and choose plants accordingly.

Mountain laurel

Identify the characteristics of the soil—is it shallow or deep; all mineral or amended with organic matter; acid, neutral, or alkaline? Some evergreens need acid soil; if you don't have that, you may be able to compensate by adding peat moss and mulching with pine bark. Or you could choose more adaptable shrubs. As for soil moisture, if the tree survives without supplemental watering, you can probably find shrubs that will, too, once they're established.

The three shrubs shown below need part sun and tolerate fairly dry, acid soil. Mountain laurel (*Kalmia latifolia*) has white, pink, or rose flowers in June. The popular new cultivars grow 4 to 8 feet tall. Zone 4. Cherry laurel (*Prunus laurocerasus*) can be a tree, but 'Schipkaensis', 'Zabeliana', and 'Otto Luyken' are low, spreading cultivars, all with very fragrant white flowers in late spring. Zone 7 or 6. Creeping holly grape (*Mahonia repens*) has yellow flowers in spring and grows 1 to 2 feet tall and 3 to 4 feet wide. Zone 4.

Planting container-grown shrubs

Most shrubs today are grown and sold in plastic pots. It's a dandy system, convenient and reliable, if you take some precautions at planting time. When you lift the shrub out of its pot, study the roots. If you see any coarse roots circling the sides or bottom of the pot, cut them off short, leaving stubs that point out like whiskers. If the rootball seems to be a mass of fine roots, take a sharp knife and cut three or four grooves from top to bottom. This pruning or slicing may seem drastic, but it forces the shrub (or any other container-grown plant, for that matter) to send its new roots out into the surrounding soil. Otherwise, they might keep circling for years as if they were still confined by the pot.

Cherry laurel

Vines

If you're tempted to think of your tree's trunk as a vacant trellis that needs to be decorated with a vine, think twice. There are vines, and there are vines. Only a few stay small. Although they may need help getting started up a tree, once they're underway, most vines grow faster than you expect, get bigger than you want, and respond to pruning with increased vigor. And once a vine has climbed up into the canopy of a tree, it's hard to pull it back down.

Vines that can overtake a tree

Have you ever seen whole trees buried under a snarl of vines? Contrary to folklore, vines rarely choke a tree, but a big vine can certainly weaken a tree by shading its leaves and competing for water, and the extra mass of the vine makes the tree more susceptible to wind and ice damage.

The following vines are potential trouble-makers, especially across the southern half of the United States. It's okay to plant them against a sturdy fence or arbor or beside a building, but don't encourage them to run up into your trees. This group includes: five-leaf akebia (*Akebia quinata*), trumpet creeper (*Campsis radicans*); Oriental bittersweet (*Celastrus orbiculatus*); vigorous clematis such as *Clematis armandii* and *C. montana*; violet trumpet vine (*Clytostoma callistigioides*); blood-red trumpet vine (*Distictis buccinatoria*); creeping fig (*Ficus pumila*); common, large-leaved forms of English ivy (*Hedera helix*); Algerian ivy and Persian ivy (*H. canariensis* and *H. colchica*); Japanese honeysuckle (*Lonicera japonica*); passionflowers (*Passiflora*); silver fleece vine (*Polygonum aubertii*); massive climbing roses such as *Rosa banksiae* or *R. filipes* 'Kiftsgate'; grapes (*Vitis*); and any wisterias (*Wisteria*).

Creeping holly grape

Nonthreatening vines

Not all vines are nuisances. Some are compact, slow-growing, or easily managed, and—this is an important point when planting under a tree—they tolerate part shade. The following examples grow well in containers or in the ground. They shouldn't need it, but keeping them potted is a way to limit their growth.

Confederate jasmine (*Trachelospermum jasminoides*) has wonderfully fragrant white flowers in late spring or summer and neat, glossy, evergreen leaves. It isn't a vigorous climber and usually doesn't grow taller than 15 feet (it can also be used as a ground cover). Zone 8. 'Buttercup' and other fancy-leaved cultivars are much more manageable than common English ivy (*Hedera helix*). They'll slowly climb 5 to 15 feet, but rarely higher. Most are hardy to Zone 6.

A few other mild-mannered vines for part shade under a tree are: downy clematis (*Clematis macropetala*), double flowers in shades of blue and white, deciduous, climbs to about 10 feet, Zone 5; decumaria (*Decumaria barbara*), white flowers, deciduous, climbs to about 20 feet, Zone 7; Carolina jasmine (*Gelsemium sempervirens*), fragrant yellow flowers, evergreen, prune to keep it below 10 feet, Zone 7; climbing hydrangea (*Hydrangea petiolaris*), white flowers, deciduous, slowly reaches 25 feet or taller, Zone 5; and woodbine honeysuckle (*Lonicera periclymenum*), fragrant flowers, semi-evergreen, climbs 10 to 20 feet, Zone 6.

Confederate jasmine

'Buttercup' ivy

Gardening without digging

If a tree's roots are crowded near the surface of the soil or exposed on top of the soil, digging underneath it spells hard work for you and trouble for the tree. Worse yet, shallow or exposed roots are often a symptom of a more basic problem: terrible soil. This situation calls for a different approach. Instead of digging holes and planting down into the ground, start at ground level and build upwards.

Deciding what to do

You could cover part or all of the area with raised beds or a simple topping of fresh soil, and plant a tough ground cover or a combination of sturdy ferns, perennials, and shrubs. A new planting like this would be a welcome addition to a tree that's exposed to public view in your front or side yard. But if the tree shades your back yard, the area underneath might be private enough to treat as an outdoor "room," with a simple floor, limbs for a ceiling, some furniture, and potted plants for decoration. This would be a pleasant place to eat, relax, play, or entertain.

Along with location, here's another basis for deciding what to do. If the tree drops messy or annoying litter, don't make a room under it. An outdoor room under a messy tree means one more floor to clean, and that's no fun. Make a room under a neat tree. Put a loose, informal planting under a messy tree, so the litter can sink down into it and disappear.

Making raised beds

Raised beds look impressive, but they're easy to make. You can do it yourself in a weekend or two.

First, decide what size and shape you want the bed(s) to be. Mark the corners and curves with stakes or spray paint. Decide how high you want to raise the bed. Measure the area and depth of the bed, and calculate how much soil you'll need to fill it. One cubic yard—about a pickup load—will cover 100 square feet to a depth of 3 inches. Any local landscape contractor can deliver soil to you.

Choose an edging material— stones, bricks, landscape timbers, bender boards, prefab edgings, or whatever suits your design and budget. Install the edging. Be sure it's sturdy and secure.

Spread plenty of newspapers on the ground inside the bed as a temporary barrier to keep the tree roots from rushing up into the new soil, then shovel the soil into the bed. The soil will settle partway after a few weeks, so heap it up a little higher than the edging at first. Use a rake or board to smooth and level it.

Water the bed right after you plant it and as often as needed afterwards. Use mulch to help keep the soil moist.

Making an outdoor room

First raise the "ceiling" then surface the "floor"—you're ready to move in.

Prune off any limbs that make you duck or get in your way. The higher you prune, the better—it's makes the difference between having your room feel like a basement or an atrium.

The ideal "floor" surface is level and pleasant to walk on, doesn't scatter when you rake or blow leaves away, and lets rain soak through. Bare, swept earth is fine in hot, dry climates but gets muddy elsewhere. Wood or bark chips are loose at first, but gradually compress into a quiet, resilient carpet. Like other mulch, chips decompose into the soil. That's good for the tree, but means you have to add a fresh layer every few years. Pea gravel is

Hostas

Caladium

Coleus

Tuberous begonia

noisy, hard to walk on, and doesn't stay put, but crushed or "processed" rock packs as solid as a granola bar. You could lay bricks or pavers under a tree, over a sand base. A wooden deck raised a few inches off the ground is the ultimate floor, and not too difficult or expensive to build.

Choose some weatherproof outdoor furniture—a table and chairs, bench, or hammock. Start collecting planters and pots big enough to stand on the ground. Buy or build some shelves or a platform where you can display smaller plants.

Plants for a shady room

Your houseplants would love to spend the summer outdoors under a shady tree. Just be very careful, when you first bring them out, not to set them in a sunny place even temporarily. Even a few minutes of sudden exposure to full sun can burn a houseplant's leaves, making big bleached spots that never go away.

Wax and tuberous begonias, caladiums, calla lilies, coleus, fuchsias, Martha Washington geraniums, regular and New Guinea impatiens, and petunias thrive in containers and are colorful all summer. Although we call them annuals or bedding plants, all of these plants are actually tender perennials, so you can keep them from year to year as houseplants if you choose. But it's easy to buy new ones each spring.

Many of the ferns, shrubs, and vines named earlier grow well in large pots or planters. Several popular shade-loving perennials such as hostas and astilbes do, too. When they outgrow their pots, you can divide and replant them or move them to the ground. To protect the plants through cold winters, move the containers into an unheated building. Or, choose plants that are hardy in zones colder than yours.

Houseplants

A row of lilacs makes a fragrant hedge, or you can train a single plant into an upright, treelike shape.

SHAPING YOUR
GARDEN WITH SHRUBS

Shrubs are the basic building blocks of a garden. Use them to enclose an area, edge a bed, mark a transition, screen a view, or hug a building. Feature individual shrubs as specimens or accents, mass them to cover or fill big spaces, design beds and borders around them. Shrubs can be background or foreground, the picture or the frame. They're the most versatile and varied group of plants.

What counts as a shrub?

Any plant that's commonly called a bush, such as a rose bush or lilac bush, illustrates the basic concept of a shrub—a medium-sized plant with several woody stems. But those familiar, bushy shrubs are just the beginning. There are treelike shrubs tall enough to shade a patio. Wee dwarf shrublets you can grow in flowerpots. Floppy shrubs that sprawl like vines. Creeping shrubs that cling to the ground. Stiff, angular, shrubby palms and yuccas and bamboos. Sub-shrubs, dieback shrubs, and shrubby perennials have stems that freeze back partway in cold winters, because they are woody at the base but soft on top. All of these plants are shrubs.

Celebrate diversity

Shrubs can be tall or short, stiff or floppy, fat or skinny. Some grow fast (several feet a year!); others just inches per year. Their leaves can be tiny or huge, thick or thin, shiny or dull, evergreen or deciduous, in shades of green, gray, gold, purple, and vivid fall colors. Different shrubs bear colorful flowers and fruits in every season. Shrub flowers (and leaves, too) can be sweet- or spicy-scented.

With so much to choose from, it's disappointing that a limited number of cheap, fast-growing, stereotyped shrubs dominate the marketplace. But thousands of kinds of outstanding shrubs *are* available, if you seek them out from top-quality local and mail-order nurseries. To distinguish your garden, plant the most wonderful shrubs you can find. They'll grow into living treasures.

Shrub life spans

Some shrubs could live as long as trees do, but that usually doesn't happen. Pests, diseases, storms, and accidents take their toll, or we remove old shrubs to try something new.

Also, most modern landscapes are designed to look "full" as soon as possible. After 10 or 20 years, a planting can get so crowded that it has to be replaced. Right now, your lot may be overgrown and brushy, bare and undeveloped, or in-between and just right. In any case, you'll want to work with the shrubs you have, and to add more shrubs to your garden.

Choosing and buying plants

It's worth planning ahead before you go shopping for shrubs. If you usually buy plants first and decide where to plant them later, taking a more deliberate approach—first itemizing your growing conditions and design goals, then picking shrubs to meet them—may seem difficult. But compare it to shopping for a particular item of clothing, such as a casual jacket, size 12, that's warm but lightweight, with a zip front, in dark blue.

Picking shrubs can work the same way. With clothes or plants, if you can say exactly what you want, you're more likely to find it. For example, you might want a shrub for a sunny site with good soil, that's hardy to

Zone 5, gets 4 to 6 feet tall, has showy flowers or colorful foliage, and does not get eaten by deer. In this case, variegated red-twig dogwood, 'Miss Kim' lilac, and 'Snowmound' spiraea are three shrubs that would meet all the qualifications.

There are "plant-finder" books and electronic media designed to help you choose plants for particular situations, or you can compile your own lists by reading about and observing plants. If you're uncertain, check your ideas by discussing them with other gardeners, or seek advice from professional landscape designers.

When you decide on a certain kind of shrub, if you can't find one at your favorite garden center, ask if they can order it for you from a wholesale grower. It may take awhile, but a good shop will try to get you what you want. Or you can order shrubs by mail. Mail-order plants are typically smaller than shrubs you'd find locally, but they cost less, and they soon grow to catch up.

Planting shrubs

If you allow enough space for a shrub to develop and reach its typical mature width, the area will look bare for the first few years. It's okay to use other plants to fill the space around a young shrub, as long as they're shorter than it is. Start a low-growing perennial ground cover, for example, perhaps adding some small bulbs for spring flowers.

Short annuals, such as sweet alyssum, wax begonia, lobelia, pansies, annual phlox, and portulaca make good temporary fillers that you can replace as needed until the shrub has filled out. Don't let annual fillers or any other adjacent plants get taller than the shrub or flop against it. Cut them back if this happens, so the shrub can get light and air. When planting or removing annuals, be careful not to disturb the shrub's roots.

Lilac

Holly

Boxwood

Geometry in the garden

These two paintings illustrate different approaches to gardening with shrubs. In the formal garden above, the shrubs are sheared into uniform, geometric shapes. In the informal garden below, the shrubs are hand-pruned just enough to clarify their natural shapes. Both gardens are neat, and all the shrubs look healthy and cared for, but the pictures give you different feelings, don't they?

Shape is so important. Much more than the details of their flowers and foliage, it's how you shape your shrubs that determines the character of your garden, and communicates your attitude toward plants. You probably have a preference for one approach or the other—either the closely sheared, controlled look or the lightly groomed, natural look, but it's worth considering them both.

Why shear?

Many suburban homeowners routinely shear all their shrubs. Why? For convenience (shearing is faster than hand-pruning, and requires less knowledge and skill), control (the fast-growing shrubs used to landscape

most subdivisions will take over if you don't keep whacking them back), and conformity (if all the neighbors shear their shrubs, you might think you should, too). As a result, boring blobs of sheared shrubbery have become a cliché in American landscapes. Shearing is overdone, and it's often badly done. Still, it's the perfect style for some situations. Sheared shapes can provide:

Structure. Shearing unites a group of matching shrubs into a single large shape, and makes it easy to see the shape as a whole. Sheared hedges and edgings are quiet markers that clarify boundaries and transitions without calling attention to themselves.

Stability. Landscape architects like sheared shrubs because they're static shapes that can be maintained at a certain size for many years, preserving the proportions and intent of a design.

Contrast. A plain green sheared hedge is the traditional backdrop for a perennial border, because its uniformity and simplicity makes an array of flowers look all the more colorful, varied, and fascinating.

Mood. This is tricky. Most people respond strongly to sheared shapes, but we react in different ways. Do you think a garden surrounded by sheared

hedges, like the one above, feels calm and dignified, or stuffy and old-fashioned? Do specimens sheared into topiary shapes make you sigh, chuckle, or scoff?

Pointers on shearing

To maintain sheared shrubs that are already in good shape, use *sharp* hedge shears or electric trimmers, remove new growth before it gets tough, and follow the established contours. Shearing once a year is enough for some shrubs; others need repeated trims. What about salvaging an old sheared shrub or hedge that's overgrown, dead inside, bare at the bottom, crooked, ugly, or worn out? Sometimes you can restore it over a few year's time, but often it's better to remove it and start again.

To create a new sheared planting, choose a shrub that's well adapted to the soil and site, has small leaves, branches repeatedly in response to pruning, and grows naturally to approximately the shape that you desire. Cultivars of various hollies, boxwoods, ligustrums, arborvitaes, and yews are traditional favorites, but there are other possibilities.

Begin shearing regularly as soon as you plant new shrubs, to promote bushy growth. Use string and stakes to make straight, level guidelines for shearing a hedge into shape. Cut cardboard or plywood templates for curved shapes, and have a helper hold the template in place as you shear to match it.

Training shrubs into shape

Training means straightening, bending, or steering a shrub's main trunks or stems, in order to refine its natural shape or to create a standard (like the lilac in the formal garden opposite), an espalier (a flat, two-dimensional shape), or other special shapes. Most shrubs are amenable to training.

Choose healthy, young, pliable stems, and tie them loosely to a stake or framework for a year or so, until they're stiff enough to stay put. Once you've chosen and trained some main stems, make a habit of removing any other shoots that sprout up from the base.

Natural shrub shapes

Any shrub has an innate tendancy to reach a certain size and develop a certain shape and appearance; this is called its *habit*. Acknowledging the natural habits of shrubs and choosing and combining them accordingly appeals to avid gardeners who really love plants. The result looks casual, relaxed, and contemporary. Shrub habits are so varied that you can compose an all-shrub garden, as shown below, or combine shrubs with perennials, grasses, and ground covers for even more variety.

The catch is that this isn't as easy as it looks. Gardening with natural-shaped shrubs requires research, planning, and patience. The most common problem is underestimating how fast your shrubs will grow and how big they will get, and planting them too close together. Crowding distorts their shape and means you have to prune to control their size, not just to keep them beautiful. (For more about pruning, see p. 71.)

Terms for typical habits

Knowing some key terms will help you visualize shrubs as you read catalogs and reference books. For example, the rose-of-Sharon (*Hibiscus syriaca*) shown here is *upright* and *treelike*, trained to a few strong main trunks. *Leggy* shrubs are also upright, but their bare stems are skinny and don't look as nice.

This camellia is so *dense* or *full* that you can't see through it. By contrast, a see-through shrub is called *loose*, *open*, or *airy*.

Bearberry cotoneaster and other low shrubs that grow horizontally are called *flat*, *creeping*, *trailing*, or *prostrate*. 'Crimson Pygmy' barberry (*Berberis thunbergii*) is *compact*, *bushy*, and *rounded*. Larger rounded shrubs often spread sideways into *broad mounds*.

Many popular shrubs, such as this variegated weigela, form a short or tall *clump* of equal-length stems that fan out in all directions in an *arching*, *fountain*, or *vase* shape.

Suckering shrubs like summersweet (*Clethra alnifolia*) spread underground to form an ever-widening *patch* of short or tall stems.

Camellia

Summersweet

Rose-of-Sharon

Bearberry cotoneaster

'Crimson Pygmy' barberry

Variegated weigela

Working with existing shrubs

What about the bushes that are already growing on your land? Foundation plantings, hedges, ground covers, lawn and garden specimens, native brush—perhaps you're surrounded by shrubs you didn't choose and can't name, plants that simply "came with the house," or maybe you're looking at a collection of shrubs that you yourself have purchased and planted over a period of time.

It's easy to take shrubs for granted as the weeks and years go by. They're kind of like furniture that you live with but don't really look at. But unlike furniture, shrubs grow and change. Sooner or later you realize that it's time to *do* something. But what should you do?

Take inventory

Walk around your property, considering each shrub. Ask yourself: What's good about it, what's bad about it? How's it doing? Is it vigorous and healthy? Are its leaves pretty? Does it flower abundantly? Is it a pleasing shape? What about size and placement? Does it look lonely, comfortable, or crowded? Now review your options.

The shrubs you like best deserve the most attention. If you don't already know their names, ask someone to help you identify these shrubs, so you can look them up in books and learn more about them and how to care for them.

Any shrub that's healthy and problem-free deserves consideration. Even if it's not an exciting shrub, it has two advantages: it's bigger than what you could buy to replace it, and it's proven its suitability to your site. You may as well make the most of having it there.

A shrub that's puny or weak may deserve a second chance. Maybe it was planted in the wrong place and would flourish if moved to a site with more or less sun, shade, or moisture. Or, you could give up and replace it.

Target any shrub you think is ugly, prickly, smelly, disappointing, demanding, or annoying, and get rid of it. You'll appreciate having an open space where you can plant something you like better. Removing a shrub you dislike is sweaty but quite satisfying work. Hiring someone else to clear it away feels good, too.

Build on what you've got

Anywhere healthy shrubs abut lawn, there's an opportunity to expand your garden. You could dig a bed in front of or around the shrub(s), and fill it with more shrubs, perennials, grasses, ground covers, and bulbs. Put a flower border in front of your foundation planting or inside a boundary hedge, or make an island bed around a lawn specimen. Building on the established shrubs will give your new garden a head start—there's already some height.

An expanded planting compliments a fine shrub, of course, but even a common shrub looks better as part of a group than on its own, as long as it's healthy and in good shape. If it's sturdy but too plain, decorate the shrub by training a non-aggressive vine such as Carolina jasmine (*Gelsemium sempervirens*), golden clematis (*Clematis tangutica*), or trumpet honeysuckle (*Lonicera sempervirens*) up and over it.

Turn a shrub into a "tree"

Any shrub that's basically upright and taller than you can reach, and that has some main trunks (not just lots of skinny stems) can be pruned into a treelike shape. This usually gives it more character, especially if the trunks bend in an interesting way or have conspicuous bark. It also lets you see through to what's beyond the shrub, and opens some space around the base for growing other plants.

To do this kind of pruning, choose the trunks you want to expose, follow them upward to make sure they support a healthy growth of foliage, then mark them with tape or string so you won't accidentally cut them as you proceed. Remove all the weaker trunks by cutting them as close to the ground as possible, and trim all the lower side shoots and branches back to the main trunks. After you've removed the obvious limbs, keep stepping back and forth to check the overall shape; this will help you decide what to cut next and when to stop pruning.

Pruning simplified

Don't be intimidated by pruning. Basically, there are just two techniques: heading back and thinning. You don't need a different strategy for each kind of shrub. The following simple guidelines cover most situations.

HEADING BACK

Heading back means cutting off the end of a limb, twig, or branch, like cutting hair. Use hand pruning shears, sharpened so the blade makes a clean slice, and cut just above a healthy leaf or pair of leaves (if you're heading back a dormant deciduous shrub, look for a healthy bud or pair of buds and cut there). Use the heading-back technique to:

- Encourage young, skinny, or leggy shrubs to branch out and get fuller and thicker. New shoots will sprout from buds below the cut. Do this anytime from late fall to early summer, but not in mid- or late summer; new growth needs time to "harden" before cold weather.

- Control overall size and shape. Compared to simply shearing the shrub, heading back individual limbs takes longer but produces a much more natural look. As you work, keep stepping back, walking around, and looking at the shape to review what you've done and decide if or where you should make more cuts. For shrubs that flower in late winter or spring, do this kind of pruning right after they bloom. For shrubs that bloom in summer or fall, wait until spring to prune them.

- Remove faded flowers. Do this if the dead flowers or developing fruits are ugly, or to prevent unwanted seedlings. Many roses and other summer-blooming shrubs will re-bloom the same year if you trim off the old flowers. Lilacs, rhododendrons, azaleas, mountain laurels, and some other spring-blooming shrubs will bloom more abundantly *next* year if you remove flowers promptly so they can't go to seed.

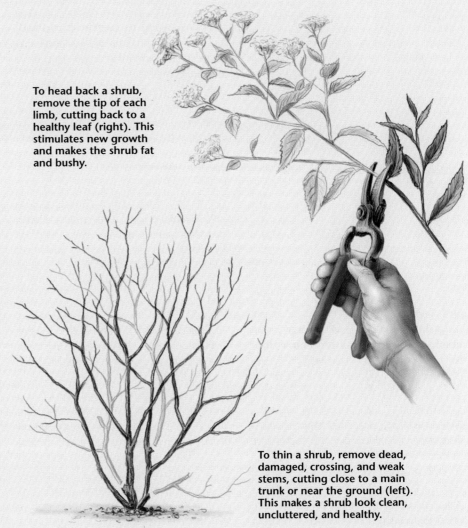

To head back a shrub, remove the tip of each limb, cutting back to a healthy leaf (right). This stimulates new growth and makes the shrub fat and bushy.

To thin a shrub, remove dead, damaged, crossing, and weak stems, cutting close to a main trunk or near the ground (left). This makes a shrub look clean, uncluttered, and healthy.

- Trim individual branches that are too long or stick out too far. You can cut an occasional stray limb at any time.

- Rejuvenate older shrubs or remove the frozen tops of die-back shrubs. Do this in spring, just as the buds swell. Cut each stem down to healthy wood, leaving stubs under 1 foot tall.

THINNING

Thinning means cutting whole limbs back to a main trunk or off at the ground. Thinning almost always improves the looks and health of a shrub, but it doesn't affect subsequent growth as much as heading back does. You can thin a shrub at any time of the year.

Use pruning shears for small limbs, and long-handled loppers or a pruning saw for large limbs. Wear long sleeves, gloves, and comfortable pants, because you'll have to crouch down under the shrub and reach up inside it. Thin away:

- Dead wood. To identify dead wood, look for brittle shoots with pale dry bark and no sign of leaves or buds.

- Old tired stems that are thick but barren and have only a few leaves or buds near the top.

- Weak and skinny stems.

- Crossing stems. Wherever you see two stems rubbing each other, remove the lesser one.

- Shoots damaged or broken by deer, storms, accidents, etc. If a shoot is broken partway, you'd better cut it all off.

- Suckers, sports, or reversions. If you find shoots coming up from the base with leaves that are different from the rest of the shrub, cut them off immediately.

Rejuvenating a shrub

If an older shrub has gotten sparse and straggly, sometimes you can make it good as new—or better than new!—by cutting all its stems close to the ground in late winter. More often than you'd expect, a shrub responds to this drastic treatment by sending up lots of new shoots. Months later, it looks eager, bushy, and fresh. Admittedly, the technique doesn't always work (some shrubs resprout sparsely or not at all), but if a shrub looks so ratty that you're about ready to uproot it, you might as well try rejuvenating it instead—it's worth the risk. A tip: be brave enough to go all the way. Cut the trunks off close to the ground; don't be timid and leave waist-high stubs. A shrub looks best if new growth sprouts up from the base.

Transplanting shrubs

If you have a shrub that's in the wrong place or is too crowded, consider moving it. Move deciduous shrubs just before the leaves emerge in spring, or just as they drop in fall. Move evergreen shrubs in cool weather, when their leaves are firm and leathery, and spray them with an anti-transpirant such as WiltPruf to reduce wilting and stress.

Work on a cloudy or overcast day. Decide where you want to put the shrub, and prepare a wide but shallow (about a spade's depth) hole for it there. To dig the shrub, slice straight down with a sharp spade, cutting a circle as big as the shrub's crown. Dig

a working trench outside that circle so you have room to cut the bottom of the rootball by jabbing the spade underneath it, working from the sides toward the center.

Soil is very heavy. Get help for lifting any rootball more than two feet wide. You may have to rock it from side to side and slide a tarp underneath, then pull on the tarp to drag the rootball up and out of its hole. *Don't* pull the shrub by its stems. Move the shrub immediately to its new hole, lower it into place, check that the top of the rootball is at or slightly above ground level, and refill the hole with soil. Water it right away, and again during dry spells for the next year or so.

Basic care, special care

If they're properly sited and have had a year or so to get established, many shrubs need minimal care—just a few minutes now and then spent pulling weeds, renewing the mulch, removing dead or damaged limbs, or trimming off faded flowers. Other shrubs, especially in marginal situations, may need to be watered, fertilized, sprayed, pruned, shaded in summer, wrapped in winter, etc. I wouldn't want a whole garden full of fussy shrubs, but it's fun to pamper a few favorites. It's a joy, not a chore, to care *for* the plants you care *about*.

Adding shrubs to your garden

Is there empty space on your lot? Too much lawn? Bare walls? Not much to look at, and no privacy either? Rough or remote areas, dry ground or wet spots, places that are hard to maintain? Situations like these call for shrubs!

Why shrubs instead of perennials? Of course you can combine the two groups, but I emphasize shrubs instead of perennials because they stand up all year instead of hiding underground for months at a time. Shrubs offer more variety of size, habit, texture, and foliage. If you're mostly interested in flowers, shrubs can provide just as much color and fragrance as perennials do, over a longer season, and they may produce colorful fruits also. As for cost, there's no comparing shrubs and perennials, because it depends on which particular plants you buy and where you buy them, but in terms of maintenance, shrubs typically need much less time and care than perennials do.

Seeking specific qualities

One way to design a garden is to itemize qualities you're looking for, shortlist plants that meet those requirements, and select finalists as you

Japanese holly

Planting a variety of shrubs fills this corner with color, texture, and fragrance.

'Somerset' daphne

please. As an example, I invented this situation (shown here in late spring, about five years after planting)—a corner along the east side of a house somewhere in the eastern United States; in Zones 5, 6, or 7; with slightly acid, well-drained soil. Choosing from trouble-free shrubs adapted to that kind of climate and site, I listed a few top candidates for each of the following roles and picked my favorites.

Height. I wanted an upright, tree-like shrub for the corner, something that would grow 10 to 15 feet tall, with multiple charms. Blackhaw viburnum (*Viburnum prunifolium*), an adaptable native, meets those conditions, providing white flowers in late spring, colorful berries later, and burgundy fall foliage.

Ground cover. Under the tall shrub, I wanted a low, suckering evergreen ground cover. Sweet box (*Sarcocca hookerana* 'Humilis') has slender glossy leaves and spreads to form a dense patch.

Evergreen structure. 'Chesapeake', 'Jersey Pinnacle', or hardy, upright-growing cultivars of Japanese holly (*Ilex crenata*) are fine candidates for a low, sheared hedge along the property line. Along the house, for a looser, unsheared look, I chose rhododendron 'Olga', a compact, upright, small-leaved hybrid with pink flowers in early spring.

Winter interest. Dwarf Hinoki cypress (*Chamaecyparis obtusa* 'Nana'), a dwarf conifer, has curly, overlapping fans of thick, lustrous foliage that looks especially rich in winter. Winter heath (*Erica carnea*) is a low mound covered with rose, pink, or white flowers for many weeks, starting in late winter. Sweet box blooms about the same time, and its flowers smell wonderfully sweet.

Fragrance. 'Somerset' daphne (*Daphne × burkwoodii*) perfumes the garden in late spring and early summer, following the sweet box. Its dense, rounded habit looks neat next to the bench, and it won't outgrow that space.

Good looks all summer. Front center position goes to 'The Fairy' rose, which forms a low fountain of arching stems, each branching into a spray of miniature pink roses. It blooms almost continually from late spring though late fall. Variegated hydrangea (*Hydrangea macrophylla* 'Mariesii Variegata') rarely blooms in Zones 6 or 5, because it freezes down to the ground in hard winters, but its large, green-and-white leaves look fresh and bright all summer, and stand out against the neighboring plants, which all have much smaller leaves.

Blackhaw viburnum

Variegated hydrangea

Winter heath

'The Fairy' rose

Sweet box

Dwarf Hinoki cypress

'Olga' rhododendron

Building a knee-high drystone retaining wall transformed an inconvenient slope into a safe, flat path and a level, easily planted terrace.

HILLSIDE GARDENING

You don't have to live in the mountains to face the task of landscaping a slope. Even in flatland, small hills and banks are common features on residential lots. The ground might drop abruptly to the street or driveway, rise like an amphitheatre behind the house, or taper from a first-floor entry to a walk-out basement. In any case, developing a sloping site is more challenging than gardening on level ground, but the opportunities are more exciting, too.

Respond to the challenges

All too often, sloping sites are weedy and neglected because their owners are frustrated by these common problems.

Working on a slope is uncomfortable and inconvenient. The footing is uncertain, using tools feels clumsy, and you can't set anything down without its rolling away. One solution is to choose plants that need minimal care. Another is to terrace the slope, making level beds that are easy to tend.

Sloping ground is typically hard and dry, often just subsoil with little if any loose-textured, humus-rich, water-absorbing topsoil. Despite these conditions, weeds often thrive. The good news is that many desirable perennials, grasses, and shrubs will also thrive on a dry slope once they get established.

Manmade slopes—those angular cuts and lumpy piles left by earth-moving equipment in the course of building houses and roads—pose a particular design challenge. It takes imagination and effort to transform an awkward bank into a graceful garden, but fortunately, these sites are often small enough that you can remodel them yourself.

Consider the opportunities

Landscaping a slope adds a new feature to your property. What would you like that to be?

If you regularly climb up and down the slope, building safe, convenient, attractive steps is a high priority. Their simple geometry gives structure and interest to a garden, and once the steps are in place, you'll enjoy planting beside and around them.

If you just want to make the slope more interesting to look at and don't have to walk there, cover it with plants. If the slope rises up from your house and looms outside a window, turn it into a mural by "painting" it with plants. Anything with trailing or arching stems or nodding flowers looks good when viewed from below. But if the slope drops away from the house and you look down at it like a rug, include some plants that form rosettes, have large horizontal leaves, or bear upfacing flowers.

If you'd like more space for growing flowers or vegetables or a place to display a special plant collection, build one or more retaining walls and terrace the slope.

Should you hire help?

Even if you've done everything else in the garden yourself, consider hiring expert help if the hillside is very steep, if the soil is unstable, if the slope is adjacent to a street or waterway, or if you need retaining walls built more than waist-high. Aside from the practical difficulties, you may have to comply with local codes in these situations.

Also, get help if you're not strong enough to move the necessary rocks or soil, if you can't decide what plants to buy, or if you're uncertain about any other phase of the project. Before hiring anyone, be sure to check their references, look at photos of their previous work, and get a written estimate of their fee.

Coral bells is an ideal perennial for slopes and terraces; it blooms for months and needs only minimal care.

Spirea

Miscanthus

Perennial
candytuft

Spirea

Perennial
candytuft

Dianthus

Lilies

Artemisia

Juniper

Planting
on a slope

Deciding what to grow on a hillside is different from designing a bed for level ground. Before you do any planting, here are some practical factors to consider:

• Tilling and amending the soil over a whole slope is impractical and can lead to erosion, so choose plants adapted to the existing soil and prepare individual planting holes. Avoid annuals that need to be replanted each year and perennials that need frequent division.

• Rely mostly on plants with foliage that is evergreen or nearly so, partly for year-round beauty, and also to protect the soil from winter winds and storms.

• Hillsides dry out faster than level ground, so choose plants that can tolerate dry spells. Also, help slow runoff and encourage water to soak in by carving a little terrace for each plant, so the top of its rootball is surrounded by an area of level soil. Then use stones, a piece of wood,

or a berm of soil to make a low dam on the downhill side of the plant.

• The right mulch can inhibit weeds, keep the soil moist, and reduce erosion, but not all mulches are suitable on hillsides. Coarse-textured shredded bark works best, because it tangles together and stays put, and water soaks through easily. Bark decomposes slowly, so a single application should last until the plants have grown into a solid cover.

Big lamb's-ears

Rose

Bigroot geranium

Euonymus

Landscape contractors sometimes use big strips of coarse, biodegradable netting or excelsior on slopes. If you see someone using such material in your area and want to try it, ask if they'll sell you some. You stake it in place first, then cut holes and plant down through it.

• Most plants need a spring cleanup, but you can reduce subsequent maintenance to a minimum by avoiding plants that need frequent grooming, deadheading, trimming, or staking and tying.

A hillside garden plan

This garden plan is designed for a sunny slope with average soil. The area measures 8 by 12 feet and the slope rises 4 feet from bottom to top. The plants are shown to scale as they would appear in early summer two or three years after planting. All are hardy to Zone 5 and tolerate fairly hot and humid summers. Once established, they need watering only during long dry spells. Maintenance consists of pruning, shearing, or grooming each plant once or twice a year.

Miscanthus sinensis 'Sarabande' forms a vase-shaped clump of very slender silvery leaves and bears fluffy seedheads in fall and winter. Cut it down to the ground in late winter. Other clump-forming grasses also develop quickly into impressive specimens, and their fibrous roots are excellent at penetrating and stabilizing hillside soil.

Perennial candytuft (*Iberis sempervirens*) makes a mat of glossy evergreen foliage and is covered with bright white flowers in spring, before the 'Sarabande' grass sprouts up. Shear candytuft after it blooms to keep it neat and bushy. Set plants 15 to 18 inches apart for a dense, weedproof ground cover.

Spiraea x bumalda 'Anthony Waterer' and related cultivars are dome-shaped shrubs with dainty twigs and foliage and fuzzy-looking clusters of bright or pale pink flowers. Prune in spring, removing the oldest stems and cutting others back by one-third.

'White Meidiland' rose displays its double white flowers and glossy foliage over a very long season from spring to fall. A low, spreading shrub, it's hardy and carefree with excellent disease resistance. Prune out old, weak, or damaged shoots in early spring. 'Pearl Meidiland', 'Seafoam', 'The Fairy', and the memorial rose (*Rosa wichuriana*) are other good roses to plant on hillsides.

Big lamb's-ears (*Stachys byzantina* 'Helene von Stein') makes a fuzzy gray carpet around the edge of the rose bush. Space plants 2 to 3 feet apart to form a living mulch that protects the soil and suppresses weeds. Gently rake away the old leaves in early spring.

Dianthus 'Itsaul White' forms dense mats of grassy, evergreen, blue-green foliage and has sweet, vanilla-scented flowers. Shear off the flowerstalks and half of the foliage after it blooms. Most other kinds of *Dianthus* also thrive on sunny hillsides. Space plants 1 foot apart.

Asiatic hybrid lilies (*Lilium*) are very easy to grow and bear big bright flowers in all colors but blue. Choose short-stalked cultivars for hillsides so they won't flop over. Plant the bulbs in late fall or early spring. Lilies can grow up through a patch of dianthus, lamb's ears, candytuft, or similar ground covers.

Artemisia 'Powis Castle' is a shrubby perennial with beautiful silvery foliage. Unlike many artemisias, it doesn't "melt down" in humid weather. Cut it back one-third or more in early spring to keep it bushy. Plant some crocuses or dwarf narcissus underneath; they'll bloom before the artemisia resumes growth.

Bigroot geranium (*Geranium macrorrhizum*) has pink or mauve flowers and soft-textured, richly scented leaves that turn bright shades of red, orange, and purple in the fall and winter. Cut away old growth in spring. Space plants 18 inches apart.

Juniperus squamata 'Blue Star' forms a dense, irregular, prickly-textured mound of sparkling blue-purple foliage. It needs no pruning or other maintenance, and unlike many junipers, it grows slowly and never gets too large for its site. Space plants 2 to 3 feet apart.

Euonymus fortunei 'Emerald Gaiety' is a carefree shrub with floppy stems that creep or climb, rooting as they go. Its smooth little evergreen leaves are bright green and white. Related cultivars with plain green or green-and-gold leaves do just as well. Prune any time, if it spreads too far.

Thyme   Rosemary   Sage

Mint   Chives   Parsley

Building walls and terraces

You don't have to accept your slope the way it is. You can change its shape by rounding off sharp corners, cutting down high spots, or filling hollows.

This may seem like a daunting task, but in many cases a few hours with a shovel and rake can do the job. The hard part is not the actual earth-moving (and anyway, you can always hire someone to do that). What's hard is eyeing the contours and envisioning the possibilities. Most people aren't used to looking at land this way, as something that can be sculpted.

For example, stand at the base of your hill and imagine that instead of sloping ground, there's a vertical retaining wall supporting a nice level bed (or a staircaselike series of walled beds) filled with well-tilled soil and overflowing with beautiful plants. Think how convenient and pleasant it

would be to tend those plants. And you'd enjoy looking at the wall itself.

Designing a retaining wall

A wall can be straight and run parallel to a nearby building or street, or curved to follow the contour of the ground. It can turn a corner, connect to another structure, or taper off at the ends. In any case, it usually looks best if a wall is level on top or "stepped" to go up a slope.

How high to make the wall(s) and how wide to make the terrace(s) depends on the overall size and height of the hill. Make a mock-up with stakes and string or arrange boxes, buckets, or what-have-you to test your ideas about the wall's placement and proportions. Examine it from all sides and adjust the design before you start to dig and build.

If you want to make a wall yourself, you can find books with detailed instructions for working with timbers, blocks, etc., at any home improvement center. Whatever material you

use, the important thing is to make the wall sturdy enough to support the weight of the soil behind it, and safe enough for people to step, sit, or lean on. Be sure that water can drain through the wall, and anticipate frost-heaving in cold climates.

How to cut and fill

This is how to carve a whole hillside into a series of terraces without hauling in truckloads of extra soil. Start at the bottom, on firm level ground, and build the first retaining wall as high as you want it. Pull enough soil downhill to fill the space behind the wall. Pack the soil in firmly or pile it high, expecting it to settle. Build the next wall on the level area where you pulled away the soil. Fill behind that wall, and continue on up the slope. Terracing a hillside in this way is one of the most satisfying things a gardener can do, especially in rocky areas where you can use the stones you dig out of the terraces to build the adjacent walls.

Plants for walls and terraces

A hillside terrace has all the advantages of a raised bed. It's a defined area where you can easily amend and improve the soil. Water soaks in quickly and drains away well. You don't have to stoop to tend or admire the plants. Along the edge of the terrace you can grow some creeping or trailing plants to hang over the retaining wall. Set plants that need or tolerate extra water at the base of the wall, where the soil is typically wetter than in the terrace above.

Planting into a rock wall

Most plants that can spill over a wall can also grow out from a wall, poking through the cracks between rocks. This often happens naturally when seeds germinate and grow in the crevices. Sowing seeds (best done in fall or spring) is a good way for you to start plants in an existing wall.

If you're building a wall, you can set plants in place as you go. Tease apart the bottom of the rootball and guide some of the roots into the soil behind the wall. Fill all the space around the rootball with soil, packing it firmly between the rocks. Use a piece of dead sod to make a little collar around the crown of the plant that will keep soil from leaking out the front of the wall. Water frequently until the plant is established.

A sunny terraced slope

A sunny terrace is easy to fill. You could have a kitchen or cutting garden there; a collection of succulents, alpines, dwarf conifers, or gray-foliaged plants; a "meadow" of wildflowers and grasses; or, as shown on the facing page, make an herb garden.

Thyme, rosemary, and common sage thrive in the well-drained soil of a sunny terrace, along with oregano, lavender, and many other herbs. Mints, chives, and parsley enjoy the extra moisture at the base of a wall.

If you'd like to see masses of flowers tumbling down the front

of a sunny wall, try basket-of-gold (*Aurinia saxatilis*), creeping baby's breath (*Gypsophila repens*), rock rose (*Helianthemum nummularium*), Missouri evening primrose (*Oenothera missouriensis*), moss phlox (*Phlox subulata*), or rock soapwort (*Saponaria ocymoides*).

A shady terraced slope

As always, there are fewer choices for shade than for sun, but a shady, rock-edged terrace like the one shown below is ideal for ferns, moss, and wildflowers such as dwarf crested iris (*Iris cristata*), which can have violet, blue, or white flowers; creeping phlox (*Phlox stolonifera*), with sweet-scented blue, pink, or white flowers; foam-flower (*Tiarella cordifolia*), which makes a cloud of tiny white blossoms; and wintergreen (*Gaultheria procumbens*), with tiny flowers but bright red berries and wonderfully fragrant and glossy evergreen foliage. These four spring-blooming wildflowers do well in all but the hottest climates, climbing up, down, or through a shady rock wall. If there's room, add hollies, hydrangeas, azaleas and rhododendrons, or other shade-tolerant shrubs.

Wood fern

Dwarf crested iris

Creeping phlox

Wintergreen

Foamflower

Comfortable steps and paths

One of the most important things to think about in landscaping a hillside is whether you need to walk around on the slope, or simply look at it. If you need a walkway, spend some time planning how to make it as safe, practical, and lovely as possible.

Depending on where it leads and who goes there, a hillside walkway can take many forms—a cut-stone stairway that welcomes guests at your front door; wooden steps with a decklike landing where you can look out over a sloping back yard; a grassy ramp that lets you roll a lawnmower or cart between two levels in the garden; a gravel path that switchbacks up the face of a slope, guiding you from one favorite plant to the next.

What route to take

A walkway can run straight up a hill if it's not too steep or too high, but the climb is more pleasant and interesting if you include a curve, a turn, or a landing. Stake a tentative route and use it awhile to see how it feels. Watch other people follow that route and monitor their movements—where do they pause, watch their step, or hurry ahead? Use this feedback to decide where a resting point would be welcome, where a turn would point you the right way, where to build steps, whether to add a handrail.

Specs for steps

It's nice for steps to *look* interesting, but they should *feel* ordinary and predictable underfoot—sturdy, flat, level, equally spaced, matched to an average stride, and big enough for your foot. It's disorienting or dangerous if steps are slippery, crooked, irregular, too steep or shallow, or too small. Other parts of your garden can be picturesque. Steps should be safe, especially if you use them in bad weather or at night.

Landscape designers use a formula to make steps that match your stride: twice the riser (the height of the step) plus the tread (the width of the step) should total between 24 and 28 inches. A 5-inch riser and 16-inch tread are common proportions that fit the formula. Vary the proportions as you choose, as long as the total stays within the limits.

Unless you're strong and handy, you'll probably need help building outdoor steps, but you can plan ahead and decide where you want them to go by cutting into the soil or stacking up boards and bricks. The actual steps can be built from stones, bricks, concrete, timbers, or other heavy, durable materials. Be sure the treads are rough-surfaced, not smooth, for steady footing.

Hillside paths

A path can zigzag up a hillside or traverse it, but wherever the walkway is steep, use steps instead a path—steps feel more secure underfoot, especially when you're going downhill. Unless you need room for two people to walk side by side, a hillside path can be narrower than most garden paths, only 12 to 18 inches wide. Cut far enough into the hill to make the path level from side to side, so one foot isn't higher than the other as you walk. You may need a low rock, brick, or wood edging along the uphill side of the path to retain the soil there.

The surface of hillside path should be firm and stable. Avoid loose gravel or bark nuggets that roll like ball bearings and deliver you over the edge. Try trodden dirt, crushed rock packed into a porous pavement, or hardwood chips that form a spongy mat as they rot. Flagstones or precast pavers set in sand also make a good path. Rake the sand smooth, walk back and forth through it, and use your footprints to decide where to set the stones. Bury them almost flush with the sand, and be sure they are level.

Nandina

Bergenia

Edging plants

Certain plants are just right for edging steps and paths—they're compact, touchable, neat and good-looking most or all year, with features that reward a close look or change surprisingly with the seasons. A few widely adapted favorites are shown here as they look in midsummer.

Dwarf cultivars of nandina (*Nandina domestica*) are spherical bushes with fine-textured foliage that turns garnet in winter. Bergenia (*Bergenia*) forms stout clumps of big glossy leaves that turn red in winter, with pink or white flowers in spring. Coral bells (*Heuchera*) has evergreen leaves and tiny red, pink, or white flowers. Blue oat grass (*Helictotrichon sempervirens*) makes a dense evergreen tuft of blue leaves. Succulent hens-and-chicks (*Sempervivum*) forms endearing rosettes that nestle in crevices. Another succulent, October plant (*Sedum sieboldii*), has round blue leaves in neat whorls of three and pretty pink flowers in fall.

Blue oat grass

Hens-and-chicks

October plant

Coral bells

Gold-variegated forms
of oregano, thyme,
and sage are as colorful
as they are tasty.

STARTING AN HERB GARDEN

Herb gardens are intimate places, meant not for viewing from afar but for appreciating up close. That's because the beauty of herbs goes more than skin deep. Looking isn't enough. You want to touch, sniff, and nibble these fascinating plants. Even more, you want to bring them into your home and your life, using them to flavor your food, pamper your body, lift your spirits.

Of course, you can grow herbs by mixing them among your other plants (see p. 90), but it's convenient and fun to group them together. Creating an herb garden helps focus your interest and makes it easier to learn about, tend, and harvest the plants. It gives you a project to plan, a place to go, and something to point to as you share your interest in herbs with family and friends.

Three theme gardens

To give you some ideas, we've designed three garden plans featuring the best and most popular herbs to grow for cooking, remedies, or fragrance. All of the herbs shown in these plans can be grown in most parts of the United States (except where summers are extremely hot and/or humid) and require similar growing conditions. Some herbs, such as sage, basil, and lemon balm, can be used in more than one way, so feel free to switch plants from one design to another to suit your tastes and interests.

Planning your own design

If you want to design your own herb garden, here are some helpful guidelines.

Put it next to something. Choose a site near a building or wall, or a long a paved walkway. A small new garden usually looks best if it's anchored to an existing structure, rather than floating in a lawn.

Plan for convenient access. Don't make the beds too wide, and do position paths and steppingstones so you can comfortably reach every plant to admire, tend, and harvest it.

Go for variety, not quantity. Why waste space growing more than you'll use of any one herb? It's more fun to collect different kinds and compare them. For perennial herbs, one plant of a kind is usually enough; for annuals, try a small patch or short row of each kind.

Show how they contrast. An herb garden looks more interesting if adjacent plants differ in size, shape, color, and texture. Also, you'll find it easier to keep track of similar-looking herbs if they aren't planted side by side.

Include some potted specimens. Many herbs thrive in containers, making ideal portable ornaments.

Buying herb plants and seeds

It's rarely worthwhile to grow perennial herbs from seed. A packet of seeds costs almost as much as one plant, and the best cultivars are propagated by cutting or division, not by seed. But it makes sense to grow annual herbs from seed, because you often want several plants. Also, more kinds of annuals are available as seeds than as plants, and some annual herbs do grow better if sown directly in the garden, not transplanted.

For plants, most garden centers carry a basic assortment of annual and hardy perennial herbs in spring, but after those plants are sold, they don't restock until next year. Go shopping and see what you can find. This is a way to get started, but you'll soon want more.

Nurseries that specialize in herbs offer a much wider selection, have more interesting and unusual varieties, including tender perennials, and sell from spring through fall. Watch for advertisements in local newspapers and magazines to see if there's an herb specialist in your area; if so, it's worth driving there to shop. You'll find plants with outstanding flavor and fragrance, and get advice tailored to your climate and growing conditions.

Basic care

Many common herbs require similar conditions and care.

Sun. Locate your herb garden in a site that gets direct sun for at least six hours a day during the growing season. Full sun all day is best, except in extremely hot climates. If planted where it's too shady, herbs grow thin and floppy, with sparse flowers and weak flavor.

Soil. Prepare the soil for growing herbs as you would for other garden plants (see p. 9). For herbs in containers, use your favorite brand of potting soil, and apply liquid fertilizer, diluted to one-half the recommended strength, every two weeks throughout the growing season.

Watering. Some herbs thrive in arid climates or dry soil; others don't. In general, you should water as often and as much as needed to prevent wilting.

Weed control. In a new garden, weeds may grow faster than the herbs. Keep hoeing or pulling them out, or spread a thin layer of mulch to shade the soil and prevent weed seeds from sprouting. Herbs themselves can be weedy. Some spread by seeds, others by runners; for tips on dealing with these plants, see p. 26.

Herbs for cooking

Choose a sunny site close to the house for growing culinary herbs. You'll use them more if they're nearby, where it's handy to run out and pick a few sprigs at the last minute as you cook. A small area will provide all you need. In this design, a bed only 2 feet wide edges a 6-by-10 foot patio, with perennials on the left, annuals on the right, and tender herbs in pots.

Hardy perennials

When buying plants of these perennial herbs, choose them by sniffing a leaf. If it doesn't have a distinct, appetizing aroma, don't buy that plant. Garden centers sometimes sell inferior, seed-raised plants or ornamental cultivars that lack flavor.

If you can't find tasty plants locally, mail-order them from herb specialists. Start with one or two plants of each kind. They will soon fill the available space, and should be divided and replanted every three years, in spring.

(A) French tarragon (*Artemisia dracunculus* var. *sativa*) forms a patch of slender stems with anise-scented foliage you can pick from spring through fall. Zone 3. Where summers are hot and/or humid, substitute Mexican mint marigold (*Tagetes lucida*), a prettier plant with similar flavor, hardy to Zone 8 or grown as an annual.

(B) Chives (*Allium schoenoprasum*) sprouts in early spring and bears pretty flowers a month or so later. After the flowers fade, shear the plant hard to make it neat again and stimulate new growth. Zone 3.

(C) Sage (*Salvia officinalis*) leaves are good fresh or dried, as seasoning or in tea. The plant is semi-shrubby and semi-evergreen, with lovely blue flowers in late spring. Prune every year in early spring. Zone 5.

(D) Common thyme (*Thymus vulgaris*) forms a bushy mound of wiry stems with tiny leaves. There are many cultivars with slightly different flavors. Other species of thyme are

good, too, so compare aromas as you shop and choose your favorite(s). Prune in spring. Zone 4.

(E) Greek oregano (*Origanum vulgare* subsp. *hirtum*, a.k.a. *O. heracleoticum*), with white flowers, has excellent flavor and is hardy to Zone 5. In Zones 8 and warmer, you can grow other tasty species of *Origanum*, plus some quite different plants that also have the "oregano" flavor, such as Mexican oregano (*Poliomintha longiflora*), a shrubby perennial with fragrant, shiny leaves and pretty pink-purple flowers.

Annuals

These herbs are grown as annuals. Since you replant them each year, you can keep trying different kinds and rearranging them, too. More annual herbs are listed on p. 90.

(F) Parsley (*Petroselinum crispum*) looks good all summer and fall and doesn't freeze down until hard frost. There are two common forms of parsley: flat-leaved types, which have more flavor, and curly-leaved types, which look more decorative. Use three plants here.

(G) Summer savory (*Satureja hortensis*) has slender, gray-green leaves with a pleasant, spicy taste. Sow

seeds where you want it to grow. It may self-sow in subsequent years. Use three plants here.

(H) Chili peppers (*Capsicum annuum*) are pretty plants and it's fun to watch the peppers turn from green to red as they ripen. Try different kinds to compare their hotness and flavors. Start seeds early indoors or buy transplants. Don't set them out until after the last frost, when the soil is warm. Use five plants here.

(I) Basils (*Ocimum basilicum*) likes heat, as peppers do, so start them the same way. Also like peppers, there are many kinds of basil to choose from, all pretty and tasty. Try lemon- and cin-

namon-flavored basils and the purple-leafed forms, as well as the common green kinds. Use four plants here.

(J) Garlic (*Allium sativum*) stores very well, but it's even better fresh. Plant cloves a few inches deep in fall or very early spring, then harvest the new bulbs when the leaves and flowerstalk wither in summer. Set one or two bulbs aside to break apart and replant, then enjoy the rest right away or braid them to save. Use 16 plants here.

Try these in pots

Where they are hardy, you can leave the following evergreen herbs out-

doors all winter. Otherwise, bring them into a cool sunny room. Most other culinary herbs can also be grown in outdoor pots if you water and fertilize them. Replace annual herbs and divide and replant hardy perennial herbs every spring.

(K) Rosemary (*Rosmarinus officinalis*) is a shrub. There are many cultivars, with blue-purple or white flowers and upright or creeping growth; any one is okay for cooking. Pick the fragrant, gray-green, needle-like leaves at any time. Prune rosemary after it quits blooming in spring, and again in summer if needed to keep it compact and shapely. Zone 8.

(L) Lemon grass (*Cymbopogon citratus*) forms a dense clump of arching leaves. Cut them to use in Thai cooking or to brew a delicious tea. This plant grows fast, so you'll need to cut it back, divide, and repot it at least once a year, in spring or fall. Zone 10.

(M) Bay laurel, or sweet bay (*Laurus nobilis*) is a tree, but it grows slowly, so you can keep a potted specimen for many years, gradually moving it from smaller to larger pots. Bay needs decisive pruning. Whenever a stem shoots out too far, cut it right back. Pick the stiff, glossy, dark green leaves at any time. Zone 8.

Remedies you'll really use

Think of these herbs as natural alternatives to over-the-counter remedies for minor ailments such as scratches, sores, colds, upset stomaches, and headaches. They're effective, but mild and pleasant to use. As noted below, many are versatile plants that can be used in different ways or to treat different problems. You can gather them fresh during the growing season and preserve them for later use.

Hopefully, you won't be using these herbs as often as you do culinary herbs. Also, although the garden shown here is colorful in early sum-

mer, muted shades of green, gray, and white predominate later. Some of these healing herbs can be invasive. For all these reasons, consider planting this garden away from the house, perhaps near a garden shed with a worksbench and and drying racks inside. For a sense of scale, refer to the elderberry bush, which is 8 feet tall and wide. Use one of each plant, except as noted.

Remedies for external use

Use these for minor wounds, soreness, and skin problems.

(P) Aloe vera. Grow this tender (Zone 9) perennial in a pot. Break off a leaf and rub the fresh sap directly onto burns, sunburns, insect stings, and nicks.

(A) Comfrey (*Symphytum officinale*). The variegated form, shown here, is slightly less robust but just as indomitable as the common green form of this hardy (Zone 3) perennial. Crush the leaves into a gooey mass and plaster it on the skin to relieve swelling and speed healing of cuts, sores, and sprains. Do not take comfrey internally.

(C) St.-John's-wort (*Hypericum perforatum*). Pick the golden flowers as they bloom and drop them into a jar of olive oil or vodka. The fluid will soon turn red. Strain it off a few weeks later; it's good for a year or more. Paint it on minor wounds and sores to speed healing. St.-John's-wort is also used to relieve depression. Perennial, Zone 3.

(E) Calendula (*Calendula officinalis*). Pick, prepare, and use calendula flowers like St.-John's-wort. The dried flowers also make a natural yellow food coloring. Annual, prefers cool weather. Use six plants here.

(H) Yarrow (*Achillea millefolium*). Crush a handful of blossoms and leaves and hold them against a scratch or cut to stop the bleeding. Perennial, Zone 3.

(O) Elder or **elderberry** (Use *Sambucus canadensis*, native throughout eastern North America, or the European elder, *S. nigra*). Pour boiling water onto a cupful or fresh or dried flowers or leaves, cool, strain, and use it to wash wounds or soothe rough skin. This fast-growing shrub should be pruned hard every few years, in spring. Zone 4.

Soothing and stimulating teas

To use these herbs, pour a cupful of boiling water onto one tablespoon of fresh leaves or flowers or one teaspoon of dried parts, let it steep about ten minutes, then strain off the tea and drink it hot or iced. Sweeten it if you choose. Except for the annual German chamomile, the following herbs are all perennials, hardy to Zone 5.

(B) Lemon balm (*Melissa officinalis*). The leaves make a tasty, lemon-scented tea that has a calming effect. Brew an extra-strength batch and dab it on cold sores or acne to reduce infection and relieve pain. Shear plants in midsummer, removing the flowers.

(F) Catnip (*Nepeta cataria*). The soft, gray-green leaves make an aromatic tea that relieves cold symptoms and congestion. Shear plants in midsummer, removing the flowers.

(G) Chamomile. Chamomile flowers make a soothing, apple-scented tea. Harvest every few days and dry them on a screen. Sow seeds here to make a patch of a dozen of so plants. Choose either the upright, annual German chamomile (*Matricaria recutita*), shown here, or the spreading, perennial Roman chamomile (*Chamaemelum nobile*), which has similar herbal uses.

(J) Betony (*Stachys officinalis*). Use the scalloped, semi-evergreen leaves to brew a mild-flavored tea which helps relieve headaches, anxiety, and stress.

(L) Sage (*Salvia officinalis*). Sage is a remedy as well as a seasoning. Tea brewed from the leaves is a traditional cure for upset stomach or sore throat.

(M) Feverfew (*Chrysanthemum parthenium*, also listed under other names). The leaf tea is a traditional cure-all, and the ferny-looking, pungent-scented leaves can also help relieve migraines.

(N) Mints. Both peppermint (*Mentha × piperita*) and spearmint (*M. spicata*) make fragrant, refreshing teas that are good for indigestion, nausea, headaches, and colds. Use either one here.

Aromatherapy

(D) Hops (*Humulus lupulus*). Harvest and dry the papery, conelike fruits in late summer, stuff them into cloth sachet bags, and breathe the aroma as a sedative. Be sure to buy a female plant of this perennial deciduous vine. Zone 3.

(I) Camphor basil (*Ocimum kilimandscharicum*). Because they contain camphor, the fresh or dried leaves have a strong, penetrating aroma. Brew a tea and inhale the vapors (don't drink it) to relieve congestion and penetrate a stuffed-up nose. Annual.

(K) English lavender. (*Lavandula angustifolia*). Use the dried flowers to fill sachets. The aroma is both sedative and refreshing. This beautiful plant has many uses as medicine, perfume, and flavoring. Shrubby, Zone 5.

Favorite fragrant herbs

Sitting in the midst of a fragrant herb garden like this is an experience to treasure, something to anticipate and to remember. If you could spend ten minutes a day here, it would change your life. Imagine turning from plant to plant, stimulated by the diversity of sweet, pungent, minty, spicy, and fruity aromas, or simply basking in the combined cloud of fragrance— either way, you'd be refreshed and revitalized by sensations only nature can provide.

This garden plan is 6 feet wide and 22 feet long, small enough to fit next to the short side of a house or along one edge of a fenced-in yard. Siting it in a sunny, sheltered location maximizes the fragrance. Use one of each plant.

Start with a rose

(H) 'Frau Dagmar Hartopp' rose. This hybrid rugosa is trouble-free, compact, and long-blooming, with sweet-scented single pink flowers. 'Betty Prior', 'Gruss an Aachen', 'Maybelle Stearns', or many other roses would all work well here, too. If you want to fill gaps around the rose, under the bench, and between the flagstones, plant Corsican mint (*Mentha requienii*) and/or any kind of creeping thyme.

Hardy plants

These herbs are more vulnerable to rotting than to cold. They survive Zone 5 winters if planted on a well-drained site.

(A) Gray santolina (*Santolina chamaecyparissus*). This little shrub has pungent, crinkly, fine-textured foliage. Its gold-colored flowers would clash with the pinks and purples here, so prune them off.

(B) Calamint. Choose either *Calamintha grandiflora*, shown here,

which has green leaves and bright, showy flowers; or *C. nepeta*, with gray-green foliage and pale, dainty flowers. Both are compact, carefree perennials with pleasantly mint-scented leaves.

(D) 'Six Hills Giant' catmint. This hybrid *Nepeta* smells similar to its cousin, catnip, but is less magnetic to cats. It blooms continually or repeatedly from late spring to frost.

(I) Russian sage (*Perovskia atriplicifolia*). Although not a traditional herb, this popular perennial has a nice aroma, and its silvery leaves and stems are topped with stunning blue-purple flowers from midsummer until frost.

(K) Bergamot (*Monarda fistulosa*). This native perennial has lavender-pink flowers in summer and gray-green leaves with a minty yet sweet aroma. It adapts well to dry, sunny sites. Related species and hybrids smell good, too, but need moister soil and tend to spread.

(L) 'Powis Castle' artemisia. This popular, widely adapted hybrid makes

a broad mound of pungent, lacy, silvery foliage. Southernwood (*Artemisia abrotanum*) has thinner leaflets and a sweeter aroma; wormwood (*A. absinthium*) has darker, gray-green leaves with a bitter, medicinal scent. Take your pick; all are shrubby perennials that should be pruned hard every spring, before new growth starts.

(M) Clary sage (*Salvia sclarea*). The rich, alluring aroma of this striking plant is especially pervasive after a rain has washed the bold, crinkled, silver-gray leaves and papery pink-and-white flowers. Be sure to grow the true clary sage, which is a robust biennial; not annual clary (*S. viridis*, a.k.a. *S. horminum*), a thin plant that's valuable for everlasting arrangements but virtually scentless. Clary sage regularly self-sows; watch for a seedling you can transplant to replace the mother.

(N) Bigroot geranium (*Geranium macrorrhizum*). Touch the sticky, semi-evergreen leaves of this carefree, clump-forming plant, and the sweet, musky aroma will linger on your skin for hours.

(O) Hyssop (*Hyssopus officinalis*). Hyssop has a clean, bitter, medicinal, smell. It's a shrubby perennial with erect stems, slender dark leaves, and blue, pink, or white flowers. It blooms nonstop from summer to fall.

Tender plants

These survive outdoors in mild regions. Otherwise, winter them indoors or treat them as annuals. Any of these can be grown in a pot or in the ground.

(C) Pineapple sage (*Salvia elegans*). A bushy perennial with soft green leaves that really do smell like pineapple, this also bears long spikes of vivid red flowers during the short days from fall to spring. Cherry sage or autumn sage (*S. greggii*) has fragrant, semi-evergreen leaves and blooms from spring to fall, with pretty flowers in many colors.

(E) 'Tutti Fruti' agastache. Rub a leaf to enjoy its fruity fragrance, then step out of the way to watch hummingbirds visit the colorful flowers, which bloom profusely from June until frost. Other new hybrid *Agastache* cultivars are just as bright and fragrant.

(F) Eucalyptus. These trees grow so quickly that you can use seedlings as annuals or keep them in pots for a few years. *Eucalyptus cinerea, E. globulus,* and *E. polyanthemos* all have aromatic "silver-dollar" foliage. Prune young plants often and hard to keep them bushy.

(G) Lemon verbena (*Aloysia triphylla*). This fast-growing shrub has thin, bright green leaves that smell intensely lemony. When dried, they retain more fragrance than other lemon-scented herbs do. Prune this plant hard to keep it compact and bushy. Often drops its leaves in winter, but recovers in spring.

(J) 'African Blue' basil (*Ocimum*). This gorgeous hybrid forms a big, bushy mound of dark foliage with a spicy, penetrating aroma. If you can't find it, use three seedlings of 'Purple Ruffles' or any other purple-leaved basil here instead.

Landscaping with herbs

An alternative to grouping herbs in a special garden is to spread them throughout your landscape. Once you start thinking this way, possibilities are everywhere. Include herbs in your flowerbeds and vegetable garden. Use herbs as ground covers. Plant some herbal shrubs and trees.

Landscaping with herbs is especially helpful if your property is small, because it helps you pack more beauty and enjoyment into limited space. By choosing an herb, you get more than just a pretty plant, you get a plant with fragrance, or flavor, or an interesting story, too. Herbs have an added dimension that makes mere ornamental plants seem boring by comparison.

MIX HERBS WITH VEGETABLES

Annual herbs—and other herbs that grow so quickly from seed that you can treat them as annuals and replace them every year—are best for inter-planting with vegetables, because they don't interfere with garden cleanup, soil improvement, and crop rotation, three important considerations in vegetable growing. These herbs also combine well with bedding plants in annual flowerbeds.

Along with the herbs shown on p. 85, this group includes **borage** (*Borago officinalis*), **mustards** (*Brassica*), **epasote** (*Chenopodium ambrosioides*), **cilantro** or **coriander** (*Coriandrum sativum*), **dill** (*Anethum graveolens*), **fennel** (*Foeniculum vulgare*), **sweet marjoram** (*Origanum majorana*), **breadseed poppy** (*Papaver somniferum*), **perilla** (*Perilla frutescens*), **salad burnet** (*Poterium sanguisorba*), and **nasturtium** (*Tropaeolum majus*).

PLANT AN HERBAL MEADOW

These herbs, mostly used for fragrance or as herbal remedies, are native or naturalized wildflowers that combine well with grasses in casual prairie- or meadow-style plantings. All are sun-loving perennials that bloom between late spring and fall. Most of these plants tend to spread by seed or by runners, which can be a problem in flowerbeds, but not in a "wild" garden. All are hardy at least to Zone 4, and grow well in most regions.

Yarrow (*Achillea millefolium*): white flowers, all summer, 3 feet tall.

Anise hyssop (*Agastache foeniculum*): purple, late summer, 3 to 4 feet.

Pearly everlasting (*Anaphalis margaritacea*): white, summer, 1 foot.

Dyer's chamomile (*Anthemis tinctoria*): yellow, summer, 2 feet.

Butterflyweed (*Asclepias tuberosa*): orange, early summer, 3 feet.

Purple coneflower (*Echinacea purpurea*): rosy pink-purple, midsummer, 3 feet.

Joe-pye weed (*Eupatorium purpureum*): dusty pink, late summer, 5 to 8 feet.

Meadowsweet (*Filipendula ulmaria*): white, summer, 4 to 6 feet.

Lady's bedstraw (*Galium verum*): yellow, early summer, 2 feet.

St-John's-wort (*Hypericum perforatum*): yellow, early summer, 3 feet.

Motherwort (*Leonurus cardiaca*): pink, late summer, 4 feet.

Great blue lobelia (*Lobelia siphilitica*): clear blue, late summer, 3 feet.

Dill

Joe-Pye weed

Bergamot (*Monarda didyma*), **bee balm** (*M. fistulosa*), and **horsemint** (*M. punctata*): red, purplish, and pink, mid-summer, 3 to 4 feet.

Soapwort (*Saponaria officinalis*): pale pink, all summer, 2 to 3 feet.

Tansy (*Tanacetum vulgare*): yellow, mid-summer, 3 to 4 feet.

Valerian (*Valeriana officinalis*): dirty white, early summer, 3 to 5 feet.

Blue vervain (*Verbena hastata*): blue-purple, late summer, 3 feet.

Two hardy perennial native grasses to include in an herbal meadow are **sweet vernal grass** (*Anthoxanthum odoratum*) and **sweet grass** (*Hierochloe odorata*). Both grow 1 to 2 feet tall, with slender leaves that smell like vanilla when cut and dried.

HERBS FOR SHADY SITES

The following herbs—mostly fragrant and medicinal plants—tolerate or even prefer sites that are shaded part or all of the day by surrounding trees or adjacent buildings. All are perennials, hardy at least to Zone 4.

Sweet flag (*Acorus calamus*) prefers damp soil and forms a dense patch of slender, fragrant leaves 3 to 4 feet tall.

Angelica (*Angelica archangelica*) needs moist soil and can't take much heat. A big, bold plant, 4 to 6 feet tall. Short-lived, but self-sows.

Wild gingers (*Asarum* spp.) form a carpet of rounded gray-green or glossy leaves.

Sweet woodruff (*Galium odoratum*) makes a good groundcover, with fine-textured leaves and tiny white flowers.

Wintergreen (*Gaultheria procumbens*) has glossy evergreen leaves and bright red berries. Spreads slowly and hugs the ground.

Alumroot (*Heuchera americana*) forms low clumps of semi-evergreen foliage. Usually has plain, dark green leaves, but new cultivars have gray, silver, or maroon markings.

Goldenseal (*Hydrastis canadensis*) forms a patch of attractive, lobed leaves and holds its berrylike fruits for weeks in fall. Under 1 foot tall.

Wild ginger

Bearberry

Sweet cicely (*Myrrhis odorata*) makes a mound of ferny foliage about 3 feet tall and wide, topped with white flowers in spring and conspicuous dark fruits later.

Yellowroot (*Xanthorhiza simplicissima*) spreads slowly to form a bushy patch, 2 to 3 feet tall, of neat, fine-textured foliage.

HERBAL SHRUBS

Not all herbs are herbaceous plants; that is, plants with soft stems that die down to the ground in winter. Rosemary, bay laurel, lavender, lemon verbena, eucalyptus, and many other herbs mature into fine shrubs or trees when grown outdoors in mild climates.

There are fewer choices for colder regions, but the following herbal shrubs are all attractive plants, readily available and easy to grow, with fragrant or medicial uses.

Bearberry (*Arctostaphylos uva-ursi*) is an evergreen ground cover with neat small leaves and red berries in fall. Hugs the ground and spreads several feet wide. Zone 3.

Junipers (*Juniperus communis, J. scopulorum, J. virginiana*) have aromatic foliage and fruits. Named cultivars have the best forms and foliage color. Zone 4.

Spicebush (*Lindera benzoin*) has tiny gold flowers in early spring, red berries in late summer, and yellow fall foliage. All parts are fragrant. Grows 8 to 10 feet tall and wide. Zone 5.

Bayberry (*Myrica pensylvanica*) has glossy aromatic leaves and waxy gray berries. It spreads underground to form a patch, 4 to 8 feet tall. Zone 4.

Rosemary willow (*Salix elaeagnos*) and other species of willow are natural sources of the pain-killing ingredient contained in aspirin. Annual pruning keeps this graceful, narrow-leaved willow under 8 feet tall. Zone 5.

Arborvitae (*Thuja occidentalis*) cultivars have fragrant, evergreen foliage and make excellent hedges. Height varies. Zone 3.

Cranberry-bush viburnums (*Viburnum opulus, V. trilobum*) grow 8 to 12 feet tall, with doily-like clusters of white flowers in spring and clear red berries that hang on the bare limbs all winter. Zone 3.

Nothing rivals the clear, glossy colors of tulip blossoms.

ADDING BULBS TO YOUR GARDEN

There are many reasons why planting bulbs is such a popular garden project. The bulbs themselves are intriguing objects, egg-like in shape and function, each with its own food supply and baby plant hidden inside. Planting bulbs is a breeze—the only hard part is figuring out which end is up. Afterwards, there's little to do but wait. Success is nearly certain. Bulbs almost always bloom a few months after you plant them. Showy, colorful, and fragrant in some cases, bulb flowers would be delightful anytime, but they're especially welcome as a sign of spring.

Crocus, daffodils, tulips, hyacinths, and other spring-flowering bulbs grow well in most parts of the United States, except where winters are extremely cold (most kinds of bulbs are hardy to Zone 4) or not cold enough (most bulbs need several weeks of cool weather to stimulate root growth and bud development). Bulbs are inexpensive and readily available from local and mail-order suppliers, and the quality is generally good.

But despite their many charms, bulbs aren't perfect. In fact, most gardeners have a love-hate relationship with spring-flowering bulbs. We love the flowers but hate the leaves. Bulb leaves are typically floppy and lazy-looking. They're out of synch with the rest of the garden—they get weather-beaten and start turning yellow when everything else looks fresh and eager. Worse yet, although bulb flowers last only days or weeks, the leaves persist for about two months before finally withering away. To find happiness with bulbs, you need to reconcile this difference.

Bulbs as annuals

One approach is to treat bulbs as annuals, planting new ones each fall and discarding them after they bloom in spring. Tulips, in particular, are often grown as annuals, especially in public gardens or commercial landscapes. This makes a gorgeous display, but it's too expensive and labor-intensive for most home gardeners.

A variation on bulbs-as-annuals is the old English estate-garden technique of digging bulbs after they bloom, transplanting them to an out-of-sight nursery bed where the leaves can mature, then replanting the bulbs in the flower beds in fall. Another option is to grow bulbs in containers which you can move to and fro as you choose. Although either of these techniques gives you a way to keep the bulbs rather than throwing them away, bulbs that have been relocated or confined to a pot usually don't bloom as well in subsequent years as bulbs left undisturbed in a bed.

Bulbs as perennials

My favorite way to use bulbs is to think of them as perennials that just happen to come in a convenient package. I look for situations where bulbs can become a permanent part of the garden, choosing sites where their flowers will add welcome color in spring and their leaves will be hidden soon afterwards by perennials, grasses, shrubs, or annuals. This chapter features a plan showing how to include bulbs in a mixed border, and gives other ideas for treating bulbs as trouble-free, long-lasting perennials.

Snowdrops pop up in late winter, weeks earlier than most other bulbs.

Bulb basics

Daffodils, tulips, snowdrops, and other spring-flowering bulbs are all perennial plants that come back year after year, sprouting up in cool weather and dying down again in hot weather. What distinguishes these plants from other spring-blooming perennials? Simply this: unlike other plants, which form a more or less organized crown or patch of buds and roots, daffodils, etc., form a distinct, compact, swollen organ called a bulb.

What is a bulb?

Botanically, the swollen organ can correspond to leaves, stems, or roots. Depending on their origin, these parts have different names, such as bulb, corm, rhizome, or tuber; for convenience, it's okay to call them all bulbs. Bulbs can be smooth or lumpy, rounded or angular, as small as a pea or as large as a peach. They're usually white or cream-colored inside, but the outer skin may be any shade of tan, brown, gold, red, purple, black, or white. In any case, making a bulb is a way for a plant to store energy and nutrients from one year to the next. It is also a means of propagation; if divided from its mother, a bulb can grow into a separate plant.

A seasonal growth cycle

Hardy bulb-forming perennials that bloom in spring have a predictable growth cycle that corresponds to seasonal changes in temperature. For example, the illustration below shows (from left to right) how a crocus plant looks in summer, fall and winter, and at several stages from early to late spring.

Summer: dormancy

During the heat of summer a crocus plant is totally dormant. All you see is a plump, dry bulb (technically a corm in the case of a crocus). Any leaves or roots are totally withered. During dormancy, which lasts for several months, crocus bulbs don't need watering, light, or care. If you already have crocuses in your garden, you can ignore them all summer—simply let them rest in place.

For commercial bulb growers, summer is the busy season. While they are dormant, bulbs can easily and safely be dug, sorted, packed, stored, and shipped cross-country or around the world. Crocuses and other spring-flowering bulbs are always harvested in summer and sold in fall.

Buy fresh bulbs as soon as they are available. Choose ones that are plump, firm, and clean—not at all withered, mushy, or moldy. Any leaves sprouting out from the top of the bulb should still be very short (less than $\frac{1}{4}$ inch long). Usually there won't be any sprouts visible at all.

Cool weather: root growth

In the fall, when the soil temperature drops below about 60°F, a crocus plant comes out of dormancy. New roots emerge from the base of the bulb and start absorbing water and nutrients from the soil. These roots grow slowly all winter, pausing if the soil freezes. Meanwhile, buds that will turn into flowers and leaves are developing inside the bulb. It takes at least two or three months of cool weather for most spring-flowering bulbs to complete the process of root and bud development.

Plant newly purchased bulbs as soon as the soil cools off—sometime between Labor Day and Thanksgiving, depending on where you live. Don't wait too late, because the sooner you plant them, the more time they have to grow roots and get established. Between purchase and planting, store bulbs in a dry, dark place at room temperature.

Choose or prepare a site with loose, deep, well-drained soil. Make planting holes two to three times as deep as the height of the bulbs. Space small bulbs 3 to 5 inches apart, and larger bulbs 4 to 8 inches apart, depending on how dense you want the

planting to look. As you plant each bulb, look for whiskers left from last year's roots, and set the whiskery end down. Refill the planting holes with soil, then cover the area with a few inches of mulch.

Fall is the best time to fertilize bulbs, because that's when the roots start growing. Use any commercial bulb fertilizer at the rate recommended on the package. Sprinkle it on the soil where bulbs are already growing, or after planting new bulbs. Normally, rainfall will dissolve the fertilizer and soak it into the soil, but if the weather is dry, give the area a good watering after you plant or fertilize bulbs.

Spring: flowers and seeds

After a two- to three-month cold period, a crocus is ready to grow rapidly as soon as the soil warms up again. There's progress from day to day as first leaves and then flower buds poke above the soil. Typically a single bulb produces two or more tufts of leaves and flowers.

The flowers open wide on sunny days and close at night or during cloudy weather. They stay fresh-looking for a week or so in hot, dry climates and for up to a month in cool, moist climates, then flop over and fade away. You don't have to remove the fading flowers of crocuses and other bulbs, but you can if you want to.

Crocuses and similar plants may or may not bear seeds, depending on the kind of plant and whether or not the flowers get pollinated. If you're lucky and conditions are right, a species such as winter aconite (*Eranthus hyemalis*) or spring snowflake (*Leucojum vernum*) may self-sow and form a glorious patch in your garden.

Cultivars of daffodils, tulips, and hyacinths, however, rarely bear seeds unless the flowers are hand-pollinated. That's how breeders develop new cultivars of these bulbs, but plant-breeding takes patience and optimism. A bulb seedling has to grow at least three years to reach flowering size, and most hybrid seedlings are inferior to their parents—only rarely is one worth naming and propagating.

Spring: leaves and bulbs

The leaves of a crocus, daffodil, or similar plant continue to elongate after the flowers fade, and stay green for about two months before they gradually turn yellow or brown and die down. Meanwhile, the old bulb shrinks and new bulbs form. Food produced by the leaves is stored in these new bulbs. The longer the leaves grow, the bigger the bulbs get, and the more flowers they can bear the next year, so let the leaves mature at their own pace—don't be too quick to pluck them off.

Over the years, the offspring from a single bulb can form a crowded clump. As long as the plant flowers abundantly, leave it alone. To expand or revitalize an older clump, divide it in late spring, as soon as the leaves turn yellow. Replant the separate bulbs right away in freshly prepared soil (see p. 34).

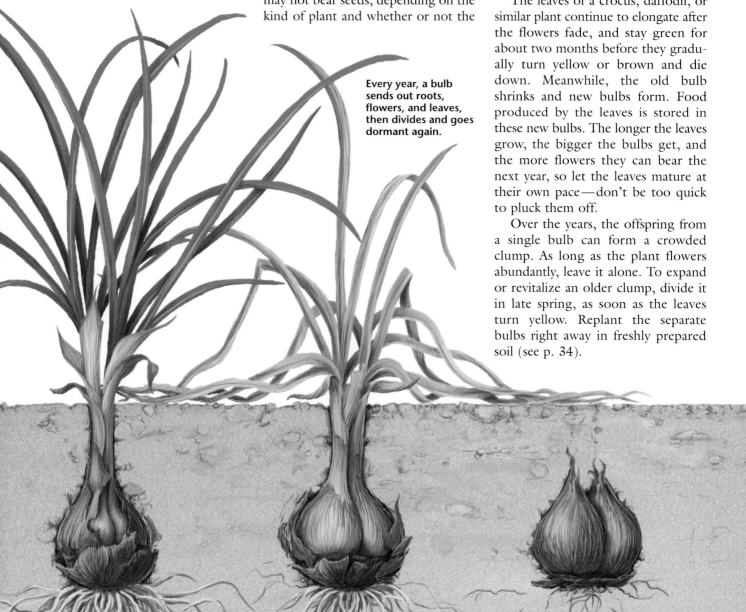

Every year, a bulb sends out roots, flowers, and leaves, then divides and goes dormant again.

A border designed for bulbs

Shown here in late summer, this mixed border features several kinds of plants—clump-forming perennials, clumping grasses, shrubs that need a hard spring pruning, and annuals—that combine well with bulbs. The border is designed for a sunny site in Zones 5 to 8, and measures 6 feet deep by 19 feet long. Turn the page to see what the same border would look like in spring.

Not all plants combine well with bulbs, and vice versa. Things to think about are timing, plant size, and growth habit. For example, surrounding bulbs with other plants that bloom at the same time makes a dis-

play that's impressive for a few weeks in spring but boring afterwards. In this design, the bulbs and other plants complement each other by flowering in alternate seasons.

Bulbs combine best with vigorous plants that emerge later and get taller than the bulb leaves do. Dainty or prostrate plants can get hidden or even smothered by a mass of floppy bulb foliage. Combining bulbs with plants that form clumps (as opposed to plants that spread into patches) makes it easier to divide or relocate the bulbs or the other plants without damaging either of them. As for spacing, you can arrange several bulbs under and around a single shrub or a large perennial or grass, or alternate clumps of bulbs with smaller perennials or annuals like squares on a checkerboard. In the following descriptions, the letters refer to the plan at right. Unless otherwise noted, use one of each plant.

Shrubby plants

Bulbs combine well with shrubs or shrubby perennials that need annual pruning to remain neat and vigorous, filling the "down time" in spring when the shrubs are mere stubs. This plan includes three shrubs that bloom over a long season in summer and early fall. Prune them each year in late winter or early spring, leaving stubs less than 1 foot tall. New growth will begin in late spring and develop fast enough to hide the maturing bulb foliage.

Russian sage (*Perovskia atriplicifolia*) forms a vase-shaped clump 3 to 4 feet tall, with fine-textured, aromatic

Russian sage

Butterfly bush

Lilies

Vinca

Dwarf fountain grass

gray foliage and long thin spikes of small blue flowers. **Butterfly bush** (*Buddleia davidii*) cultivars grow 4 to 8 feet tall, and have arching stems tipped with spikes of fragrant pink, blue, purple, or white flowers. **Tree mallow** (*Lavatera thuringiaca* 'Barnsley') grows about 4 feet tall and has pink flowers that look like hollyhocks or hibiscus.

Clump-forming perennials

Small, early-blooming bulbs are good for filling the spaces around and between perennials whose stems emerge from a compact central crown in late spring and branch or arch in all directions to form a bushy mass later in the season. **Balloonflower** (*Platy-*

codon grandiflorus) blooms over a long season, with puffy buds that open into star-shaped flowers. Depending on cultivar, the flowers are blue, white, or pink, on stems 1 to 3 feet tall. Use three plants of a compact cultivar to fill the area shown in this plan. **Nippon daisy** (*Chrysanthemum nipponicum*) forms a dome-shaped clump of glossy foliage, 2 to 3 feet tall, and bears daisies from mid-fall until hard frost.

Lilies (*Lilium*) are hardy summer-blooming bulbs that combine well with spring bulbs. There are hundreds of wonderful hybrid lily cultivars, with large flowers in a wide range of colors on stalks 1 to 6 feet tall. For this plan, choose pink or white Asiatic or Oriental hybrid lilies that grow about 3 feet tall. Plant two groups of six bulbs each.

Clumping grasses

Bulbs combine well with any ornamental grasses that need to be cut to the ground in winter or early spring and form a fountainlike clump in summer and fall.

Dwarf fountain grass (*Pennisetum alopecuroides* 'Hameln') grows about 2 feet tall and 3 to 4 feet wide, with slender leaves and bottlebrush-like flowerheads.

Annuals

Spring bulbs finish blooming before it's safe to plant frost-sensitive annuals, so this makes a timely combination. For this plan, use six plants of **vinca**, or Madagascar periwinkle (*Catharanthus roseus*), which can have shiny white, rose, or pink flowers; and six plants of **flossflower**, or ageratum (*Ageratum houstonianum*) which has fuzzy blue, white, or purplish flowers.

Lilies

Tree mallow

Nippon daisy

Flossflower

Balloonflower

The same border in spring

The same border looks dramatically different in spring, when the shrubs, perennials, and grass have been cut off short and the annuals discarded, and flowering bulbs paint a colorful picture. Of course, these bulbs would actually flower in sequence over a span of many weeks, not all at once as shown here. Precise timing varies from place to place and year to year, but in most situations, the shorter plants shown across the front of the border would bloom earlier than the taller plants shown in back.

When designing a mixed border like this, arrange the larger plants— the shrubs, grasses, and perennials— first, spacing and positioning them according to their size, then decide which bulbs to add and how many of each to use. It's easier to keep track of what's where if you make the areas coincide. Here, for example, there are hyacinths in the area under and around the Russian sage, tulips interplanted with the lilies, etc.

Daffodils

Daffodils or narcissus (*Narcissus*) are the most popular and reliable spring bulbs. These troublefree plants thrive throughout the United States, need minimal care, and bloom year after year, often surviving for decades. There are hundreds of excellent cultivars. Most have yellow or gold flowers, but some are all or part white, and a few kinds have orange or pink cups. The flowers range from 1 to 5 inches wide, on stalks 6 to 20 inches tall, and can be scentless or very fragrant, and single or double. Daffodil season begins in very early spring and continues, with one cultivar following another, through late spring.

Any and all daffodils do well in a mixed border. This garden plan uses **'Ice Follies' daffodils** (ivory flowers on 18-inch stalks, midseason, plant 12 bulbs in front of the butterfly bush), and **'February Gold' daffodils** (yellow flowers on 6-inch stalks, very early, plant 18 bulbs in the left front corner, where annual vinca blooms in summer).

Tulips

Tulips (*Tulipa*) are almost as popular as daffodils, and they come in many more colors, including all shades of red, pink, purple, orange, gold, and white. The flowers vary in shape and size and can be single or double, on stalks 6 to 36 inches tall. Although they are beautiful, tulips can be disappointing. Typically, they bloom well the first spring after you plant the bulbs but have fewer, smaller flowers afterwards. The petals drop quickly in hot, dry, windy, or stormy weather, and the plants are vulnerable to deer, rodents, and diseases.

This plan uses **'Pink Impression' tulips** (pink flowers on 20-inch stalks, midseason, use two groups of 12 each among the lilies), and *Tulipa bakeri* **'Lilac Wonder'** (pink-and-yellow flowers on 6-inch stalks, midseason, plant 24 bulbs in the right front corner, where flossflower blooms in summer. As tulips go, these two kinds are relatively long-lasting.

Dutch iris

Hybrid Dutch iris *(Iris)* have elegantly shaped blue, yellow, purple, white, or bicolor flowers on stiff stalks 18 to 24 inches tall. There are several named cultivars. They typically bloom in May. This plan uses **mixed Dutch iris** (plant 24 bulbs behind the butterflybush).

Hyacinth

Garden, or Dutch, hyacinth *(Hyacinthus orientalis)* produces short, chubby, densely packed spikes of very fragrant blue, purple, violet, pink, pale yellow, or white flowers. Typically each bulb produces a single flowerstalk and reblooms for a few years but doesn't multiply. There are a few dozen named cultivars. This plan uses **'Delft Blue' hyacinth** (blue flowers, 10 inches tall, mid-spring, plant 24 bulbs around the Russian sage).

Bluebells

Spanish bluebell, or wood hyacinth (now *Hyacinthoides hispanica,* but often listed under *Scilla* or *Endymion)* has scentless flowers that are shaped like hyacinths but are arranged more loosely on several stalks. The flowers are typically blue, but there are pink and white forms. English bluebell (*H. non-scriptus)* has smaller, blue, fragrant flowers. Both species are carefree, inexpensive, and long-lived plants that multiply quickly and adapt to sun or part shade. This plan uses **Spanish bluebell** (blue flowers on 12-inch stalks, mid-spring, plant 24 bulbs around the tree mallow).

Crocus

There are many species and cultivars of spring-blooming crocus *(Crocus)*, but the most common and widely available types fall into two groups: snow crocus *(C. chrysanthus)*, which bloom very early and have smaller flowers, and Dutch, or hybrid, crocus *(C. vernus)*, which bloom a few weeks later and have larger flowers. Both kinds are sold in mixed bags or by separate color, and come in shades of yellow, blue-violet, purple, white, and striped or bicolor. A single bulb produces three or more flowers, and the bulbs multiply quickly and bloom year after year, unless they are discovered by rodents, who eat crocus bulbs like candy. This plan uses **mixed snow crocus** (4 inches tall, very early spring, plant 24 bulbs around the three balloonflowers).

Other small bulbs

Windflower *(Anemone blanda)* has daisylike flowers on short stalks and lacy foliage. The flowers come in shades of white, pink, or blue, all with yellow "eyes." The plants are carefree and adaptable and spread quickly. This plan uses **'White Spendour' windflower** (white flowers on 4-inch stalks, mid-spring, plant 24 bulbs around the fountain grass).

Glory-of-the-snow *(Chionodoxa luciliae)* has sprays of starry blue, pink, white, or two-tone flowers in early spring. It's easy to grow and multiplies quickly. This plan uses **'Gigantea' glory-of-the-snow** (blue flowers on 8-inch stalks, early spring, plant 24 bulbs around the Nippon daisy).

Instead of windflower or glory-of-the-snow, you could substitute other small bulbs such as snowdrops *(Galanthus nivalis)*, with nodding white flowers; winter aconite *(Eranthis hyemalis)*, with buttercup-like flowers on a leafy collar; dwarf iris *(Iris reticulata)*, with small blue, purple, yellow, or white flowers; or grape hyacinth *(Muscari)*, with very fragrant purple, blue, or white flowers arranged in grapelike clusters.

'Pink Impression' tulip

Spanish bluebell

'Lilac Wonder' tulip

'White Splendour' windflower

Snow crocus

Where else can you plant bulbs?

If you'd like to add more bulbs to your garden but can't decide where to put them, here are some ideas and suggestions for how you can tuck spring-flowering bulbs around and be-tween your existing plants. When you add extra plants to a garden, the soil may not provide enough nutrients for everything to reach its full potential, so it's a good idea to apply bulb fer-tilizer every year in late fall, and spread a balanced, slow-release, or-ganic fertilizer in spring, too.

Bulbs and sun-loving shrubs

Bulbs combine well with shrubs or shrubby perennials that should or can be pruned hard each spring. Along with the butterfly bush, Russian sage, and tree mallow shown on p. 96, other plants in this category include south-ernwood, wormwood, and other shrubby artemisias (*Artemisia*), blue-beard or blue mist (*Caryopteris* × *cladonensis*), red-twig dogwoods (*Cor-nus alba*, *C. sericea*), shrubby St.-John's-worts (*Hypericum*), shrubby indigos (*Indigofera*), lavenders (*La-vandula*), bush clover (*Lespedeza thunbergii*), bush cinquefoil (*Potentilla fruticosa*), most roses (*Rosa*), shrubby willows (*Salix*), summer-blooming spiraeas (*Spiraea japonica*), tamarisk (*Tamarix*), and germander (*Teucrium chamaedrys*). Any of these shrubs can be cut close to the ground in late win-ter, so it will be out of the way when the bulbs flower; it will grow back in late spring and look better than ever.

Combinations for shady sites

Most bulbs grow and flower well on sites that are sunny in spring but turn shady in summer when decidu-ous trees leaf out overhead or nearby. Whether you have a single tree or a woodland garden, try interplanting bulbs with hostas, astilbes, goatsbeard (*Aruncus dioicus*), black cohosh (*Cimicifuga racemosa*), Solomon's-seals (*Polygonatum*), or false Solo-mon's seal (*Smilacina racemosa*); with any ferns that grow taller than the bulb foliage; or with Northern sea oats (*Chasmanthium latifolium*), a shade-tolerant grass.

Also, bulbs are good companions for shade-tolerant deciduous shrubs that leaf out late, such as bayberry (*Myrica pensylvanica*) or fringetree (*Chionanthus virginicus*), or that need hard pruning in early spring, such as *Hydrangea arborescens* 'Annabelle' or snowberry and coralberry (*Sym-phoricarpos*).

Bulbs and ground covers

Planting bulbs to add seasonal color to a bed of low evergreen ground covers might sound like a good idea, but it usually doesn't work well. At best, the bulb foliage is con-spicuous for weeks; at worst, a floppy mass of dying bulb foliage can actu-

Grape hyacinths bloom amidst emerging hostas.

Dutch irises accompany sun-loving shrubs.

ally smother a prostrate ground cover, leaving bald spots that may or may not fill in later in the season.

It works better to combine bulbs with deciduous ground covers that are dormant or still short when the bulbs bloom but grow tall enough to hide the bulb foliage soon after. Also, if you ever need or want to divide either the bulbs or the ground cover, it's easier if the ground cover stays in clumps and doesn't form a continuous mat. Some herbaceous perennials that make good ground covers and can combine well with bulbs are dwarf plumbago, (*Ceratostigma plumbaginoides*), pinks (*Dianthus*), bishop's hat (*Epimedium*), hardy geraniums (*Geranium*), daylilies (*Hemerocallis*), hostas (*Hosta*), catmints (*Nepeta*), and violets (*Viola*).

Bulbs and ornamental grasses

Many ornamental grasses should be cut off close to the ground during the winter or early spring, and don't resume growth until the weather gets warm. Spring-flowering bulbs are perfect for filling this gap. Plant bulbs around or between clump-forming grasses such as feather reed grass (*Calamagrostis* × *acutiflora*), ravenna grass (*Erianthus ravennae*), miscanthus cultivars (*Miscanthus sinensis*), switch grass (*Panicum virgatum*), the various kinds of fountain grass (*Pennisetum*), and little bluestem (*Schizachyrium scoparium*). Every few years, you can dig and divide both the grasses and the bulbs at the same time, in spring.

Bulbs and turf grasses

Most bulbs grow very well in association with common lawn, pasture, or meadow grasses. If you wait until the bulb foliage has matured before mowing the grass, the bulbs may persist for many years, gradually spreading by division and by seed. If you (and your neighbors) are open-minded about unmown grass, give this combination a try. Plant inexpensive, old-fashioned cultivars or assorted "landscape-quality" bulbs of crocus, snowdrop, grape hyacinth, squill, bluebell, or daffodil.

Pheasant's eye narcissus and ajuga brighten a shady site.

Daffodil 'Hawera' combines well with violets and other deciduous ground covers.

A well-planned vegetable garden looks neat and full and provides a steady, varied harvest.

VEGETABLES

To most Americans a generation ago, the word "gardening" meant "growing vegetables." Now many gardeners focus on flowers instead, and don't grow any vegetables at all.

That's a loss, because growing vegetables offers a satisfaction that flowers can't match. It's a miracle, really, and much too precious to overlook or take for granted, that you can sow a few pinches of tiny seeds, no bigger than the letters on this page, and watch those plants develop into bushels of food. This happens *fast!* Most vegetables grow from seed to harvest in just two or three months. And they're so *good!* Garden-fresh vegetables set the standard for flavor and quality. I think it's important to stay in touch with all this, and to teach children about it, too.

Choosing what to grow

When you decide to grow some vegetables, the first question is what kinds to plant. Here are some tips:

- Grow what you love to eat. Tomatoes, snow peas, sweet corn, whatever it is, a homegrown serving of your favorite vegetable is a treat worth working for.
- Grow what you can't buy. Seed catalogs offer hundreds of vegetable varieties—both old heirlooms and new hybrids—that you'll never find in a supermarket. Read the descriptions closely, and choose kinds recommended for their taste and tenderness. Also, grow perishable crops that bruise easily and don't ship well, such as spinach, butterhead lettuce, or baby squash.
- Experiment. Compare different vegetables, and different varieties of the same vegetable, to see which ones grow best for you and which taste best to you.

- Branch out. Try uncommon vegetables such as kohlrabi, horticultural beans, or tomatillos. Try vegetables in unfamiliar colors, such as white eggplants, ruby chard, or yellow beets.

How much to plant?

Crop yields and people's appetites vary so much that you'd think there's no answer for this question, but actually it's simple. Whatever your first estimate might be, divide it in half. No kidding, gardeners almost *always* plant too much of any vegetable. Those jokes about zucchini are so funny because they're so true. Sometimes you can preserve or give away extra vegetables, or you can always compost them, but growing too much of one thing wastes space that you could have used for something else.

Unless you feed many mouths or want to do some preserving, plant just small quantities of each crop at any one time. Combine varieties that mature at different rates, or make successive plantings every few weeks, to sustain the harvest. If you haven't grown vegetables before, start with numbers like this:

Assorted greens. Sow 2- to 4-foot rows of each kind. Replant often.

Cabbage, broccoli, and cauliflower. Three or four plants of any one.

Carrots, beets. Plant 4-foot rows.

Peas. One 8-foot row.

Snap beans. One 4-foot row of bush beans, or one teepee of pole beans.

Tomatoes. A total of three or four plants, of different varieties.

Pepper. A total of six to eight plants, of different varieties.

Eggplant. A total of two or three plants, of different varieties.

Sweet corn. About two dozen plants, arranged in a square block.

Squash and cucumber. One or two hills of each kind you grow.

Potatoes and sweet potato. A dozen plants of either or both.

Succession planting

This is a strategy for producing fresh vegetables over as long a season as possible, by timing crops to ripen in sequence, not all at once. It's also a way to multiply the amount you can harvest from a single plot of land. Working out the details depends on your climate and which vegetables you want to grow, but here are some typical examples:

- Plant both "early" (fast-growing) and "late" (slower-growing) varieties of tomatoes; they'll ripen at different times.
- Plant short rows of peas or beans every two weeks; when you finish harvesting one batch, the next will be ready.
- Fill gaps fast by planting a small patch of lettuce, other salad greens, or radishes in any empty space.
- Alternate crops that prefer cool weather, such as peas and carrots, with warm-weather vegetables such as tomatoes and peppers. When one crop is done, pull it out and plant the other.

Days to maturity

Take these numbers, which are given in seed catalogs and in this article, as general guidelines, *not* as guarantees. (Also, when reading catalogs, be sure to distinguish whether the day numbers refer to starting from seeds or transplants.) How long it takes any particular vegetable variety to mature in your garden depends on how warm the soil and air are, how long the days are, and whether you have more sunny or cloudy days. If you keep track, you'll find the actual number of days to maturity is occasionally a few days less than the stated number, and often many more than predicted.

Wall-o-Water

Cold frame

Keys to success

Almost all common vegetables require similar care and growing conditions. The only major difference is that some vegetables grow better in cool weather, and others in warm weather; for more about that, see the following pages.

Choose a sunny site

Plant vegetables in a site that's not shaded by trees or nearby buildings. In summer, vegetable plants need at least six to eight hours of sun a day. From fall to spring, when the days are shorter and the sun is lower in the sky, full sun all day gives best results. Without enough sun, vegetable plants grow weak and floppy and their yield is greatly reduced.

Loosen the soil

The job of transforming plain old worn-out dirt into rich, soft, fertile soil is easier and faster than you'd think, and it's very impressive and gratifying to see how vegetables respond to your efforts. When starting a new vegetable garden, dig or till the soil 6 to 8 inches deep, removing any rocks, roots, or debris. Then spread a 2- to 4-inch layer of compost, shredded leaves, rotten manure, peat moss, or other organic matter over the bed, and work it into the soil. As time goes on, keep adding more organic matter at least once a year, or whenever you pull out one crop and plant another.

Consider raised beds

Raised beds can simply be soil raked or hoed into broad, shallow mounds, or you can build wooden or masonry frames 6 to 12 inches tall and fill them with a mixture of topsoil and organic matter. Either way, the advantages of a raised bed are that the soil warms up faster, drainage is better, you don't have to bend over so far, and you're less likely to step onto the soil and compact it.

Note, though, that raised beds can dry out *too* fast in hot, arid climates or where the soil is sandy. In those conditions, you'd better plant on the level, or in depressions called sunken beds.

Fertilize thoughtfully

Various kinds of manure and other organic and natural fertilizers are all good for vegetable gardens, but don't guess at how much to use. Recommendations are usually given in pounds per 100 or 1000 square feet, so measure the area of the garden and weigh out the appropriate amounts. Spread the materials as evenly as possible and work them into the soil.

Vegetable plants also respond quickly and well when you sprinkle or spray dilute fertilizer solutions onto their leaves. Products made from fish and seaweed seem especially helpful. Measure and apply as directed on the label.

Water generously

Don't wait until the soil gets so dry that plants wilt. If it doesn't rain enough, use a sprinkler, soaker hose, or drip system to wet the soil several inches deep. (Check this by digging test holes to see how far the water has soaked in.)

Allow enough space

Use a yardstick (or paint stripes every 6 inches on your rake or hoe handle and use that) when you're sowing seeds, thinning seedlings, or setting out transplants, and follow the spacing guidelines on the seed packets or in the catalog. At the time, you'll think everything is way too far apart, but they'll grow to fill the whole area sooner than you can imagine. Give vegetable plants enough space and they will yield more, be healthier, and be easier to tend and pick.

Stay ahead of the weeds

Don't let weeds overwhelm you and our garden. First, keep your garden small enough that you can do a thorough weeding once a week, removing every single sprout. Then, from day to day, pull stray weeds as soon as you spot them.

Mulching greatly reduces the job of weeding. Between rows and around the plants, use straw (but not hay, since it often introduces more weeds than it suppresses), lawn grass clippings, tree leaves, compost, etc. These materials decompose fast, so you can work them into the soil between crops. Use longer-lasting materials like wood chips or shredded bark to surface the pathways.

Defend against pests

Plant some vegetables, and you'll soon realize how much wildlife, like this fat woodchuck, is present in your neighborhood, and you'll be amazed how much these creatures can eat. If woodchucks, rabbits, deer, gophers, or other critters find your garden, you'll probably have to put up a fence, try repellents or noisemakers, leave a dog out, or set traps.

Meanwhile, bees, wasps, bugs, beetles, flies, caterpillars, earwigs, slugs, and mites will be buzzing and crawling all over the place, but don't be alarmed—not all of these are bad. Many are harmless, and some are beneficial. Before you try killing any supposed pest, make sure you've identified the actual culprit.

You can repel or control almost all vegetable insect pests with safe-to-use, environmentally responsible products made from soaps, oils, and botanical extracts. These "new" (actually, some are as old as the sky) insecticides were sold only by mail a few years ago, but now local garden centers stock them, too. You may have to dust or spray the infested plants more than once; follow directions on the label and monitor the results.

Avert diseases

Vegetable plants are subject to several kinds of blights, spots, wilts, rusts. To prevent or reduce disease problems, choose resistant varieties (these are noted in catalog writeups), space plants far enough apart that air can circulate between them, water regularly so the plants aren't stressed by drought, and dispose of any plants that do get infected by putting them in the trash, not the compost. In humid climates, where disease problems are most severe, you can dust or spray with sulfur- or copper-based fungicides. These work better if applied in advance, to prevent disease, than for treating a problem that's already evident.

Extend the season

If you've set aside part of your property for growing vegetables, it makes sense to use that space for as many months as possible, not just in summer. You can extend the growing season in both spring and fall by growing cool-weather crops, and also by using protective coverings and enclosures such as Wall-o-Waters (clear plastic cone-shaped tubes that you fill with water) and cold frames, shown opposite. For example, you can plant tomatoes in Wall-o-Waters a month before the last frost in spring, or pick spinach and other salad greens from a cold frame all winter.

Try row covers

These are big white sheets of synthetic fabric that protect plants from frost in spring or fall but let light, air, and water through. There are different weights, offering protection down to 30°F, 28°F, or even 25°F. These fabrics are inexpensive, and you can re-use them several times. Buy a big piece and cut it to size with scissors. Lay it directly on the plants and hold it down with stones, or support it with hoops of plastic pipe. Row covers look very tacky, but they work better than you'd dare to hope, protecting plants not only from cold weather, but also from insects and varmints.

Keep a garden journal

If you grow vegetables for a few years and keep track of what you do, you can really fine-tune your system and become quite expert at growing just the right amounts of the crops you love best, and timing them for a steady harvest over as long as season as possible. Make notes of when you plant each crop, when you start picking it, when it's finished, how much you plant and pick, which varieties you like best, whether the plants need more or less space than you allowed, and ideas for improving your garden in the future.

Make a pretty garden

Vegetables combine well with annual flowers, such as calendulas, marigolds, cosmos, zinnias, and sunflowers; with annual herbs, such as parsley, basil, and dill; with everlastings such as strawflowers and statice; and with novelties such as gourds, pumpkins, and broom corn. A mixed planting is more colorful and attractive than a garden of vegetables only, and you'll have more fun designing, planting, and tending it.

Woodchuck

Cool-weather crops

These vegetable prefer cool weather. They grow fastest when daytime temperatures are in the 60s or low 70s and nights dip into the 50s or upper 40s, but tolerate much cooler temperatures, including light frosts. What they can't take is heat—they stop growing or die when temperatures reach into the 90s.

Timing

You can start planting cool-weather vegetables when the early daffodils bloom; depending on where you live, that may be late January or late May. Enjoy these early crops until you've used them up or they wither in the heat, then plant again later in the year.

For a second crop in cold climates, count backward from the average first hard frost date, and time plantings so they'll mature around or soon after that date. Use row covers to protect the plants, and you can continue harvesting throughout the fall and early winter, until you've eaten all there is to pick.

Where winters are mild, you can start in late summer and plant a succession of cool-weather crops to harvest through the fall and winter. Because the days are shorter and the sun is lower, vegetables grow slowly in winter, and they'll stop altogether during chilly, dreary weather, but they start right up again at the first sign of spring.

A medley of greens

Almost all kinds of leafy vegetables that you eat raw or cooked grow best in cool weather. This includes lettuce,

Plant peas, beets, and carrots in early spring or in fall, as they prefer cool weather.

spinach, mesclun mixes, arugula, endive, mache, radicchio, Oriental greens, mustard greens, and Swiss chard. These are all easily raised from seeds, sown directly where you want the plants to grow. You can start picking most greens about 40 to 60 days after sowing the seeds. Plant small patches or short rows of several different kinds and combine them for interesting salads and stir-fries. If you have a long cool season, replant every few weeks to prolong the harvest.

The cabbage clan

The various kinds of cabbage, broccoli, Brussels sprouts, cauliflower, collards, kale, and kohlrabi all belong to a single species, *Brassica oleracea*. Often called cole crops, these tasty, nourishing, healthful vegetables all grow best in cool weather. The plants get larger than you expect—much wider than the part you harvest, so space them about 2 feet apart. You can direct-seed any of them, or save space by sowing them in small pots or in a nursery bed and transplanting the seedlings when they are four to six weeks old. Most kinds are ready to pick about 60 to 90 days after transplanting in spring. Fall and winter crops develop more slowly than that.

Peas

English or shelling peas (the kind you shell out of their pods), snap peas (with thick, succulent pods that you eat like snap beans), and snow peas (the kind with flat, tender pods, used

in Chinese food) all taste especially sweet and tender when picked fresh from the garden. Pea plants thrive in cool, but not *cold* weather. They languish if planted too early, and can be damaged by hard frosts. From sowing to harvest takes about 60 to 90 days.

Unlike most vegetables, peas grow best if the plants are crowded close together, so sow the seeds about one inch apart in bands 4 to 6 inches wide. English peas do not yield much—a short row only supplies a few servings, and the pods all mature within a week or so. By contrast, edible-pod peas seem to produce all you can eat, and the plants may continue bearing for a few weeks or more if you keep picking them.

Carrots

You can sow seeds in early spring and harvest crisp, tender carrots about 65 to 75 days later. These will be lots better than what you buy at the store, but not as good as carrots can be. The *best* carrots are timed to mature in fall, as the weather cools off, and you can leave them in the ground until the soil freezes (or all winter in mild areas). Grown this way, carrots become as sweet and juicy as apples.

Carrot seeds are tiny and you inevitably sow them too thick. When they're about 1 inch tall, thin the seedlings to stand about 3 inches apart. (If thinning by hand is too tedious for you, run a rake down the bed to comb out some of the seedlings.) Diseases cause problems in some areas, but where carrots grow well, they're very productive, yielding more food per square foot than almost any other vegetable.

Radishes, beets and turnips

These crops are all sensitive to heat and drought, which stunt the plants and make the roots tough and woody. But in cool, moist weather they grow very quickly and make tender, juicy roots. You'll be eating regular or "breakfast" radishes within 25 or 30 days of sowing the seeds. "Winter" radishes, beets, and turnips are ready in 50 to 70 days.

Although called root crops, these plants are dual-purpose. Steamed beet greens or turnip greens are wholesome and nourishing; cut them off when you harvest the roots. And let a few radish plants go to bloom, then pick the immature seedpods—they're as tender and tasty as the roots.

Onions and their kin

Growing good onions is tricky, because the plants are sensitive to daylength as well as being fussy about soil and vulnerable to several diseases and pests. Growing scallions (green onions that are pencil-thick, with no swollen bulb), however, is easy. Sow seeds of "bunching" onions to harvest as scallions about 90 to 100 days later, or plants sets of regular onions and harvest them after 45 to 60 days.

Homegrown leeks and garlic have great flavor, but they're slow. Sow leek seeds in early spring, and harvest in fall. Plant garlic cloves in early fall, and harvest them the next summer.

Potatoes

Potatoes are an intermediate crop; they can't take frost *or* extreme heat. Plant "seed potatoes" (pieces of sprouted tuber) when the dandelions bloom in spring, a few inches deep and at least 18 inches apart, and pile soil or mulch around the stems as the plants grow. Watch for the pretty flowers; about a month later you can dig small "new" potatoes. Wait until the vines wither to dig mature, full-size potatoes. One plant can produce a few pounds of potatoes.

Warm-weather crops

Wait until the soil feels warm against your bare hands or feet before planting these vegetables in the garden; otherwise, seeds will rot and transplants will sulk. Warm weather crops grow best when both soil and air (day and night) temperatures average 60°F or higher.

Where summers are long and hot, you can (in fact, you'll have to) make successive plantings of most warm-weather crops, as the first plantings will wear out or succumb to the heat by midsummer. If your frostfree season is shorter than four months, you'll only need to (or get to) make one or two plantings of these crops.

Get a head start

If you want to pick warm-weather crops as early as possible—in any region, but especially where summers are short—use these techniques:

• Buy transplants at a garden center, or grow your own by sowing seeds indoors under fluorescent lights (see p. 41). From sowing seeds to transplanting (including a few days for hardening-off the seedlings), allow six to eight weeks for tomatoes and eggplants; eight to ten weeks for peppers; and three weeks for corn, squash, and cucumbers. (It's debatable whether you gain much by

starting this last group indoors, but it doesn't hurt to try.) Don't bother starting beans indoors; it doesn't work well.

• Make raised beds, so the soil warms up faster. Don't apply any organic mulch until after the soil is warm—bare soil heats up faster.

• Although it's ugly, and installing and removing it is an annoying job, plastic mulch really works great for warming the soil. You can use either clear or black plastic. Prepare the bed and install the mulch a week or so before planting, to preheat the soil, then leave the mulch in place throughout the season.

• If the soil is warm enough for planting but nights are still chilly, use fabric row covers or enclosures to protect seedlings and transplants. Monitor the weather, and be sure all tender plants are covered if a late frost is forecast.

Tomatoes

Try growing different kinds of tomatoes—large and small, juicy and pulpy, sweet and tangy, red and golden. One or two plants of each kind is enough, unless you plan to can, freeze, or dry them. In seed catalog descriptions, look for disease resistance (especially if you live in a humid climate), growth habit (determinate plants are compact and bushy; indeterminate plants are big heavy

vines that need a strong stake or a cage 4 feet tall), and estimated days from transplanting to first ripe tomato (this ranges from about 60 to 90 days).

Peppers and eggplants

Sweet, or bell, peppers and hot, or chile, peppers all grow a little more slowly and are more sensitive to cold than tomatoes, so start them earlier indoors and don't set them out too soon. After transplanting, it takes at least 70 to 85 days of warm weather for bell peppers to ripen from green to red, gold, or whatever their mature color is, or for chile peppers to develop their "hot" flavor. Don't pick them too soon; peppers taste best when fully mature. The plants need rich soil and constant moisture, but aren't troubled much by insects or diseases.

Grow eggplants like peppers, but harvest the fruits while they are still small and shiny; don't wait too long or they get tough and seedy. Each plant bears many fruits over a span of several weeks. Eggplants and peppers are both pretty plants, bushy and upright, and you'll enjoy watching their colorful fruits form.

Sweet corn and pop corn

You don't need a big garden to grow some corn. You can succeed with a patch as small as 6 by 6 feet, holding about two dozen plants spaced about 18 inches apart. (Arrange the plants in a square block for good pollination.) Each plant bears one or two ears, and corn tends to ripen all at once, so a patch that size may produce all you can eat fresh. If you have space, plant several patches of varieties that ripen at different times (the range is from about 60 to 90 days).

Pop corn grows just like sweet corn, but requires at least 90 days. Wait until the stalks turn brown before husking out the ears, then let them dry a few weeks indoors before shelling off the kernels.

All kinds of beans

Snap beans, with crisp, edible pods that can be green, yellow, or purple, round, flat, or skinny, and stringy or stringless, grow in two forms: "bush" plants, which grow knee-high, and "pole" beans, which climb 6 to 8 feet up a trellis or teepee of poles. Bush forms are ready to pick about 55 to 65 days after planting and produce generously for two or three weeks. Pole forms start bearing after about 70 days, and continue for several weeks; their productivity will astound you.

Beans that you shell out of the pods—dry beans, horticultural beans, and lima beans—take longer to mature (at least 80 days), and it always seems as if the yield is rather low for the space, time, and effort involved, but if you love eating these beans, then try growing them.

Squashes, pumpkins, and cucumbers

These plants, sometimes called cucurbits, are usually grown in "hills" of two to four plants apiece, spaced at least 4 feet apart. Make the actual hills by raking the soil into low, flat mounds; this helps it get warm so the seedlings will grow faster. Summer squashes, such as zucchini, yellow crookneck, and pattypan, start producing about 50 to 60 days after you sow the seeds and continue until you don't want them anymore. Pick them while they're still small and tender.

Cucumbers can be as fast and productive as summer squash, but are more vulnerable to diseases which reduce yield or kill the plants. Winter squashes and pumpkins are less prolific and require at least 90 to 100 days of warm weather to fully mature.

Southern favorites

These are best known and most loved in the South, but they grow well wherever summers are long and warm.

Okra grows tall and narrow, with stiff stalks and flowers like yellow hollyhocks. Pick the tender, finger-sized pods daily from July until frost.

Field peas are bushy, beanlike plants that make long skinny pods filled with cream, brown, or "black-eye" peas. Wait until the peas reach full size and make bumps in the pods before picking them.

Sweet potatoes are vigorous vines that can creep or climb. Plant rooted slips in spring, and harvest by digging the tubers before frost in fall.

Peanuts are bushy plants that prefer sandy soil, as their pods form in an odd way—after flowering, the stems bend over and burrow into the ground! Dig the peanuts when the plants wither in fall.

Corn

Peppers

Squash

Strawberry plants are pretty, and they grow quickly and bear abundant crops.

FRUITS AND BERRIES

Everyone appreciates the difference between a luscious, tender, homegrown tomato and those pulpy, anemic surrogates from the supermarket. Fewer people realize that the same comparison applies to most fruits. You don't know how sweet and juicy a peach can be until you've eaten one right from the tree, or how fragrant ripe cantaloupes are until you've picked one on a sunny day. Homegrown fruit offers flavors, textures, and aromas that you'll never find at a grocery store.

Unlike money, fruit really does grow on trees (and bushes and vines), but you still have to work for it. A bountiful harvest is the reward for planning ahead, choosing fruits suitable for your climate, learning what care the plants need, and providing it on a regular schedule. Growing fruit can be a very satisfying hobby, and you may enjoy the process as much as the results. Here's what you need to get started.

Get local advice

The details of fruit-growing vary widely from place to place, but fortunately there's a lot of reliable, regularly updated, regionally specific information available. Contact your local Cooperative Extension Service to find out which particular fruits are recommended for your area and which you should avoid because they're prone to troublesome insects and diseases.

Choose a suitable site

You don't need an orchard to grow fruit. A 10-foot-square plot is big enough for a dwarf fruit tree, a grape vine, a few hills of melons, or a patch of berries. Many fruit plants are attractive enough to plant as lawn specimens, near the house, or in mixed borders.

Large or small, the site must be sunny throughout the growing season (it can be shaded in winter). Nearly all fruits need full sun all day to develop good color and flavor. The soil should be deep, fertile, and well-drained. If your soil is shallow, poor, or soggy, build raised beds and fill them with better soil.

Buy from a fruit specialist

Garden centers usually don't stock many kinds of fruit plants. For more variety and better quality, it's worth ordering by mail or planning a trip to nursery that specializes in fruit. Most fruit nurseries have catalogs that are informative and tempting. Get catalogs early so you can study them and place your order in time for spring planting.

Be patient and persistent

Melons ripen a few months after planting, and berries in a year or two, but you'll probably have to wait three to five years before picking much fruit from a tree. Tasks such as pruning, mulching, spraying, and thinning have to be done repeatedly, and always at appropriate times. These tasks aren't difficult, but you can't postpone or ignore them if you want top-quality fruit. Plan to protect your fruit from birds and varmints. You may need netting, a fence, or scare-away devices.

Pray for good weather

Most fruits are vulnerable to factors you can't control—late frosts, cloudy spells, too much rain, hail, severe wind, droughts, etc. Some years you lose the crop. Other years everything goes just right and the harvest is magnificent.

A dwarf apple tree can produce up to a bushel of apples every year.

Berry bushes and grapes

Raspberries, blackberries, and grapes are good fruits to start with. The plants do well in all but the coldest and hottest parts of the United States. They grow quickly, bear abundantly, and are relatively trouble-free.

Bramble basics

Raspberries, blackberries, and their kin, collectively called brambles, are vigorous shrubs, usually thorny or prickly, with erect, arching, or trailing stems. Most kinds of raspberries are hardy to Zone 5 or 4; blackberries to Zone 6 or 5. Check catalog descriptions for hardiness of specific cultivars. Brambles tolerate more shade than most fruits and bear well with just a half day of sun; they prefer afternoon shade where summers are hot.

Brambles are self-fertile, so a single plant can bear fruit. A healthy bush produces about two quarts of berries per year. Most kinds of brambles ripen between June and August. Individual plants bear for about three weeks, depending on climate and cultivar. Some kinds of red and gold raspberries ripen in fall, usually beginning in September and continuing until frost.

Most brambles produce a crop the second year after planting, but fall-bearing raspberries bear the first year if planted in spring. With good care, bramble plants live ten years or longer.

Tending brambles

It's easier to maintain a berry patch and to pick the berries if you support the stems or canes with wires, as shown below, or tie them to a wire or rail fence.

Fall-bearing raspberry plants require less care than other brambles. Simply cut or mow the canes close to the ground in late winter. Berries form on new shoots which grow 3 to 5 feet tall by fall.

Summer-bearing brambles need more deliberate pruning, done in three installments. New canes emerge from the ground each spring but do not make berries until the second year.

(1) In early summer, as soon as the new shoots reach 3 to 5 feet, cut off their tops to make them branch out.

(2) Later in the summer, as soon as you finish picking, cut all the older, berry-producing shoots to the ground.

(3) In late winter, cut back the side branches on the new canes, leaving them 1 to 2 feet long. These side branches are where the berries grow.

Pruning thorny brambles is rough work. Wear denim clothes and leather gloves. Don't neglect it, though, or your berry patch will turn into a jungle.

Brambles don't suffer much from insect pests and diseases, but you may have to use netting or scare-away devices to keep birds from eating the berries.

Grapes for your garden

There are wild grapes in almost every state, and it seems as if most states have a winery nowadays too, so chances are good that you can grow grapes in your garden. The secret is choosing a variety that's adapted to your climate and resistant to any diseases which are troublesome in your region.

Cultivars and hybrids developed from our native wild grapes do best in most areas. For example, 'Concord', 'Catawba', and 'Niagara', developed from the wild fox grape which is native throughout the eastern United States, are generally hardy to Zone 5 and ripen in the moist, often cool summers of the Northeast, Northwest, and Midwest.

'Scuppernong', 'Magnolia', and 'Carlos' are cultivars of the muscadine grape, which is native to the Southeast. Hardy to Zone 7, these grape tolerate hot, humid summers.

European-type grapes such as 'Thompson Seedless' and 'Chardonnay' are less adaptable; they require mild winters and long, warm, dry summers. They grow well only in the western United States, particularly in California.

Read catalog descriptions carefully to choose a grape that's suited for eating fresh or making juice, jelly, or wine; only a few kinds are good for all purposes. Most grapes are self-fertile, so you only need one plant, or one of each cultivar. They start bearing in the second or third year. An established vine bears 10 to 20 or more pounds of grapes per year.

Growing grapes

Grapes need full sun, shelter from late spring frosts, good air circulation, and deep, well-drained, but not overly fertile soil. One vine can cover an arbor or spread 8 to 10 feet along a fence or trellis. Build the support first, and make it sturdy. Plant the vine in spring.

For the first few years, you work at training the vine, which means guiding its growth so it has a single upright trunk with two or more horizontal limbs or arms. In subsequent years, you prune every winter, cutting back the canes, which grow several feet long. (Grape prunings are great for making wreaths and baskets.) Reference books give detailed instructions and diagrams on pruning grapes. The process looks complicated in a book, but you soon get the knack of it.

Let grapes ripen completely on the vine before you pick them; the longer you wait, the sweeter they get. As they ripen, you may need to put up netting or fencing to keep birds, raccoons, and possoms away from your grapes. Wasps and hornets are also attracted to ripe grapes, so be careful when you do pick them.

Blueberries

Suitable soil—moist but well-drained, with acid pH (preferably between 4.0 and 5.5)—is the key to success in growing blueberries. If azaleas and rhododendrons grow well in your neighborhood, blueberries will thrive, too.

Choose cultivars suited to your climate. Highbush blueberries, erect shrubs that grow 5 to 10 feet tall; lowbush blueberries, spreading shrubs 1 to 2 feet tall; and high/low hybrids generally do well in Zones 3 to 7, depending on cultivar. Rabbiteye blueberries are larger bushes, reaching 15 feet or taller, and more adaptable plants. They tolerate hot summers and are hardy to Zone 7 or 6. Read the catalog carefully when ordering blueberries. Not all are self-fertile, so you may need to pair two different cultivars for cross-pollination.

With suitable soil and climate, blueberries grow quickly into handsome plants with lovely white flowers in spring, dense twiggy growth, and crimson fall foliage. A row of blueberries makes a good hedge. The plants need very little pruning, although if you want to, you can shear them right after the berries ripen. Blueberries rarely suffer from insects or diseases, start bearing within a few years of planting, and live for decades.

Strawberries

Strawberries grow fast and bear abundantly. You can pick about a quart of berries per plant within a year or so of setting them out. Strawberry plants are short-lived, so you have to replace them often, but they are inexpensive and readily available. They are usually sold in bundles of 25 plants.

Strawberries need full sun and moist, well-drained soil enriched with plenty of compost or aged manure and a little fertilizer. If your soil tends to stay wet in winter, plant strawberries in raised beds or hoe the soil into low ridges or mounds and set the plants on top.

Use straw or other mulch to keep the soil cool and moist and to keep the berries clean. The plants are subject to various insect pests, and slugs, rodents, and birds eat the berries, but typically the crop is so abundant that you don't mind some loss.

There are two main types of strawberries: June-bearing (sometimes called spring-bearing) and everbearing (sometimes called day-neutral). Individual cultivars differ in berry flavor, ripening time, cold-hardiness, heat tolerance, and disease resistance. Read

catalog descriptions carefully and get local advice about which cultivars do best in your area.

June-bearing strawberries

Cultivars such as 'Cardinal', 'Honeoye', 'Sparkle', and 'Surecrop' produce a big crop over a short season, usually just two to three weeks, in late spring or early summer. Then, thoughout the summer, the mother plants send runners in all directions and makes dozens of daughter plants, which all produce berries the next spring. To allow for this growth, space June-bearing plants about 2 feet apart.

There are many approaches to growing June-bearers, but typically you set out new plants in spring, remove any flowers that appear the first summer, enjoy a big crop the next spring, mow or shear off the foliage right after harvest and fertilize to promote fresh growth, pick smaller crops for another year or two, and then replace the plants.

Where winters are mild, grow June-bearers as a winter annual. Set plants out in early fall, remove flowers for part of the winter, let the plants bear a crop of berries in spring, then discard them.

Ever-bearing strawberries

Cultivars such as 'Ogallala', 'Ozark Beauty', 'Selva', and 'Tristar' are called everbearing, but they bear mostly in the cool weather of late spring and fall, and only intermittently in the heat of summer. Aside from the extended fruiting season, the big advantage of ever-bearers is that you can harvest berries the same year you set out the plants.

Ever-bearers don't make as many runners as June-bearers, so you can space the plants about 1 foot apart. Set out new plants in early spring (or fall where winters are mild), remove all the blossoms for about two months while the plants grow roots and get established, then let them start bearing fruit. Depending on climate and conditions, everbearers produce for one or two years; after that, discard them.

Melons

Watermelons, cantaloupes or muskmelons, honeydews, and other melons are annual vines that you grow from seed, much like growing squashes or cucumbers. Most seed catalogs list several types of melons that have been developed especially for home gardens. In choosing a melon to grow, check the number of days to maturity. All melons grow best in hot weather. If your summers are short and cool, choose melons that mature in 75 days or less. Where summers are long and hot, you can grow any melon you desire.

Planting and growing melons

Don't plant melons outdoors until the soil is warm and night temperatures remain above 50°F. Three to four weeks before you expect mild weather, sow the seeds in peat pots. Grow the seedlings indoors on a sunny windowsill.

Meanwhile, prepare a planting site. You can grow melons in rows (space plants 2 feet apart, rows 6 feet apart) or hills (space hills 4 to 6 feet apart.) Either way, till or dig to loosen the soil and work in a generous dose of compost or aged manure plus one cup of bonemeal per melon plant. Then stretch a sheet of black plastic over the soil and fasten it down. (Even if you normally shun plastic, try using it for melons—by heating the soil, it definitely improves their growth and yield. Also, it eliminates competition from weeds.)

As soon as you trust the weather, cut slits in the plastic and plant the seedlings, being careful not to disturb their roots. Water them in with a dilute fertilizer solution. Spread a fabric row-cover over the plants to keep them warm and protect them from cucumber beetles.

Water as often as needed to keep the soil from drying out as the melon plants grow. Remove the row cover as soon as they start to bloom, so pollinating insects can get to the flowers.

Keep watch as they ripen

If you didn't use black plastic, carefully lift the vines and slide a board under each baby melon to hold it away from the moist soil. As the melons enlarge, water just enough to keep the leaves from wilting. Check them every few days, but don't pick melons until they're fully ripe.

Cantaloupes are ready when the skin turns tan, the aroma is rich, and the melon slips readily off its stem. With watermelons, wait until the pale spot on the bottom turns from white to yellow and the tendril nearest the melon withers.

You might need a fence or watch dog to protect the crop, lest critters such as raccoons and possums raid the patch just when the melons reach perfection.

Favorite fruit trees

Here are specific tips about the most popular tree fruits. For general guidelines on growing fruit trees, turn the page.

Apples

Apples can be grown throughout the continental United States, but individual cultivars vary in cold hardiness and chilling needs. Most apples are hardy to Zone 5; 'Freedom', 'Spartan', and 'Wealthy' are hardy to Zone 3. Look for "low-chill" apples, such as 'Braeburn' or 'Granny Smith', if you live in Zone 8 or 9.

Apples are not self-fertile, so you need to plant a pair of cultivars that bloom at the same time for cross-pollination, unless there's already another apple or crab apple tree nearby. Many apples are susceptible to various diseases that can disfigure or destroy the fruit or even kill the tree. 'Liberty' stands out for its remarkable resistance to diseases.

Space standard, full-size apple trees 30 to 40 feet apart, give semidwarfs about 20 feet, and dwarfs 10 to 15 feet. When mature, standard trees can bear five bushels of apples per year. Semidwarfs and dwarfs bear one to two bushels a year. Trees start bearing in three to five years and live for decades.

Pears

Pears are almost as widely adapted as apples and are generally more carefree. They tend to be narrow, upright trees. Dwarfs grow 10 to 15 feet tall. Standard pears reach up to 30 feet tall. The trees start bearing after about five years and live for decades. The main problem with pears is fire blight, a common and promptly fatal disease. Plant only blight-resistant varieties.

Plant two pear trees for good pollination. Choose two European pears, which have the familiar pear shape and soft flesh, or two Asian pears, which have larger, rounded, crisp-textured fruits.

Cherries

Cherries tolerate cold winters but not hot summers, and do best in Zones 4 to 7. Sweet cherries are more temperature-sensitive and disease-prone than sour cherries. A dwarf sour cherry such as 'Meteor' or 'North Star' is a good choice for most home gardens. You only need one of these trees. They grow about 10 feet tall and wide, start bearing after three years, and produce 10 to 20 quarts of cherries per year. Let the cherries ripen on the tree until they're dark red and ready to drop—they get much tastier and sweeter in those last few days.

Citrus

Aside from bearing delicious fruit over a conveniently long season, lemons, oranges, mandarins, grapefruit, and other citrus are beautiful trees with glossy leaves and heavenly fragrant flowers. If you live in a suitably mild climate, you should definitely plant a citrus tree. Get local advice about which citrus do best in your area.

Citrus are subject to many pest and disease problems, but you might never encounter them, and if you do, local experts can help you diagnose and treat your tree. Your main concern will be watering and fertilizing enough, but not too much, to keep the tree healthy.

Most citrus are small trees, under 25 feet tall and wide, and several kinds are bush-sized, only 6 to 12 feet tall. Dwarf citrus grow very well in containers and make beautiful, fruitful specimens. Where it's too cold to plant citrus in the ground, you can grow one in a pot and bring it into a sunny room for the winter.

Depending on kind and size, individual citrus trees can bear a few pounds or several bushels of fruit every year. Unlike most fruits, you don't have to pick citrus all at once. You can leave ripe fruit on the tree, where it stays fresh for many weeks or even months.

Figs

Figs, like citrus, thrive where summers are hot and winters are mild. They grow best in Zones 8 to 10, although devoted fig lovers grow 'Brown Turkey', a particularly hardy and adaptable cultivar, in containers as far north as Zone 5.

Established fig trees require less care than most fruits. Just prune as desired to control the tree's size and shape and water during long droughts. Fig trees grow 10 to 30 feet tall and wide, are self-fertile, and bear within a year of planting. One tree bears more figs than you can eat fresh, but it's easy to dry the extras.

Peaches and nectarines

Peaches are fast-growing but short-lived trees that thrive in Zones 6 to 9. Hardy cultivars can be grown in Zone 5. Dwarf trees grow up to 10 feet tall and wide; standard trees can reach 20 feet. Peaches are a vulnerable crop, easily damaged by bad weather and susceptible to countless pests and diseases. But the trees are beautiful, with pink flowers and slender glossy leaves, and in good years, the fruit is not only delicious, but abundant. Even a dwarf tree can bear one to two bushels of peaches, starting three years after you plant it. Peaches are self-fertile, so you only need one tree. Nectarines are like peaches but have fuzzless skin, and the trees are generally weaker and more prone to trouble.

Apricots, plums, and prunes

These are all small trees, usually 10 to 20 feet tall and wide. They're as pretty as peach trees, but not quite as susceptible to pests and diseases and generally longer-lived. Hardiness and heat-tolerance vary, but most kinds grow well in Zones 5 to 9 and some survive in Zone 4.

This group includes dozens of appealing cultivars, including many hybrids, such as plumcots. Consider hardiness, sensitivity to late spring frosts, and disease resistance when choosing what to grow. Normally you need a pair of trees for cross-pollination. Check catalogs for specific recommendations. Most apricots, plums, and prunes start bearing the third year after planting. One tree can bear two bushels or more fruit.

Tree fruits

Plant a pine or oak tree, and you can sit back and watch it grow to maturity without lifting a hand to care for it. Most fruit trees aren't like that. A fruit tree needs your help. You have to train and prune its limbs, protect it from insects and diseases, keep the weeds away, give it fertilizer and mulch, thin and pick its fruit, and pick up litter. Granted, you may have seen a wild or abandoned tree that was laden with beautiful fruit, but those are the exceptions. Normally, a fruitful tree is the sign of a devoted gardener.

Although indispensable, the work isn't tiring or difficult, and it isn't time-consuming. Caring for a fruit tree takes only a few hours a year, much less than tending a flowerbed or keeping up with your houseplants. And probably you'll find that the more time you spend caring for the tree, and the longer you've had it, the more pleased you'll be when it rewards you with bushels of fruit.

Adopting an existing tree

You may have a fruit tree that "came with the house." With luck, it's healthy and productive and the previous owners told you how to keep it that way. Or it may be a good tree, but overgrown or neglected. In that case, ask around until you find someone who can help you prune it and bring it back to shape. However, if the tree is sick, ugly, or unproductive, you might as well cut it down. Just because it's alive, you don't have to keep it. You'd get more and better fruit, and have more fun, too, by starting over with a new tree.

Choose a reliable tree

If you're thinking about planting a new fruit tree, the first consideration is picking a tree that's suitable for your climate. Climate affects the tree's survival and the yield and flavor of its fruit. Get local advice, read catalog descriptions, and monitor your weather patterns. Factors to consider include:

Cold-hardiness. Catalogs and reference books state either the USDA hardiness zone, or the absolute minimum temperature that a tree or its flower buds can survive.

Chilling requirement. Apples, cherries, peaches, and pears require a certain amount of cool weather in order to complete their dormancy and be ready to grow again in spring. Breeders have developed special "low-chill" cultivars that are adapted to mild-winter climates.

Susceptibility to late spring frosts. If frost strikes when a tree is in bloom, that year's crop is usually lost. Apricots and peaches are especially sensitive to this problem.

Summer heat. Hot sunny days improve the sweetness and flavor of most fruits. (Cherries, however, can't tolerate hot weather.)

High rainfall and humidity. Too much rain leads to watery fruit, but there's not much you can do about that. You can, however, avoid some of the disease problems caused by high humidity by choosing disease-resistant cultivars.

Climate. Along with climate (the general weather patterns in your area), study the microclimate—the particular conditions right where you want to plant the tree. For example, if you're thinking about training a tree against a wall or fence, it makes a big difference whether the site faces north, south, east, or west.

Choose an exciting tree

Be sensible and get a tree that will do well in your garden, but just as important, choose a fruit that you love, and pick a cultivar that's reknowned for its beauty, flavor, and quality. This is especially important if you have limited space and time. Devote your effort to growing something wonderful. You can always buy ordinary fruit.

Planting a fruit tree

Citrus trees, which are evergreen, are usually grown and sold in containers. They're available all year, but seem to do best if you plant them in early spring.

Deciduous fruit trees, such as apples, are typically field-grown, dug when dormant, and sold bare-root in early spring by mail-order or local nurseries. Bare-root trees may look skimpy and abused, but typically they grow very well.

Be prepared to plant a bare-root tree as soon as you get it home. In advance, choose a site with good soil and dig a hole about 1 foot deep and 3 feet wide, and set the soil aside. When planting the tree, spread its roots across the width of the hole. Look for a change of color on the trunk bark that indicates how deep the tree was planted at the nursery, and position it at the same depth as you refill the hole with soil.

Routine care

Water deeply once a week during dry weather, especially during the first year after planting. Depending on your tree and your soil, you'll probably need to apply compost, manure, or fertilizer once or twice a year, using enough to promote vigorous growth, rich green foliage, and abundant yield. Keep weeds under control by pulling them often, spreading a layer of mulch around the tree, or planting a ground cover there.

Training and pruning

Young fruit trees need training, which means establishing a sturdy trunk and a framework of major limbs. Older trees need pruning once or twice a year to maintain their shape and size. Reference books give detailed instructions on when and how to prune each kind of fruit tree.

An espaliered tree like the pear shown below takes extra attention for the first few years, but once you get it trained, it's no more difficult to maintain than a regular tree, and it makes a great focal point for your garden.

Pests and diseases

Get local advice, and don't bother planting fruit trees that are susceptible to pests and disease problems which are serious in your area. You'll probably still have to spray for minor problems, but you can usually treat them with nontoxic remedies such as insecticidal soap, horticultural oil, and lime-sulfur fungicide.

Plant a varied collection of annuals, perennials, and herbs, and you can pick a different bouquet every week from spring through fall.

FLOWERS FOR BOUQUETS

What brings more joy than a bouquet of fresh flowers? On the dinner table or nightstand at home, on your desk at work—wherever you put it, a vase of flowers will brighten your day, especially if you've grown them yourself.

Picking flowers from your own garden is like harvesting your own vegetables. You get freshness and quality for a bargain price. There's a satisfying seasonal progression, from peas and peonies in spring to asters and acorn squash in fall. And it makes you proud and grateful to realize how much you can harvest from even a small plot.

Deciding what to grow

The floral industry has come alive in the last decade, breaking away from its tradition of stiff roses and dyed carnations to offer an amazing variety of flowers. This change has affected what's available to amateur arrangers. Now mail-order catalogs call attention to flowers with unusual details, tall stiff stalks, and a long "vase life." Every year there are more kinds of cutflower plants to try—heirlooms that have been rediscovered, new introductions from plant breeders, and exotic treasures from all around the world.

Cutflowers can come from annual, biennial, or perennial plants; tender and hardy bulbs; grasses; trees, shrubs, and vines. In other words, you can pick here and there from around the garden. You probably have some potential bouquets growing already. But if you crave carefree, pick-all-you-want abundance, designate a special cutting garden and stuff it full of plants that bloom generously over a long season, so you can cut them heavily and repeatedly. Annuals are the mainstay of a cutting garden, but this is also a good place for tender bulbs that you have to dig every fall, for biennials like sweet William that make great cutflowers but are hard to place in a border, and for most kinds of everlastings, which often look more interesting after they're cut and dried than when they're growing in the garden. Long-blooming perennials such as yarrow and feverfew are useful in cutting gardens, too.

Tips on cutting flowers

When and how you cut flowers affects how long they will last in a vase. For best results, gather bouquets in early morning, late evening, or on overcast or rainy days, when plants are turgid (full of water), not wilted. Use sharp, clean pruning shears to cut the stems. Don't pluck them off by hand, as that can damage or uproot the plant.

Some people recommend carrying a deep bucket of water into the garden so you can immerse the cut stems immediately. I find it easier, and just as effective, to carry a shallow basket or tray lined with a damp cloth big enough to fold over the flowers.

After picking, remove any leaves that would be underwater in the vase (or strip them all off) and trim the stem shorter if you want to. It's sometimes recommended that you recut every stem while holding it under water to prevent air from entering the cut end, and there are special gizmos to help you do this. I'm not convinced that it matters, so I just trim them with sharp pruning shears.

Conditioning

Most flowers look better and last longer if you "condition" them before arranging them in a vase. Conditioning stops sap from leaking out the cut ends of the stems and saturates the stems and flowers with water.

To condition most kinds of annual, perennial, and bulb flowers, immerse them neck deep (up to but not covering the flowers) in a jar or pail of tepid fresh water and let them soak there all day or overnight. Do this indoors or in a shady place, away from direct sun.

Making arrangements

Don't be intimidated by the prospect of making arrangements. If you just want to stick some flowers in a jar of water, that's fine. Or you can learn more about arranging by reading books, attending classes, or joining a garden club. If you do pursue it, you'll find that the art of flower arranging compliments the art of garden design—both are concerned with color, texture, line, form, and style. Studying arrangement can help you refine your borders, and vice versa.

Enjoying cutflowers

Artist Georgia O'Keeffe wrote that, "Nobody sees a flower, really—it is so small—we haven't time, and to see takes time, like to have a friend takes time." It's true: what gardener takes time to examine a flower when there are chores such as weeding and watering to do? But when you come in and sit face to face with a bouquet, you tend to slow down and appreciate details that go unnoticed in the garden—a scallop along the edge on the petals, fuzzy sepals, bright-colored pollen, or subtle fragrance. This heightened awareness is part of the joy of bringing flowers indoors. Like painting or photography, making bouquets can change the way you look at plants and remind you how beautiful they are.

Flower forms

Thinking of flowers in terms of their basic form or shape is a good way to add variety to your arrangements and also to your garden. For example, the bouquet shown here uses popular biennials and perennials that bloom in late spring to illustrate seven common flower forms.

The form categories useful to arrangers are looser than those defined by botanical terms such as raceme or cyme, or those applied to particular flowers such as daffodils or dahlias. This isn't a scientific system; it's just a handy way of talking to yourself about what flowers you have or don't have and what you like or don't like.

Spikes

Foxglove (*Digitalis purpurea*) is an example of the spike form, which is basically a cylinder made of many small or medium-size flowers crowded close together at the top of a stalk. Spikes can be blunt or pointed, short or long, as thin as a pencil or as thick as your arm. Like exclamation points, they grab your attention in arrangements or in the garden.

Many plants bear spikes of flowers. Some examples good for cutting are: delphiniums, blazing-star (*Liatris spicata*), cardinal flower (*Lobelia cardinalis*), obedient plant (*Physostegia virginiana*), tuberose (*Polianthes tuberosa*), 'May Night' and other cultivars of *Salvia × superba*, and upright-growing veronicas (*Veronica*).

Daisies

Shasta daisy (*Chrysanthemum × superbum*) illustrates this form, along with many other plants in the daisy or composite family. Daisies can be borne singly on long stalks or in small groups on branched stalks. This simple, natural, unsophisticated shape is always popular. Examples good for cutting are: gerbera daisy (*Gerbera jamesonii*); painted daisy (*Chrysanthemum coccineum*), gloriosa daisy and black-eyed Susans or coneflowers (*Rudbeckia*); purple coneflower (*Echinacea purpurea*); cosmos and calendula; annual and perennial sunflowers (*Helianthus*); and single forms of dahlia, zinnia, and chrysanthemum. Although unrelated to true daisies, many kinds of anemones and clematis also have daisylike flowers.

Balls

A double peony (*Paeonia*) is a good example of the ball form, as are plump old-fashioned roses and dou-

Foxglove

Columbine

Baby's-breath

Shasta daisy

Sweet William

ble forms of poppies (*Papaver*), dahlias, and chrysanthemums. Mophead-type hydrangeas, most rhododendrons, and some kinds of camellias and magnolias are ball-shaped too. Some of these big, fluffy, ball-shaped flowers or flowerheads occur in nature; others were developed by plant breeders. Most make opulent bouquets, but are vulnerable in the garden. Too much rain makes them flop over, collapse, or rot.

A few other plants produce spherical flowerheads that are natural but *look* artificial. Think of angelicas, for example, or those ornamental alliums that make perfect, giant balls. These are exciting alone, but hard to combine with other forms.

Siberian iris

Peony

Sculptural flowers

Siberian iris illustrate a form I call sculptural. They're large flowers with a bold, simple shape made from just a few parts. Other kinds of iris, daffodils (*Narcissus*), tulips (*Tulipa*), lilies (*Lilium*), daylilies (*Hemerocallis*), magic lilies (*Lycoris squamigera*), and calla lilies (*Zantedeschia*) also have sculptural forms. These showy flowers stand out from a distance in the garden and look fascinating up close in a vase. Although quite distinctive, sculptural-form flowers are perfectly natural and very versatile. They combine easily with other flowers.

Taking a step beyond these familiar sculptural flowers, you reach the more exotic forms of tropical plants such as bird-of-paradise (*Strelitzia reginae*), bromeliads, and orchids. Except as houseplants, you probably won't get to grow or use any of these, and they tend to look weird combined with other flowers.

Flat-tops

Sweet William (*Dianthus barbatus*) is an example of the form I call flat-top, with dozens of small flowers crowded together in a cluster that's flat or somewhat rounded on top and round or irregular in outline. Many plants have flowers arranged in the flat-top form, because it makes a good landing pad that attracts butterflies and other pollinating insects. Pollinators appreciate that flat-tops include many small flowers, each providing a sip of nectar, but we people tend to perceive a flat-top cluster as a single unit when we're making bouquets or designing garden. We look at the overall size and shape, not the individual elements.

Along with sweet William, other plants that produce flat-tops good for cutting are: yarrows (*Achillea*), butterflyweed (*Asclepias tuberosa*), many kinds of asters, fleabanes (*Erigeron*), hardy ageratum and Joe-Pye weeds (*Eupatorium*), many kinds of euphorbias, 'Autumn Joy' sedum, and tansy (*Tanacetum vulgare*).

Dill (*Anethum graveolens*), Queen Anne's lace (*Daucus carota*), bishop's weed (*Ammi majus*) and many other plants in the carrot family produce flat or gently rounded clusters of flowers. Pollinating insects regard these as flat-tops but flower arrangers sometimes use them as "fillers" because the individual flowers are quite tiny, so the overall effect is more delicate and dainty than other flat-tops.

Fillers

Baby's-breath (usually the perennial species, *Gypsophila paniculata*, but the annual *G. elegans* is used, too) is the epitome of fillers—plants that bear thousands of tiny flowers in cloudlike masses, airy sprays, or loose clusters. In bouquets, fillers do just what the name says—they fill in the gaps between larger individual flowers. In the garden, plants with fillerlike flowers can form specimens big enough to be quite showy, even from a distance, with a soft, billowy profile.

For a change from baby's breath, try some of these other fillers: calico aster (*Aster lateriflorus* var. *horizontalis*), lady's-mantle (*Alchemilla mollis*), calamint (*Calamintha nepeta*), coral bells (*Heuchera*), catmints (*Nepeta*), Russian sage (*Perovskia atriplicifolia*), mountain-mints (*Pycnanthemum*), bridal-wreath and other kinds of spirea (*Spiraea*), meadowrues (*Thalictrum*), and fine-textured grasses such as switch grass (*Panicum virgatum*).

Branched clusters

Columbines (*Aquilegia*) are an example of the branched-cluster form. They bear many thimble-size or larger flowers spaced well apart from each other on a branched stalk. Plants like this are very common and indispensable in the garden, but branched clusters can be hard to fit into a bouquet—they often look crooked or unbalanced, and it's hard to fit other flowers around them. Try using them alone or in simple assymetric designs.

Boughs cut from flowering trees or shrubs are often branched clusters. Other examples good for cutting are Canterbury-bells (*Campanula medium*) and other bellflowers, balloonflower (*Platycodon grandiflorus*), alstroemerias, and hellebores (*Helleborus*).

Plant a cutting garden

If you're reluctant to pluck flowers from your formal beds and borders for fear that you'll ruin the display, you might enjoy the freedom of having a special cutting garden, where you could pick all the flowers you want with no hesitation, as freely as you pick ripe vegetables in a kitchen garden. Having a cutting garden is really liberating. With flowers to spare, you can put arrangements in every room of the house and pick extras to give away.

Cutting garden basics

Plenty of sun, fertile soil, and regular rain or watering are ideal conditions for growing cutflowers. If you have a large vegetable garden, borrowing part of it for cutflowers would be convenient. If you have to dig up lawn and start a new bed, take time to prepare the soil well, digging at least 8 inches deep and adding plenty of organic matter and some balanced fertilizer, before planting flower crops.

You could grow cutflower plants in rows, but it saves space to group them in beds 3 to 4 feet wide, spacing individual plants about 6 to 18 inches apart in all directions, depending on how wide they grow. Make the beds as long as the garden, with 2-foot-wide paths in between and on all sides. Mulch both the paths and the beds to control weeds.

Choosing plants

Many annuals make excellent cut-flowers, with the added advantage they bloom continuously over a long season. Garden centers don't always offer much choice, but if you can find them, buy tall-growing cultivars with long-stalked flowers rather than the stubby kinds bred for bedding-plant use. For a wider selection, especially if you want particular colors or unusual annuals, plan ahead, order seeds by mail, and raise your own seedlings.

Several kinds of tender bulbs produce glamorous, long-lasting cutflowers. Although some are hardy where winters are mild, in most areas these bulbs are treated as annuals. You have

to replant them every spring and dig them up in fall. That really isn't much trouble, and it's gratifying to see how fast they multiply. Buy a few to start with, and you'll soon be giving away bulbs as well as bouquets.

Of course you can grow grasses, everlastings, hardy bulbs, biennials, perennials, or whatever else you have room for in a cutting garden, too.

Tending a cutting garden

The major concern in growing flowers especially for cutting is keeping the long-stalked varieties upright. You can hope the plants will lean on each other (good luck!), tie the stalks to stakes, surround the bed with a cage

Cosmos

Calla lily

Snapdragon

Mealy sage

Dahlia

Gladiolus

Zinnia

of stakes and string, stick pea brush (twiggy shrub trimmings) around the plants, or bend 6-foot lengths of woven wire fencing over the bed to make a quonset-hut type framework for the stalks to grow up through.

Tender bulbs for cutflowers

Hybridizers have developed countless gladiolus cultivars, in all colors but blue, with dainty or mammoth flowers on stalks ranging from knee-high to over your head. Dahlias also come in all colors but blue and sizes small to huge. Calla lilies (*Zantedeschia*) can have large white flowers or smaller blossoms in bright or pastel shades of pink and yellow. These are all bold, dramatic cutflowers, but all are scentless or virtually so.

For fragrance, plant bulbs of peacock orchid (*Gladiolus callianthus*, formerly *Acidanthera bicolor*) with floppy white flowers; tuberose (*Polianthes tuberosa*) with dense spikes of very fragrant single or double white flowers; or baboon flower (*Babiana stricta*) with spikes of bell-shaped flowers in shades of white, pink, rose, and magenta.

Favorite annual cutflowers

Snapdragons (*Antirrhinum majus*) prefer cool weather and make thick spikes of velvety red, pink, orange, yellow or white flowers. Some strains are scentless, others smell like KoolAid.

Mealy sage (*Salvia farinacea*) blooms nonstop through the heat of summer, with slender spikes of white, pale blue, or dark blue-violet flowers.

Cosmos (*Cosmos bipinnatus*) bears daisylike flowers in shades of magenta, rose, pink, and white, all with yellow eyes. Sow two or three crops in succession for continuous bloom where summers are long.

Zinnias (*Zinnia elegans*) belong in every cutting garden. 'Blue Point', a new strain with 6-inch flowers in vivid colors, is highly recommended by growers and arrangers across the United States.

More annuals for bouquets

Like zinnias, gloriosa daisies (*Rudbeckia hirta*), sunflowers (*Helianthus annuus*), and China asters (*Callistephus chinensis*) produce armloads of big, round, composite flowers.

Also big and round but quite different in texture are the papery or silky flowers of Iceland, shirley, and breadseed (or opium) poppies (*Papaver*); and the glossy, mallow-type flowers of lavatera (*Lavatera trimestris*).

For contrast, be sure to include other flower forms in your cutting garden. Several annuals have spike-type blooms. Try 'Flamingo Feather' celosia (*Celosia spicata*), with thin pink plumes; fast and fragrant 'Sunrise' lupine (*Lupinus hartwegii*); spicy-scented stocks (*Matthiola incana*); old-fashioned larkspurs (*Consolida ambigua*); 'Sightseeing' veronica (*Veronica spicata*), a fast-growing perennial with slender pastel spikes; or the wonderful new hybrid lobelias (*Lobelia*) such as the 'Fan' and 'Compliment' strains, which bloom in vivid shades of scarlet, blue, purple, and pink.

Wonderfully fragrant sweet peas (*Lathyrus odoratus*), satiny godetia (*Godetia grandiflora*), and thick-petalled lisianthus or prairie gentian (*Eustoma grandiflora*) are more challenging to grow than most annuals, but with skill and luck you can pick branched clusters of exquisite, medium-size flowers.

For easy-to-grow annual fillers, try airy white annual baby's breath (*Gypsophila elegans*); bishop's flower or white dill (*Ammi majus*), which has flat white blossoms like Queen Anne's lace; 'Blue Horizon' ageratum (*Ageratum houstonianum*), with fluffy blue clusters on 2-foot stalks; and annual statice (*Limonium sinuatum*), with tiny papery flowers in many colors.

What else can you arrange?

Flowers are the main ingredient in most bouquets, but sometimes we take their beauty for granted. To make a centerpiece that will catch everyone's attention and spark dinnertime conversation, use a variety of plant parts along with or instead of familiar flowers. Even people who are normally oblivious to plants suddenly take notice when they see something unexpected up close.

It's fun to add this element of surprise to your designs, and seeking new material to use will increase your own awareness and enjoyment of plants. Once you start looking for them, you'll find botanical treasures all around your property, and you'll want to expand your cutting garden to provide more variety, too.

Berries and fruits

Fleshy berries, fruits, and pods make bright additions to a fresh bouquet and usually up to a week in water; some kinds last longer. Fresh pods of hyacinth bean (*Dolichos lablab*), a fast-growing annual vine, have a stunning color and texture; people can't resist touching them to see if they're real or plastic. Stems lined with tight clusters of violet beautyberry fruits (*Callicarpa*) provoke a similar reaction. Beautyberries are deciduous shrubs hardy to Zones 7 or 6.

Gather berry-laden boughs from chokeberries (*Aronia*), dogwoods (*Cornus*), hawthorns (*Crateagus*), hollys (*Ilex*), viburnums (*Viburnum*), and other shrubs. You can always find some lower, interior, or rear branches that won't be missed in the garden.

Two perennials with showy berries are hardy to about Zone 6. Blackberry lily (*Belamcanda chinensis)* has stiff, branching stalks topped with shiny black berries in clusters the size and shape of edible blackberries. Stinking iris (*Iris foetidissima*) bears stiff stalks of brown pods that open in fall to reveal bright orange seeds. Both have modest flowers and foliage but deserve a place in the cutting garden for their fruits.

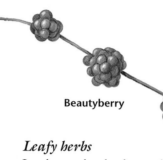

Beautyberry

Leafy herbs

Look to the herb garden for sprigs of foliage that are both colorful and fragrant. If you like the pungent, waxy, blue-gray leaves of silver-dollar eucalyptus (*Eucalyptus cinerea*), you can grow your own from seed; the seedlings grow fast enough to treat as annuals. Catalogs list several cultivars of purple basil (*Ocimum basilicum*) that you can raise from seed. All are neat, bushy plants with dark, lustrous, sweet-scented leaves.

Visit an herb nursery to buy a plant of pineapple mint (*Mentha suaveolens*), which has slightly fuzzy green-and-white leaves that smell more fruit than minty. You may find some other kinds of variegated mints also. All are beautiful and smell delicious, hardy to about Zone 5, and in general, the variegated forms are less invasive than all-green mints.

Wormwood (*Artemisia absinthium*) and most of its many relatives have finely divided, aromatic, silvery gray or gray-green foliage that's as useful in a bouquet as it is in the garden for combining with other colors, bright or pastel. Most artemisias are shrubby perennials hardy to about Zone 5.

Other herbs with fragrant, beautiful foliage that's good for bouquets include fuzzy gray horehound (*Marrubium vulgare*, Zone 5), lacy blue-green rue (*Ruta graveolens*, Zone 5), the variegated or purple forms of garden sage (*Salvia officinalis*, Zone 8), and all kinds of scented geraniums (*Pelargonium*).

Everlastings and dry pods

Most of the papery-textured flowerheads and seedpods called everlastings can be used either fresh or dried. Bells of Ireland (*Molucella laevis*), an annual, is lovely either way, bright green when you pick it fresh in summer, or tan when dry. Both love-in-a-

Hyacinth bean

Pineapple mint

Eucalyptus

Bells of Ireland

Fountain grass

Wormwood

Purple basil

mist (*Nigella damascena*), a slender, knee-high annual, and love-in-a-puff (*Cardiospermum halicacabum*), a fine-textured annual vine produce delicate, balloon-like pods that dry from green to brown. It's worth growing both plants just so you can talk about them to your friends and say those wonderful names.

So many other annuals and perennials have delightful pods that it's hard to list them all. Watch what happens when you let radishes or broccoli go to see in the veg-etable garden, or gather wild radish or wild mustard seed-stalks. Grow some breadseed, or opium, poppies (*Papaver somniferum*), shake the seeds into a bag or jar, and save the pods for arrangements.

In the perennial border, let the pods or seedheads ripen on butterfly weed (*Asclepias tuberosa*), wild indigo (*Baptisia australis*), gas plant (*Dictamnus albus*), globe thistle (*Echinops ritro*), foxtail lilies (*Eremurus*), wild buckwheats (*Eriogonum*), sea hollies (*Eryngium*), Siberian iris (*Iris sibirica*), Missouri evening primrose (*Oenothera missouriensis*), and coneflowers (*Rudbeckia*).

Graceful grasses

Seedheads from most of the perennial ornamental grasses that are so popular now add interest to fresh arrangements and dry well also. For example, fountain grass (*Pennisetum alopecuroides*, Zone 5) forms slender bottlebrush-like seedheads. To keep them from shattering, pick the seedheads as soon as they fluff out and spray them with hair spray.

Annual grasses are seen less often, because you can't buy plants and have to start them from seed, but they're fast and easy to grow. Sow the seeds directly where you want them. A few kinds of annual grasses can turn weedy if you let them self-sow, but that shouldn't happen if you pick all the seedheads for arrangements.

Hare's tail grass (*Lagurus ovatus*) makes dense, furry, pettable, creamy-white seedheads about 2 inches long. Squirreltail grass or foxtail barley (*Hordeum jubatum*) seedheads have hair-thin awns about 3 inches long, and turn from green to pink to tan as they ripen. Quaking grass (*Briza maxima*) has puffy, podlike seedheads that dangle from threadlike stalks.

Annual grain crops such as wheat, oats, rye, barley, millet, and broom corn have distinctive and interesting seedheads. Some kinds of grain have been bred especially for use in arrangements and crafts. They have larger-than-average heads or turn black, rusty, or pale as they ripen, instead of the usual gold or tan colors.

Tricolor sage and lacy
southernwood leaves
release pungent
aromas when touched.

No matter how beautiful it is, a photograph never captures the full essence of a plant or a garden. You see size, shape, and color, but what about the smell? In person, fragrance has an immediate, irresistible impact that multiplies your awareness and enjoyment.

Growing plants with sweet flowers and aromatic foliage adds so much to your enjoyment of a garden. Part of the pleasure comes from fragrance's ability to change your state of mind—to make you feel more serene, alert, or relaxed. (That's the basis for aromatherapy.) You can't help but respond to a scent. Even if it's delicate or subtle, it surrounds you like an aura, captures your attention, and makes you forget whatever you were thinking about before.

Mysteries of fragrance

I enjoy the elusive aspects of fragrance. Sometimes it's like ventriloquy—you notice a pleasant smell in a garden, but can't tell which plant it's coming from, so you sniff here and there, trying to track it down. You might have stepped on a patch of thyme or chamomile growing in a grass path, or there might be a shrubby osmanthus blooming nearby, with flowers too tiny to notice but too sweet to ignore.

Some fragrances are predictable. Whenever you touch it, peppermint smells minty. Others turn on and off. Witch hazel (*Hamamelis*) blooms for weeks in late winter. The flowers smell very sweet on mild days, but when the air is cold, they're scentless. Sweet woodruff (*Galium odoratum*) leaves are scentless when green and growing, but after they've been cut off the plant or killed by frost, they start smelling like vanilla. Consider chives: the leaves are oniony, but the flowers are very sweet. If you're curious and observant, fragrant plants will give you many mysteries to ponder.

Describing fragrance

Perfumers have tried to develop systems for describing fragrance, but most of us with untrained noses rely on comparison. We say something smells like a rose, smells lemony, etc. It's hard to be precise when describing fragrant plants, because we don't have the vocabulary, and also because a plant's aroma may vary and because people have different senses of smell. But whether or not you can describe it, you know what you like, and when you're choosing fragrant plants for your garden, the really important questions are: Does this plant smell at all? Does it smell good to me?

Don't be surprised, though, when friends and family contradict your assessment of particular plants. Some people swoon and others gag over the flowers of paperwhite narcissus. Privet flowers and marigold leaves are the subject of heated arguments. Even if you love fragrance in general, you have to admit that some plants really do stink.

'Incense' passionflower smells as rich and exotic as it looks.

Wisteria

Carolina jasmine

Flowering vines

A porch or arbor covered with flowering vines makes the perfect hideway, a place to relax, breathe deep, and forget your troubles. The vines recommended here all have delightfully fragrant flowers and are vigorous and easy to grow. They need full or part sun, something to climb on, occasional coaxing to steer new shoots in the right direction, and annual pruning to limit their size and remove old growth.

Spring-blooming vines

Caroline jasmine (*Gelsemium sempervirens,* Zone 7), shown at right, has sunny yellow flowers, dark evergreen leaves, and thin woody stems. It climbs by twining around a support, grows quickly, and reaches 15 feet or taller, but doesn't get out of bounds. Prune in early summer.

Wisterias (*Wisteria*), shown at left, have violet, lavender, pink, or white flowers in drooping clusters ranging from 6 inches to 3 feet long. There are dozens of cultivars, some mildly fragrant, some extremely so. Most are hardy to Zones 6 or 5. All have deciduous compound leaves and twining woody stems as thick and strong as a boa contrictor. A wisteria vine needs a sturdy support and can climb at least 25 feet tall, or you can train it into a small "tree." Be patient, because wisterias typically take a few years to settle in and start blooming. Prune in midsummer.

The large-flowered hybrid clematis are odorless, but cultivars of anemone clematis (*Clematis montana,* Zone 6) have vanilla-scented pink or white flowers, and the evergreen clematis (*C. armandii,* Zone 7) has fragrant white flowers. Both vines climb 15 feet or taller. Prune them right after they bloom.

Summer-blooming vines

Goldflame honeysuckle (*Lonicera × heckrottii,* Zone 5) blooms from early summer until frost, and perfumes the garden on warm evenings. It has pink-and-yellow flowers, handsome blue-green leaves that are semi-evergreen, and thin twining stems that climb to about 10 feet. Prune in winter.

Passionflowers (*Passiflora,* hardiness varies) have round, many-parted flowers in shades of purple, pink, and white. The deciduous vines die down in winter, emerge late in spring, then quickly grow at least 8 to 10 feet tall.

Chilean jasmine (*Mandevilla laxa,* Zone 8) has very fragrant white flowers and evergreen foliage. It reaches 10 feet or taller outdoors. Northern gardeners can grow it in a large container and bring it indoors for the winter. Prune anytime.

Sweet autumn clematis (*Clematis terniflora,* often listed as *C. paniculata,* Zone 5) has masses of starry white flowers in late summer or early fall. It climbs to 20 feet or higher. Prune hard in spring.

Trees with sweet-scented flowers

A specimen tree with fragrant flowers is a cherished feature in any garden. Although it takes decades for a tree to mature, the ones recommended here don't keep you waiting to inhale—they all start blooming as young specimens, sometimes the year after you plant them.

Fringe tree and sweet bay

Fringe tree (*Chionanthus virginicus*, Zone 4) and sweet bay magnolia (*Magnolia virginiana*, Zone 5), shown together below, have much in common. Both are native to the Southeast but grow well in other regions. Naturally shrubby, they tend to have multiple trunks but are easily trained and pruned into small trees 15 to 25 feet tall. Choose a site with part or full sun and rich, moist, acid soil.

Fringe tree leafs out in late spring and blooms at the same time, with fluffy clusters of white flowers that have a mild, spicy aroma. The large, smooth, deciduous leaves turn gold in fall. Fringe trees have a rounded crown and often grow wider than tall. Male and female flowers are borne on separate plants. Nurseries rarely mark which is which, as both sexes are desirable, but if you manage to get one of each, the female tree will bear blue fruits that birds love.

Sweet bay magnolia has round white flowers, about 3 inches wide, with a lemony aroma. It blooms mostly in early summer, but scattered blossoms may appear until fall. The smooth, oblong leaves are dark green above, silvery below; they may be deciduous or evergreen, depending on cultivar and climate. Sweet bay typically forms an upright oval crown.

Other fragrant magnolias

Cultivars of star magnolia (*M. stellata*) and the hybrid *M. × loebneri* bear floppy-petalled white or pale pink flowers in April, before the leaves unfurl. These are deciduous trees, 10 to 30 feet tall, and hardy to Zones 5 or 4, depending on cultivar.

Southern magnolia (*M. grandiflora*) has giant, bowl-shaped, creamy white flowers in summer and glossy evergreen leaves. Most cultivars are hardy to Zone 7 and grow to 50 feet or taller. 'Bracken's Brown Beauty', 'Edith Bogue', and 'Little Gem' are compact, usually under 30 feet tall, and hardy to Zones 6 or 5.

More fragrant trees

Black locust (*Robinia pseudoacacia*, Zone 4) is one of the most fragrant trees, with drooping clusters of white pealike blossoms in late spring. 'Frisia', a fine cultivar with golden yellow foliage, grows quickly to about 30 feet tall.

Hardy orange (*Poncirus trifoliata*, Zone 6) has fragrant white flowers in spring and aromatic but too-tart fruits in fall. It grows 15 feet tall, with deciduous leaves and thorny green-barked stems.

Littleleaf linden (*Tilia cordata*, Zone 3) has inconpicuous but very sweet-scented flowers that dangle under the leaves in early summer. A fine shade tree, it grows 40 feet or taller.

Mimosa, or silk tree (*Albizia julibrissin*, Zone 6) is a fast-growing deciduous tree, about 20 feet tall, with a shallow, open crown. It blooms for weeks in the heat of summer, and its fluffy pink flowers are fragrant at night.

Sweet bay magnolia

Fringe tree

Night-scented stock

'Royal Standard' hosta

Four-o'clock

Evening primrose

Night-scented flowers

If you spend evenings in the garden or sleep with the windows open, you would really enjoy night-scented flowers. These have some of the loveliest perfumes in the plant kingdom, and they engage your curiosity. Because of their sense of time, they seem more animated than other plants. Even if you cut stalks and put them in a vase, the flowers "remember" to "turn on" their fragrance at dusk and "turn it off" at dawn. Amazing.

Another bonus is that night-scented flowers attract pollinating moths such as the hummingbird-like sphinx moth shown here. These small moths are common around the country, and are quite tame. It's fun to watch one uncoil its hoselike mouth, probe deep into a flower, and hover, sucking nectar.

Hostas

Most hosta (*Hosta*) flowers are scentless, but some smell very sweet at night. 'Royal Standard' has glossy solid green leaves and forms a clump about 3 feet wide, with large white flowers on stalks 3 feet tall. It blooms for weeks in August and September. Other fragrant hostas that bloom in mid- to late summer include 'Fragrant Blue', 'Honeybells', 'So Sweet', and the August lily (*H. plantaginea*) and its double-flowered cultivar 'Aphrodite'. All are vigorous perennials hardy to Zone 4. If planted in rich, moist soil and generously mulched, they thrive for decades with minimal care. 'Royal Standard' can take part or full sun; the others prefer part or full shade.

Night-scented stock

Night-scented stock (*Matthiola bicornis*) looks so humble by day that you'd toss it aside as a weed, but at night its cross-shaped lilac flowers release a heavy, intoxicating aroma. An annual, it grows 12 to 18 inches tall and wide, with floppy stems and dull gray-green leaves. Direct-seed a few patches to fill gaps in your garden, between clumps of lilies, for example.

Four-o'clock

Four-o'clock (*Mirabilis jalapa*) flowers come in cheerful shades of reddish-purple, yellow, pink, white, and bicolor. They open in late afternoon and smell lovely through the evening and night. The plant thrives in hot sunny sites, tolerates dry soil, and makes a bushy clump 2 to 3 feet tall and wide, covered with flowers from early summer until frost. Hardy to Zone 8, it grows well as an annual in colder climates.

Evening primroses

Several species of evening primroses (*Oenothera*) have lovely large four-petalled flowers that are fragrant at night. *O. odorata*, shown at left, *O. lamarkiana*, and *O. biennis* all have yellow flowers. *O. albicaulis*, *O. caespitosa*, and *O. pallida* all have pale pink or white flowers.

These plants are all easy to grow on any sunny site with well-drained soil. They are usually raised from seed. Catalogs list them under various common and Latin names, but don't worry about that; read the descriptions and choose whatever plant sounds good to you. You can start the seeds indoors or sow them directly in the garden. The plants will bloom the first or second season and continue year after year in most climates, either by self-seeding or as perennials.

Tobaccos and daturas

These two groups, both members of nightshade family, include many species with white or colored flowers that release a rich, sweet fragrance at night. The plants often look ungainly and they have sticky, smelly, poisonous leaves, but many gardeners are willing to overlook those faults for the sake of the perfume.

Like evening primroses, the fragrant species of flowering tobaccos and daturas are listed under various Latin names in seed catalogs. Whatever you call them, the plants are easily raised from seed and treated like annuals, although some are perennial in Zones 8 or warmer. They all thrive on sunny sites with well-drained soil.

Among the flowering tobaccos (*Nicotiana*), I've grown seeds listed as *N. affinis*, *N. alata*, *N. sylvestris*, and *N. suaveolens*. Although the plants vary in size and appearance, they all bear white flowers that smell wonderful, and bloom steadily all summer until frost. I have never detected very much fragrance in the bright-colored day-flowering strains of *N. × sanderae* grown as bedding plants.

Daturas or angel's trumpets (*Datura*) listed under the names

D. inoxia, *D. metel*, *D. meteloides* bear incredible trumpet-shaped flowers 6 to 8 inches long, typically white but sometimes lilac or yellow, with a heavenly aroma. If you have a party when these plants are in bloom, your guests will never forget them.

Start the seeds indoors, like tomatoes, and transplant the seedlings into the garden after danger of frost. The plants get big and bushy, 3 to 6 feet tall and wide, by late summer. You can grow them in pots and overwinter them indoors, as with plants of the related genus *Brugsmansia*, but they are so susceptible to houseplant pests such as aphids and whiteflies that I'd rather discard them in fall and start new seedlings each year.

More night-scented flowers

Moonflower (*Ipomoea alba*, often listed as *Calonyction aculeatum*) is a vigorous vine with large heart-shaped leaves and white flowers that open at dusk into white disks as round as the moon and 4 to 6 inches wide. Although hardy to Zone 8, moonflower is usually grown as an annual. It climbs 8 to 10 feet tall and needs a sturdy trellis, as the mass of vines becomes quite heavy by late summer.

Many kinds of lilies (*Lilium*) are very fragrant, especially at night. Plant several for a sequence of bloom. Madonna lily (*L. candidum*) and Easter lily (*L. longiflorum*) both have white flowers in early summer; goldband lily (*L. auratum*) and regal lily (*L. regale*) have white or two-toned flowers in midseason; the Aurelian and Oriental hybrids bloom in many colors in late summer (see p. 135). Most lilies are hardy to Zone 5 or 4. Under favorable conditions—full sun; deep, rich, moist, well-drained soil; and no bulb-eating rodents—they multiply slowly into magnificent clumps.

Bouncing Bet or soapwort (*Saponaria officinalis*, Zone 4) blooms all summer, with pink or white flowers that have a spicy clovelike fragrance at night. This perennial is invasive and will grow anywhere, so tuck it out of the way, not in a flowerbed. It grows 2 to 3 feet tall.

Many kinds of fragrant leaves retain their aroma when dried and used in sachets or potpourri.

Leaves with lovely aromas

Most leaves are scentless, and plants that do have fragrant foliage typically keep it a secret. You can be standing right beside a patch of mint and not catch a whiff until you brush or bruise a leaf, instantly releasing its powerful aroma. Along with touch, certain weather conditions may reveal a leaf fragrance that's normally hidden. For example, the air around a sweetbriar rose bush (*Rosa eglanteria*) smells like tart green apples right after a rain, but you won't detect that fragrance in dry weather unless you rub the leaves.

When fragrance takes you by surprise in the garden, you get caught up in a treasure hunt, trying to figure out which plant it is that smells so good. Once you've located it, you'll sniff it on purpose the next time you pass. There's an interesting contradiction here. Although foliar fragrance often seems elusive and ephemeral, it's actually much more dependable and long-lasting than floral fragrance. A sweet flower gives just a few days of delight, but you can enjoy aromatic leaves again and again, whenever you pass by.

Drying leaves

Furthermore, some leaves smell just as good after they are dried as they do when fresh. Drying leaves is simple. The most important advice is to do it as quickly as possible by placing them in a warm dry place with good air circulation. Spread loose leaves on racks or screens that are supported so air flows underneath. Secure small bundles of sprigs or stems with rubber bands and hang them up to dry. Either way, the leaves should dry to a crisp in just a few days; if it takes longer than that, the aroma will deteriorate. Dried leaves retain their aroma for months or years.

Herbs and herblike plants

Nurseries that specialize in herbs offer the widest variety of plants with fragrant leaves. Their catalogs list countless kinds of basil, catnip, dill, fennel, lavender, mint, rosemary, sage, thyme, and other culinary and/or healthful herbs, along with fragrant plants like agastaches, artemisias, eucalyptus, santolinas, and scented geraniums, which seem herblike although they have few practical uses.

One of the many ways to enjoy growing these plants is to collect kinds that smell the same, such as lemon-scented eucalyptus (*Eucalyptus citriodora*), lemon geranium (*Pelargonium crispum*), lemon grass (*Cymbopogon citratus*), lemon thyme (*Thymus × citriodorus*), and lemon verbena (*Aloysia triphylla*). (These are all tender, except the thyme.) Other collectable groups smell like anise, mint, or vanilla; in each case, similar aromas are produced by totally unrelated plants. How mysterious, and what fun!

Most herbs and herblike plants retain at least part of their fragrance when dried, especially if you dry them very quickly. Some remain wonderfully potent.

Conifers

More often than not, conifer foliage has a fresh, resinous, woodsy aroma that's associated with Christmas trees, camping trips, and other happy memories. So many conifers are fragrant that it's hard to narrow the list. My favorites include balsam fir (*Abies balsamea*, Zone 3), incense cedar (*Calocedrus decurrens*, Zone 5), Monterey cypress (*Cupressus macrocarpa*, Zone 7), Rocky Mountain juniper (*Juniperus scopulorum*, Zone 4), all kinds of pines (*Pinus*), American arborvitae (*Thuja occidentalis*, Zone 4), and western red cedar (*Thuja plicata*,

Zone 5). Most of these are available in dwarf or compact cultivars that fit small gardens. All need full sun and most prefer well-drained soil.

You'll smell the fragrant conifers in your garden on warm sunny days or after a rain, and the old needles that drop off make an aromatic mulch. Indoors, a sachet filled with balsam fir needles will perfume a drawer or closet for years.

Bayberry and myrtles

If you like the smell of bayberry candles, grow one or another species of *Myrica*. Bayberry (*M. pensylvanica*, Zone 4) is native to the Northeast, and has broad glossy deciduous leaves that are dark green in summer, purple in fall. It's usually under 8 feet tall but spreads by suckers and grows wider than it is tall. Wax myrtle (*M. cerifera*, Zone 7) is native to the Southeast, has smooth slender evergreen leaves, and grows up to 30 feet tall, 20 feet wide. California wax myrtle (*M. californica*, Zone 7) is native to the Pacific coast, has slender evergreen leaves, and forms a bushy shrub about 10 feet tall and wide.

These plants all make fine specimens or hedges with handsome natural shapes, or you can prune or shear them as they choose. The sexes are separate; if pollinated, female plants produce heavy crops of waxy, fragrant berries. Both the leaves and berries retain their fragrance when dried.

Other fragrant natives

Spicebush (*Lindera benzoin*, Zone 5) is aptly named: all parts of it are fragrant, including the small gold flowers that bloom in early spring, the red berries that attract songbirds in fall, the bark and twigs, and the soft oval leaves that are rich green all summer, butter-yellow in fall. Native to the eastern United States, this trouble-free shrub grows 8 to 12 feet tall and wide. It adapts to most growing conditions but prefers part shade and rich, moist soil.

Sweet shrub, or Carolina allspice (*Calycanthus floridus*, Zone 5) has large glossy leaves with a spicy aroma and many-petaled maroon flowers that bloom in early summer. The flowers are very fragrant on some plants, not at all on others. The leaves are deciduous and turn gold in fall. Sweet shrub grows 6 to 10 feet tall and wide, adapts to sun or shade, and needs no routine care. Western spicebush (*C. oc-*

cidentalis, Zone 8) is a similar shrub native to the West Coast.

Florida anise (*Illicium floridanum*) is native along the Gulf coast but hardy to Zone 7 if planted in a sheltered site. It's a dense, bushy shrub reaching 10 feet or taller, with large, glossy evergreen leaves that smell like anise or licorice when crushed, asterisk-shaped maroon flowers in spring, and interesting brown seedpods in fall. It needs part or full shade and moist soil and makes a fine specimen, background, or hedge. Small anise (*I parviflorum*, Zone 8) is similar but grows more upright, has white flowers, and tolerates drier sites and more sun.

Wintergreen (*Gaultheria procumbens,* Zone 4) is a creeping perennial that forms patches of glossy evergreen leaves dotted with white flowers in summer and red berries in fall. Only a few inches tall, it can spread several feet wide. Native to the Northeast, it grows well in other regions, and makes a handsome, fragrant groundcover for sites with part shade and well-drained, acid soil. Salal (*G. shallon*, Zone 7), widespread along the Pacific coast, has taller stems and larger, glossier leaves, but it doesn't smell as good.

More fragrant flowers

The following plants are readily available, easy to grow under suitable conditions, and have flowers with strong, clear perfumes that most people find very enjoyable.

ANNUALS

You probably won't find these plants in six-packs at the local garden center, but they're listed in many catalogs and it's easy to raise them from seeds. Since some strains or cultivars are much more fragrant than others, read catalog descriptions carefully. Start the seeds indoors or sow them in the garden, following the directions on the packet. Most annuals can be grown throughout the United States if planted at the onset of cool or hot weather, whichever they prefer. The following all need full or part sun.

Sweet sultan (*Centaurea moschata*). Thistlelike yellow, purple, or white flowers on stiff, skinny stalks about 2 feet tall. Likes hot weather.

Sweet pea (*Lathyrus odoratus*). White, pink, purple, or red flowers on vines that climb 3 to 6 feet tall. Prefers cool weather and rich, moist soil.

Sweet alyssum (*Lobularia maritima*). A low mound about 1 feet wide covered with masses of white, rose, or purple flowers. Blooms month after month.

Stocks (*Matthiola incana*). Dense spikes of spicy-scented flowers in many colors, on stalks 1 to 2 feet tall. Prefers cool weather.

Mignonette (*Reseda odorata*). Plain-looking—just a leafy green mound about 1 feet tall with inconspicuous but very sweet yellow-brown flowers.

BIENNIALS

You have to plan ahead with biennials, since they germinate one year and bloom the next, but these are so fragrant, they're worth waiting for. If you let the seeds ripen, they often self-sow. The following overwinter unprotected in Zone 6 but may need shelter in colder zones.

Wallflower (*Cheiranthus cheiri*) has yellow, orange, red, cream, or apricot flowers on stalks 1 to 2 feet tall, in spring. It grows best where temperatures are mild year-round.

Sweet William (*Dianthus barbatus*) has clove-scented white, pink, rose, red, almost-black, or bicolor flowers in flat round clusters on stiff stalks 2 to 3 feet tall in early summer. Makes an excellent cutflower.

Dame's rocket (*Hesperis matronalis*) has night-scented rose-purple or white flowers on stalks 2 to 3 feet tall. It naturalizes readily and tolerates part shade.

Clary sage (*Salvia sclarea*) has showy, long-lasting pink or white flowers on stalks 3 to 4 feet tall. Although the flowers aren't very fragrant, the big, wrinkly, gray-green leaves smell great, especially after a rain.

PERENNIALS

The following are usually sold as plants, although some kinds come true from seed. The ones that are hardy in your climate are probably available at good local garden centers.

Lily-of-the-valley (*Convallaria majalis*, Zone 3). Sprays of tiny white bells in late spring. A ground cover, it spreads fast on shady sites in cool climates, but falters where summers are hot.

Pinks (*Dianthus*, Zone 5 or 4). There are many kinds of pinks, almost all with white, pink, or rose flowers on stalks under 1 feet tall. A few are scentless, but most have a sweet, spicy, or clovelike perfume. Pinks can't take extreme heat or high humidity.

Gingers (*Hedychium*, Zones 8 or 7). These are tropical perennials with sweet-scented, exotic-looking flowers in shades of white, pink, orange, or yellow. They bloom best in hot weather, and form bold clumps or

Pinks

'Hyperion' daylily

'Casablanca' lilies

patches of leafy stalks about 6 feet tall. Where winters are cold, you can dig the rhizomes in fall and store them indoors, or grow the plants in big pots.

Daylilies (*Hemerocallis*, Zone 4.) Breeders are introducing fragrant new daylilies, but they aren't widely available yet. Meanwhile, two old-timers are still excellent choices. Both have sweet-scented yellow flowers. 'Hyperion' blooms on 42-inch stalks in July. Lemon lily (*H. lilio-asphodelus)* blooms on 24-inch stalks in May or June.

Sweet iris, or orris root (*Iris pallida*, Zone 4). Sweet lavender or purple flowers on 3-foot stalks in late spring. Very adaptable; grows nationwide. Some, but not all, bearded iris cultivars are fragrant too.

English lavender (*Lavandula angustifolia*, Zone 5). A shrubby 1- to 2-foot perennial topped with slender, stiff-stalked spikes of very fragrant flowers for weeks in early summer. Most cultivars have lavender or purple flowers, but they can be pink or white. The gray-green foliage is fragrant too. Lavender loves hot dry weather but can't stand wet soil or high humidity.

Peony (*Paeonia*, Zone 3). Herbaceous peonies have huge single or double flowers in shades of white, pink, rose, and red and form bushy clumps of handsome foliage. White 'Festiva Maxima' and rosy pink 'Edulis Superba' both have very fragrant double flowers and do well in Southern as well as Northern gardens.

Garden phlox (*Phlox paniculata*, Zone 3). Blooms for weeks in late summer, with big heads of flowers on erect stalks. 'Mt. Fuji' and 'David' are especially fragrant cultivars. Both have white flowers and mildew-resistant foliage, grow 3 to 4 feet tall, and thrive in all but the hottest climates. Several other cultivars and species of phlox are fragrant, too.

Lilies (*Lilium*, Zone 4). Oriental hybrid lilies, such as 'Casablanca', 'Sans Souci', and 'Stargazer', bear large star-shaped flowers on stiff stalks 3 to 6 feet tall. Aurelian hybrids, such as 'Black Dragon' and 'Pink Perfection', have trumpet-shaped flowers on stalks 6 to 8 feet tall. All bloom for weeks in late summer.

English lavender

Tropical plants
like bougainvillea
love hot weather.

FLOWERS FOR HOT SUMMERS

By early July, temperatures are regularly reaching the 90s across the southern United States, and gardens there have reached a turning point. All the early-season plants, including spring bulbs, cool-weather annuals, many hardy perennials, and most hardy trees and shrubs, have already finished blooming and retired into the background.

So what's next? With more than half the growing season still to come, it's too soon to call it quits. If you want a garden that stays colorful all summer, you need plants that begin blooming when others have finished and continue despite the heat.

Fortunately, there are plenty of plants to choose from, including tropicals that grow well in containers, perennials that attract butterflies and hummingbirds, and low-maintenance plants for your landscape.

Rating heat-tolerance

It isn't easy to find information about whether or not a particular plant will thrive and bloom in hot weather. For years, nursery catalogs and gardening magazines and books have rated plants' cold hardiness by referring to the USDA hardiness zone system. Checking its hardiness rating helps you predict whether or not a plant is likely to overwinter in your climate, but a plant's cold-hardiness rating doesn't tell you anything about how it will perform in the heat of summer. Some plants tolerate both cold and heat; others can't stand either extreme. There's no pattern to it.

In 1997, the American Horticultural Society published *The Heat Map,* which divides the country into 12 heat zones, and Sunset published the *National Garden Book* map, which divides the country into 45 climate zones. So far, these systems are too new to be widely used, but someday they may help gardeners in hot climates choose promising plants.

Make your own list

Meanwhile, you can make your own list of heat-tolerant plants. Watch for flowers as you drive around town or visit gardens this summer. Once you start looking for hot-weather flowers, you may be surpised by how many you see. Get choosy. Keep upgrading your goals. Note plants that have healthy foliage and neat habits, along with showy flowers.

Whenever you find a plant you really like, write down its name or take a picture of it, so you can go to a garden center and say, "I want one of these." Fall is a good time for buying and planting the perennials, shrubs, and vines you want. For hot-weather annuals, of course, save your shopping list until spring.

How some flowers adapt

Some plants have special ways of coping with hot weather. For example, hibiscus makes new flowers every day. Four o'clocks stay closed until late afternoon when the air starts to cool. Butterflybush has tiny, thick petals that resist wilting. Bougainvillea has papery bracts that keep their color even when desiccated.

What gardeners can do

Most flowers, though, are stressed by heat. It fades and withers their petals. That's why florists keep their cut flowers in refrigerators. You can't refrigerate your garden, but if you can shelter plants from the heat of the midday and afternoon sun by locating them on the east or north side of a building, tree, or screen, their flowers will look brighter and last longer.

Watering helps, too. Flowers drink a lot of water—think how often you have to water a bouquet in a vase. In the garden, a flowering plant can transpire as much water through its petals as through its leaves. In hot dry weather, some plants that would otherwise continue blooming may stop in order to save water. If you can give them a good deep soaking, they may start up again.

This hardy hibiscus has saucer-size flowers.

'Incense' passionflower

'Petite Pink' oleander and 'Radicans' gardenia

'Red Riding Hood' mandevilla

Tropical flowers in containers

As you'd expect, most tropical plants thrive in hot weather. Even better, many tropicals bloom continuously or nearly so—unlike temperate plants, which tend to bloom just once a year. Because they are so showy and colorful over such a long season, tropicals are an excellent choice for prominent positions near the doors of your house or on a deck or patio.

The plants shown here, and many other tropicals, grow very well in containers, and that's a particularly effective way to display them. Putting a plant in a nice big pot lifts it up, enhances its stature, and makes it look more special.

Although some tropical plants are hardy to Zones 9 or 8, most are tender and die at the first frost. You can replace them each year or bring them into a sunny room for the winter.

Tips on container gardening

Tending plants in containers takes more time than growing them in the ground, because you have to water and fertilize more often. To brighten the routine, each time you care for a plant, take a moment to appreciate it, too. Here are some tips and reminders.

- Choose planters and pots made of whatever materials you like and can afford. Rot-resistant wood, heavy-duty plastic, fiberglass, terra cotta, metal, and concrete are all okay. Just be sure there are drainage holes in the bottom.
- Large heavy containers are more practical than small light ones, because they don't dry out so fast and don't tip over in the wind. If you want to keep a plant in a pot small enough to bring indoors easily in winter, grow it in an unglazed clay pot, and bury that rim-deep in a larger container for summer.
- Use good-quality potting soil. I find the heavier loam-based mixes are better than lightweight soilless mixes for outdoor use.
- Water as often as needed to prevent wilting—probably several times a week or even daily in hot or windy weather. Each time, add water until it runs out the bottom.
- Fertilize every week or two with your favorite soluble fertilizer, measured according to directions.
- Watch for spider mites, white flies, aphids, scales, and mealybugs. If you spot any, spray with insecticidal soap or a houseplant insecticide.

Passionflower

Passionflowers (*Passiflora*) are vigorous vines with large, lobed leaves and complex flowers in shades of violet, blue, red, pink, and white. Some kinds, such as 'Incense', are extremely fragrant. Passion flower vines grow so fast you can almost watch them climb, and their strong, springlike tendrils grip tight to any support. One plant is enough to cover a large trellis.

Oleander

Often used for hedges in hot climates, oleanders (*Nerium oleander*) are typically large shrubs, but 'Petite Pink' and other compact cultivars grow well in pots. Oleanders bloom all summer with clusters of single or double flowers in shades of pink, red, salmon, cream, or pure white. Some kinds are fragant. Note that all parts of these handsome plants are poisonous.

Chinese hibiscus

Star-cluster

Angel's trumpet

Gardenia

Like oleanders, full-size gardenias (*Gardenia augusta,* often listed as *G. jasminoides*) make dramatic hedges, but 'Radicans' is a miniature, spreading form that will trail over the edge of a pot. Its blossoms are small—under 2 inches wide, and wonderfully sweet-scented. Other good gardenias for containers are 'Veitchii', a compact, upright form, and 'August Beauty', a bigger shrub with larger flowers.

Mandevilla

Two kinds of mandevillas are very popular for patio containers; both are trouble-free and bloom nonstop. *Mandevilla sanderi* 'Red Riding Hood' is a compact climbing or trailing vine with small glossy leaves and dark pink flowers. *M. × amoena* 'Alice du Pont' is larger and wants a trellis to climb; it has ridged leaves and pale pink flowers. A less familiar species, Chilean jasmine (*M. laxa*), has fragrant white flowers. Golden trumpet (*Allamanda cathartica*) is similar to mandevillas and has big yellow flowers that smell good at night.

Tropical hibiscus

Most cultivars of the tropical hibiscus (*Hibiscus rosa-sinensis*) are sturdy, erect shrubs that grow several feet tall but are easily maintained in containers. What varies is the flowers, which can be single or double, 2 to 10 inches wide, in shades of red, orange, pink, yellow, white, and bicolor. Hummingbirds regularly visit the single red flowers, and explore the other kinds, too.

Star-cluster

Star-cluster or pentas (*Pentas lanceolata*) isn't well known, but it's compact, flowery, and easy to grow—you can even start it yourself from seeds. The clusters of small pink, red, or white flowers are very attractive to butterflies. The plants are bushy and grow about 2 feet tall in one season.

Angel's trumpet

If you want something really impressive, grow an angel's trumpet (*Brugmansia,* formerly *Datura*). Several types are available, with huge single or double flowers in shades of lavender, pink, orange, gold, and white. They release a penetrating, sweet aroma at night. Angel's trumpet plants grow fast and make bushy specimens with thick, treelike trunks. Although all parts of these plants are poisonous to humans, the leaves are particularly attractive to spider mites and whiteflies, so watch out for these pests and spray if needed.

Sedum 'Autumn Joy'

Aster 'Monch'

Spike gayfeather

Flowers for butterflies and hummingbirds

Hot weather may slow you down, but it doesn't bother these little creatures. Butterflies and hummingbirds actually prefer the heat; it's cold that slows them down. On hot summer days, they're active from dawn to dusk, flitting from flower to flower looking for nectar to drink.

How successfully you can attract them depends partly on your setting. An isolated garden that's surrounded by bare lawns or buildings may go unvisited, but if you live in a neighborhood with other gardens, parks, fields, or roadside wildflowers nearby, there are probably butterflies and hummingbirds around, and they'll soon discover any flowers you plant for them.

These lively pollinators visit many kinds of flowers. The examples shown here are all perennials, but annuals, shrubs, and vines can lure them, as well. For more recommendations, see p. 144.

Observing your visitors

Watching nectar-drinkers is a great way to spend summer days when it's too hot to do garden work. If you sit or stand quietly, most butterflies will ignore you and continue feeding. A butterfly may stay in the same area all day, or drift slowly around the neighborhood.

Hummingbirds come and go in a flash, returning several times a day to plants they know about, and constantly exploring for new flowers. More than tame, they're actually bold, and will fly close to investigate if you wear clothes with bright colors or floral patterns.

In the evening, watch for sphinx moths. Common but often unnoticed, they look and act like miniature hummingbirds, hovering in front of a flower and probing it with their tubelike tongue.

Butterfly favorites

Butterflies visit both fragrant and scentless flowers of all colors, including white. (They can see colors, but they see them differently than we do.) Butterflies seem to prefer small flowers or florets that are arranged in flat, round, or elongated clusters, like the examples shown above. (In an aster, there are dozens of tiny florets in that central yellow disk.) Their tongues usually aren't long enough to reach for nectar at the base of long or large flowers.

Sedum 'Autumn Joy' and other clump-forming sedums such as 'Meteor', 'Vera Jameson', and 'Rosy Glow' all draw swarms of butterflies for a few weeks in late summer, when the flowers first open and are still fresh and filled with nectar.

'Monch' aster (*Aster × frikartii*) blooms all summer, bearing hundreds of blue-purple asters about two inches wide. 'Wonder of Staffa' is a similar cultivar, and butterflies love them both. The many fall-blooming asters are also popular with butterflies.

Spike gayfeather or blazing star (*Liatris spicata*) is a prairie wildflower with dense spikes of purple, magenta, or white flowers that open from the top down (most spikes progress from the bottom up). Several wildflower nurseries offer this and other species of gayfeather; they're all magnets for butterflies.

One of the nice things about growing these sedums, asters, and gayfeathers is that they don't need deadheading, which is a tedious task in hot weather. The sedums and gayfeathers will grow in any average soil and tolerate considerable dryness,

but the asters prefer good garden soil and regular watering. These plants are all hardy to Zone 5.

Hummingbird favorites

Hummingbirds see colors the same as we do, but they have no sense of smell. They're drawn to bright colors like red, hot pink, fire orange, and gold, but they explore other-colored flowers, too. Hummingbirds visit both large and small flowers, wherever there's nectar.

Along with hibiscus, one of their favorite large flowers is gloriosa lily (*Gloriosa superba*). This is a vine with tendrils at the tips of its leaves; it can climb 6 to 8 feet high. Flowering lasts for a month or more in midsummer. Gloriosa lily isn't hardy, but it's easy to keep it from year to year, because it forms tubers. Dig them up in fall, keep them cool and dry all winter, and replant them in spring.

'Lucifer', with bright red flowers, is one of the most popular cultivars of crocosmia or montbretia (*Crocosmia.*

Crocosmia 'Lucifer'

Gloriosa lily

Cardinal flower

Other cultivars have orange, gold, or bicolor flowers. All are showy and easy to grow from corms that you can buy and plant in spring. Once established, crocosmias spread quickly and forms impressive clumps or patches with armloads of flower spikes and distinctive flat leaves. They're hardy across the southern United States, thriving in average soil.

Cardinal flower (*Lobelia cardinalis*) is a hardy wildflower native to wet, even swampy sites. It needs part shade, rich soil, and extra watering in the garden, but under those conditions, it's quite tolerant of heat and blooms for a month or so in late summer. Along with the wild type, there are some incredible new hybrid cardinal flowers, with very dramatic spikes of red, blue, or purple flowers. Hummingbirds love them all.

Landscape plants

A large plant or mass planting that blooms in summer is a welcome sight in an otherwise green-and-tan landscape, but the more prominent the plant, the more important that it be fully adapted to your situation. It's much more expensive and disappointing to replace a big plant that fails than to fill a little gap where a perennial disappeared. So when you're choosing major plants for your landscape, be sure to think about cold-hardiness, soil and water requirements, and potential pest and disease problems, as well as heat-tolerance.

The examples featured here are some of the most widely adapted and readily available plants for hot summer landscapes, but there are many other good plants to consider. Watch local gardens to get more ideas about what will succeed in your particular region.

Crape myrtle

The crape myrtle (*Lagerstroemia indica*) has always been a popular summer-flowering tree, but the new cultivars are better than ever—they're more compact (ranging from 10 to 25 feet tall) and hardier (to Zone 7 or 6), and their leaves are resistant to powdery mildew and often display bright fall colors. Many nurseries are now growing these new crape myrtles, which were developed by the National Arboretum and have Native American names. 'Sioux' has dark pink flowers and reaches 10 to 15 feet. Other cultivars have pale pink, lavender, rosy red, or white flowers.

Blue mist

Blue mist (*Caryopteris × clandonensis*) is a shrubby perennial that looks best if you cut it back hard every spring, leaving stubs about 1 foot tall. It will sprout back into a bushy mound about 3 feet tall and wide by midsummer, then cover itself with fluffy clusters of tiny flowers that butterflies love. 'Dark Knight'

has dark green foliage and dark blue flowers. 'Longwood Blue' has paler leaves and sky blue flowers. 'Worchestershire Gold' has cheerful yellow foliage and medium blue flowers. All are hardy to Zone 6.

Rose verbena

'Springbrook Pink', 'Homestead Purple', 'Sissinghurst' and other cultivars and hybrids of rose verbena (*Verbena canadensis*), a wildflower native

'Sioux' crape myrtle

'Dark Knight' blue mist

'Springbrook Pink' rose verbena

to the eastern United States, make colorful ground covers for sunny sites with well-drained soil. All form matted clumps under 1 foot tall and 2 to 3 feet wide. They bear round clusters of pink, magenta, or purple flowers from spring until fall. Zone 6.

Cape plumbago

Cape plumbago (*Plumbago auriculata*) is a malleable shrub with pale green leaves and ice-blue or white flowers. You can prune it into a compact bush, let it sprawl naturally over a wall or bank, or train it up a trellis or support. It blooms nonstop for months, even in the hottest weather, and tolerates poor, dry soil, but is only hardy to Zone 9.

Roses

Roses are the best known and most beloved of all summer flowers, and they're some of the most versatile landscape plants, too. Rose bushes can be miniature or giant, stiff or loose, climbing or trailing, dainty or bold. Don't abstain just because you've heard that roses are difficult to care for; that isn't necessarily true. Many roses, both heirloom and modern, are adaptable, trouble-free plants. 'Ballerina', for example, needs no spraying and minimal pruning, and blooms all summer whether you deadhead it or not.

Although they keep blooming, some roses do look bleached or faded in hot weather. If that faded look bothers you, plan a midsummer trip to the nearest rose display garden (there's one in almost every state). There you can determine which roses hold up best in your climate.

Coral vine

Coral vine or queen's wreath (*Antigonon leptopus*) is a deciduous vine that sprouts up from the ground in spring and quickly covers a fence or arbor. It blooms from late summer until frost, with slender sprays of rosy pink or white flowers that slowly fade to tan. Cut down the stems after they freeze and mulch the crown for winter. Zone 8.

More shrubs and trees that bloom in the heat

These all require well-drained soil.

Bird-of-paradise (*Caesalpinia gilliesii*) has finely-divided leaves and yellow flowers. Dies back in winter but recovers fast in spring. Zone 8.

Chaste tree (*Vitex agnus-castus*) is a shrub with slender spikes of lilac flowers and spicy-scented, gray-green compound leaves. Zone 7.

Chitalpa taskentensis 'Pink Dawn' is a fast-growing small tree with big showy clusters of ruffled lavender-and-yellow flowers. Zone 6.

Chinese flame tree (*Koelreuteria bipinnata*) is covered with yellow flowers in late summer, followed by equally showy clusters of puffy pink pods. Zone 9 or 8. Golden rain tree (*K. paniculata*) blooms earlier and has tan pods. Zone 5. Both trees grow about 30 feet tall.

Pomegranate (*Punica granatum*) is a rounded evergreen shrub with bright orange or white flowers. The cultivars with double, carnation-like flowers bloom all summer but don't bear fruit. Zone 7.

Rose-of-sharon (*Hibiscus syriacus*) is an upright shrub with single or double flowers in shades of lilac, lavender, blue, and white. Zone 5.

Yellow bells (*Tecoma stans*) is a fast-growing shrub with large, clear yellow flowers and bold compound leaves. Cut back old stalks every spring. Zone 8.

Coral vine

'Ballerina' rose

Cape plumbago

More butterfly and hummingbird favorites

This list includes annual, perennials, vines, and shrubs, grouped by flower color. All bloom in hot weather and attract butterflies (🦋) and/or hummingbirds (🐦) to your garden. Unless otherwise noted, these plants grow best in well-drained soil, need to be watered during long dry spells, and are hardy at least to Zone 7.

WHITE OR PASTEL

Glossy abelia (*Abelia × grandiflora*). Dense shrub, 6 to 8 feet tall and wide, with arching limbs. Blooms all summer, bearing thousands of pale pink flowers. 🦋

Double Japanese aster (*Kalimeris pinnatifida*). Light-textured perennial that forms an airy mound 2 to 3 feet tall. Blossoms are like miniature double daisies, about 1 inch wide. 🦋

Blackfoot daisy (*Melampodium leucanthum*). Low, mounded, shrubby perennial, usually under 1 foot tall. Abundant daisylike blossoms have white rays and yellow disks. 🦋

RED OR RED-ORANGE

Anisacanthus (*Anisacanthus wrightii*). Small evergreen shrub, 2 to 4 feet tall, with tubular red-orange flowers. Prune to keep it bushy. Zone 8. 🐦

Red bird-of-paradise (*Caesalpinia pulcherrima*). Fast-growing shrub that freezes back but recovers. Glorious clusters of red-orange flowers. Zone 10. 🐦

Cannas (*Canna* cvs.). These durable perennials form a patch of upright, leafy stems and bloom all summer in shades of red, orange, pink, and yellow. Zone 8; in colder zones, dig the rhizomes and store in a cool dry place. 🐦

Cockspur coral tree (*Erythrina crista-gallii*). Tender shrub that freezes back but blooms on new wood, with gorgeous crimson flowers. Zone 9. 🐦

Firebush (*Hamelia patens*). Shrubby perennial, 4 feet tall, with tubular red-orange flowers. Zone 9 or 8. 🦋 🐦

Red yucca (*Hesperaloe parviflora*). Succulent perennial with tough grassy foliage and spikes of showy coral flowers on stalks 4 feet tall. 🐦

Cypress vine (*Ipomea quamoclit*). Annual vine. Climbs to 10 feet, with lacy leaves and small star-shaped red flowers. 🐦

Standing cypress (*Ipomopsis rubra*). Annual or biennial. Forms a slender clump, 3 to 4 feet tall, topped with masses of red-orange flowers. Self-sows. 🐦

Coral honeysuckle (*Lonicera sempervirens*). A well-mannered vine that climbs 10 to 20 feet. Blooms off and on all summer, with clusters of red-orange, coral, or gold flowers. 🐦

Turk's cap (*Malvaviscus arboreus* var. *drummondii*). Shrubby perennial, 3 to 5 feet tall, with flowers that look like short red lipsticks. 🐦

Scarlet sage (*Salvia coccinea*). Annual or perennial, usually about 2 feet tall, with loose spikes of crimson flowers; a graceful alternative to the common bedding salvias (*S. splendens*). 🐦

California fuchsia (*Zauschneria californica*). A perennial wildflower for informal gardens. Grows 1 to 2 feet tall, with gray foliage and red-orange flowers. Zone 8. 🐦

ORANGE, GOLD, OR YELLOW

Butterfly weed (*Asclepias tuberosa*). Clump-forming perennial, 2 to 3 feet tall, with flat clusters of orange flowers. Cut it back to promote repeat bloom. 🦋

Trumpet vine (*Campsis radicans*). A vigorous vine that climbs any support and grows 25 feet or taller. Usu-

Canna

Scarlet sage

Common lantana

Butterfly bush

ally has orange flowers, but there are yellow and red forms. **Chinese trumpet vine** (*C. grandiflora*) is similar, but has shorter, wider flowers, usually orange or coral.

Candle bush (*Cassia alata*). Tender shrub, treated as an annual. Grows 6 to 8 feet tall in just a few months. Stems are topped with flamelike clusters of yellow flowers.

Yellow cosmos (*Cosmos sulphureus*). Annual with erect stems 1 to 3 feet tall and semi-double flowers 1 to 2 inches wide in shades of bright orange, orange-red, and yellow. May self-sow.

Common lantana (*Lantana camara*). Erect or sprawling shrub, 2 to 4 feet tall. Rounded flowerheads are often two-tone, in shades of orange, yellow, red, pink, and creamy white. Zone 8.

Butter daisy (*Melampodium paludosum*) is a carefree annual, under 1 foot tall, with countless small gold flowers.

Mexican hat (*Ratibida columnifera*). Perennial wildflower, under 2 feet tall, with masses of distinctive brick-red and yellow flowers.

Mexican sunflower (*Tithonia rotundifolia*). A bushy, erect annual, 4 to 6 feet tall, with long-stalked orange blossoms about 3 inches wide.

Butter daisy

Zinnias (*Zinnia*). Unlike common, upright zinnias with large double flowers, these two are low, spreading plant covered with small single blossoms. *Z. angustifolia* is an annual with orange or white flowers. *Z. grandiflora* is a perennial with yellow flowers.

PINK, PURPLE, LILAC, OR BLUE

Texas hummingbird mint (*Agastache cana*). Perennial, 2 to 3 feet tall, with fragrant leaves and disheveled spikes of showy pink flowers. Several related species and hybrids are wonderful, too.

Butterfly bush (*Buddleia davidii*). Vase-shaped shrub with spikes of vio-

let, blue, pink, or white flowers at the end of each branch. Cut it back in spring; it grows 6 to 8 feet tall by fall. There are many good cultivars.

Hardy ageratum, blue mistflower (*Eupatorium coelestinum*). Spreading perennial, 2 feet tall, with fluffy clusters of lavender flowers. Prefers damp soil.

Blue marguerite (*Felicia amelloides*). Shrubby perennial, better treated as an annual. If pruned, forms a neat mound 1 to 3 feet tall and wide. Daisylike blossoms have sky-blue rays.

Trailing lantana (*Lantana montevidensis*). Perennial groundcover, evergreen with round clusters of lilac, rose, or white flowers. Zone 8.

Pincushion plant (*Scabiosa columbaria*). Clumping perennial with round flowerheads over a long season. 'Butterfly Blue' and 'Pink Mist' are good cultivars.

Blue fanflower (*Scaevola aemula*). Spreading perennial with masses of blue-purple flowers from spring to fall. Great for containers. Zone 9.

Purple top (*Verbena bonariensis*). Perennial or annual, usually 3 to 4 feet tall. Stiff, branching stalks bear countless clusters of mauve flowers. **Rigid verbena** (*V. rigida*) is similar but shorter.

Flame grass bends
under a wet snow but
straightens up again as
soon as the snow melts.

PLANTS FOR WINTER ENJOYMENT

When you look out into your garden in winter, do you see blank spots where the perennials are dormant, the annuals have died, and the bulbs haven't come up yet? A barren garden can be quite a dreary sight.

But wait—your garden doesn't have to be boring in winter. Even in cold climates, you can create a garden that's interesting and attractive all year. The key is to look beyond flowers, and choose plants for other reasons, too—for the beauty of their foliage, for their shape and silhouette, for the color and texture of their bark and twigs, for their abundant berries or pods.

These features are less dramatic than flowers, but they last longer, and they wear well. A planting designed for winter will give you months of steady pleasure. As you survey it again and again, you'll appreciate details that you'd never notice in the rush of summer. Some people like their garden best in winter, because they have more time to look at it and less work to do.

Consider the big picture

Garden designers say that winter reveals the "bones" of a garden—the underlying proportions of its beds and paths, the lines of its fences and edgings, the placement of benches and ornaments, and the position and scale of its permanent plantings. These things are very important, and winter is the best time to think about them. You can be much more objective about the basic design of a garden when it isn't padded with billowing foliage and flowers.

Make substitutions

But if you see too many blank spots, now is the time to think about substitutions. Pick a spot, recall what you've planted there before, then consider the alternatives. For example, instead of a clump of daylilies that bloom for a few weeks in July, you could have a patch of Northern sea oats grass (*Chasmanthium latifolium*) that holds its dainty dangling flowers from July until spring, turning from green to beige in fall. Daylilies and sea oats grow about the same height and fill about the same space, but one is effective for weeks and the other for months.

Instead of sunflowers or hollyhocks, you could plant a cranberry bush viburnum (*Viburnum trilobum*) with lacy white flowers in late spring, red-purple fall foliage, and bright crimson berries all winter. Substitution is a step-by-step way to add winter interest to an existing garden. Just keep asking yourself: How often do I notice the plant that's growing here now? Would something else give me more pleasure over a longer season?

Planting outside a window

Most people spend part of each day near a particular window—over the kitchen sink, next to the breakfast table, or in the office. No matter how small, the space outside that window is the perfect place for a special winter garden. Espalier a flowering quince (*Chaenemeles*) against a wall or fence. Fill a planter with miniature wintercreeper (*Euonymus fortunei* 'Kewensis') or a sparkly creeping juniper such as *Juniperus squamata* 'Blue Star'. Make a simple grouping of upright and spreading evergreens, or combine a small tree with a few low shrubs and a ground cover. Treat yourself to some plants that really delight you, and start with specimens that are big enough to be impressive. A winter garden like this is the best Christmas present you'll ever give yourself.

Selecting plants for winter

Gardeners in Zones 7 to 11 can choose from hundreds of plants that look good all winter. There are fewer candidates for colder regions, so this chapter features plants that are hardy at least to Zone 6.

One reminder: Before buying a plant for any particular site, be sure the growing conditions are right for it. A site that is shady in winter can be sunny in summer, and vice versa. Think about soil type and moisture level, too. After all, a plant must grow well in summer in order to look good in winter.

Tiny red crab apples last all winter.

Evergreen trees and shrubs

To most people in cold climates, evergreen means a conifer; that is, a tree or shrub with needle- or scale-like leaves, such as pines and junipers. But there are also broadleaf evergreens—trees and shrubs with broad flat leaves that hang on through the winter.

Although we call them evergreens, broadleaf evergreens and conifers actually come in many colors—pale to dark green, olive, gold, silvery blue, blue-black, maroon, purple, and variegated. Their leaves often change color with the seasons, emerging in shades of pale green, gold, or red; turning green in summer; then darkening to maroon or bronze in late fall. Combining evergreens with different leaf colors and textures and different overall sizes and shapes makes a varied and satisfying winter scene. Here are some favorites to choose from, illustrated from left to right below. For more evergreens, see p. 154.

Conifers

There are dozens of species and hundreds of cultivars of conifers for cold climates. Most need full sun in summer and well-drained soil, but there are a few conifers for shaded or damp sites, too. Conifers are easy to grow. The only problem is that they may get too big, too fast, sometimes growing a foot or more each year. For small spaces, choose dwarf conifers that grow only a few inches a year and shape themselves naturally into graceful domes, cones, and columns.

'Boulevard' false cypress (*Chamaecyparis pisifera*) has luxuriously soft and fluffy foliage. The needles are bright silvery blue in summer and darker blue-violet in winter. It grows slowly into an upright cone, eventually reaching 8 to 10 feet tall. Zone 5.

Mugo pines (*Pinus mugo*) look like bushes, not trees. Some mugos are more dwarf than others, but all are slow-growing and take many years to get more than a few feet tall and wide. They form spreading mounds of rich dark green foliage, and need full sun and well-drained soil. Zone 3.

American arborvitae (*Thuja occidentalis*), a native tree, is a mainstay for hedges and foundation plantings throughout the Northeast and Great Lakes states, but wild trees and older cultivars have the drawbacks of growing too large and turning a dirty brown color in winter. New cultivars

'Blue Girl' holly

'Boulevard' false cypress

Heathers

are more shapely and compact and stay bright green all year. Many nurseries are growing 'Emerald', which makes a narrow column of beautiful green foliage. 'Nigra' and 'Techny' are broader, conical trees with darker foliage. There are also several dwarf cultivars, including some with gold foliage. Most cultivars are hardy to Zone 3.

Broadleaf evergreens

Only a few kinds of broadleaf evergreens are hardy in Zones 6 or 5, and very few are hardy in Zones 4 or colder, but even this small group offers a variety of leaf sizes, shapes, and colors. Most hardy broadleaf evergreens are slow-growing shrubs that prefer a sheltered site near a building or under a large deciduous tree, with part to full shade in winter, part to full sun in summer, and well-drained acid soil. If you can provide the right conditions, a few broadleaf evergreens will be the highlight of your winter garden.

Hollies

'Blue Girl', 'Blue Boy', 'Blue Princess', 'Blue Prince', and other "blue" hollies (*Ilex × meserveae*) have dark, glossy, blue-green leaves and purple stems, and the females bear bright red berries. Let them grow up to 8 to 10 feet tall and wide, or prune them as you choose. Zone 5. 'China Girl' and 'China Boy' are related and similar to the blue hollies, but have medium green leaves. Zone 5. Inkberry holly (*I. glabra*) is the hardiest evergreen holly, with small, spineless leaves and navy blue berries. Zone 4.

Heaths and heathers

Winter heath (*Erica carnea*) and heather (*Calluna vulgaris*) are mounded or sprawling shrubs, usually under 1 foot tall and 2 feet tall, that have twiggy stems covered with scaly leaves. There are scores of cultivars, with foliage in shades of green, gray, gold, red, and bronze; most change color in winter. Winter heaths are already blooming as the snow melts away, and have white, pink, or red flowers. Heathers bloom in summer and fall, with pink or purplish flowers. Both heaths and heathers need excellent drainage and acid soil. They make good ground covers for dry sites. Zone 5 or 4, depending on cultivar.

Rhododendrons

Rhododendrons are best loved for their flowers, but they also have glossy, dark, evergreen leaves. 'P.J.M.' and other types with small leaves are typically hardy to Zone 4. Their leaves often turn maroon or purple-bronze in winter, but they look perky even in subzero weather. Many large-leaf rhododendrons are hardy to Zone 6 or 5. Their leaves stay green all winter and look wonderful on mild days, but hang like wet laundry when temperatures drop much below freezing. All rhododendrons need moist but well-drained soil, sun or light shade in summer, and protection from winter sun and wind.

Mahonias

Oregon grape (*Mahonia aquifolia*) has fragrant bright yellow flowers in early spring; silvery blue berries in winter; and leathery, spiny leaves that are glossy green in summer, turning dark purple bronze in winter. It slowly forms a clump of stems 6 to 8 feet tall. Zone 6.

Creeping holly-grape (*M. repens*) has similar but smaller features. It spreads slowly to form a loose patch, under 1 foot tall. Zone 5.

'Emerald' arborvitae

Oregon grape

Rhododendron 'P.J.M.'

Dwarf mugo pine

Bark and twigs

Many trees develop interesting bark on their trunks and main limbs as they mature. This bark is attractive all year, but you notice it most in winter, when there's no shade from the foliage and the sun is so low that it shines directly on the trunks.

If you're planting a tree for its bark, get a head start by buying the largest specimen you can afford. It usually takes several years for trunk bark to develop its distinctive character. A clump with two or more trunks makes an especially fine specimen, because the more trunks, the more bark.

You don't have to wait long to enjoy trees and shrubs with colored twigs. You'll appreciate them the first winter after planting, because it's the newest twigs that have the brightest color. Several trees have glossy maroon, olive, or ebony twigs, but the most conspicuous twig colors are gold and scarlet. These bright twigs are cheerful even on cloudy days, and they absolutely glow when the sun shines on them.

Red-twig dogwoods

Two species of dogwoods have bright red twigs in winter: Siberian dogwood (*Cornus alba*) and the native red-osier dogwood (*C. sericea*, often listed as *C. stolonifera*). Both are easy to grow and adaptable. There are several fine cultivars, including dwarf, variegated, and yellow-stem forms.

Plant red-twig dogwoods where you'll see the sun shining on the stems in winter. They can take either sun or shade in summer.

The bark is most colorful on first-year growth, so cut old stems to the ground every year or two just before they leaf out in spring. New shoots reach 4 to 8 feet tall by fall. Zone 2.

Birches

Most birches have beautiful bark, and it starts to color, peel, and curl on trees only eight or ten years old. Unfortunately, the native canoe birch (*B. papyrifera*) and the European birch (*B. pendula*), both loved for their white bark, are very susceptible to the bronze birch borer. For that reason, many nurseries now recommend the 'Whitespire' birch (*B. platyphylla* 'Whitespire'), an Asian birch that is resistant to borers. It has beautiful white bark and a narrow, upright habit, maturing at about 40 feet tall. Choose a sunny, well-drained site. Zone 4.

River birch (*Betula nigra*), also resistant to borers, is the best birch to plant where summers are hot and humid. Native to wet sites, it adapts to average garden soil if you water deeply during summer dry spells. Seedling trees have curly, reddish tan bark. 'Heritage' is a cultivar with beautiful caramel-and-cream bark that peels off in large flaky sheets. Zone 4.

'Heritage' river birch

Red-osier dogwood

Grasses and stalks

It's pleasant to work in the garden on warm fall days, tidying up and putting things away, and doing a good fall clean-up frees time for other tasks in spring. Toss mushy frozen annuals and tender perennials on the compost pile, so you won't have to look at them all winter. But think twice before cutting back herbaceous plants that are stiff and sturdy. They may be brown, but as long as they're standing up, clumps of dry foliage and stalks add height and form to the winter landscape.

Grasses

Among the most popular ornamental grasses are various cultivars of *Miscanthus sinensis*. These form leafy clumps 4 to 6 feet tall and wide, with fluffy seedheads on stalks 6 to 8 feet tall. 'Gracillimus', sometimes called maiden grass, has thin, gray-green leaves. 'Variegatus' has broader leaves with bright white stripe along the edges. 'Purpurascens', called flame grass, has leaves that turn red-orange in fall. There are many other fine cultivars. All turn beige or tan after hard frost and hold up well to rain and dry snow. Most are hardy to Zone 5.

Other grasses that last well into the winter include feather reed grass (*Calamagrostis × acutiflora*), which forms narrow clumps 4 to 6 feet tall; ravenna grass (*Erianthus ravennae*, a giant grass with flowerstalks 8 to 12 feet tall; and switch grass (*Panicum virgatum*) which makes broad dense clumps 3 to 5 feet tall, topped with a cloud of delicate flowerstalks. All are hardy to Zone 5.

Blue fescue grass (*Festuca ovina* var. *glauca*) and blue oat grass (*Helictotrichon sempervirens*) both make dome-shaped clumps of beautiful blue leaves. Blue fescue has thin, wiry leaves and grows 1 foot tall and wide. Blue oat grass has wider leaves and grows 2 feet tall and wide. Both are hardy to Zone 4.

Bamboos

We usually think of bamboos as tropical plants, and indeed, many species are tender to frost, but some bamboos are surprisingly hardy. Their leaves and stems may freeze down, but if the underground rhizomes survive, the plant recovers and sprouts back in spring like other perennials do. Kuma bamboo (*Sasa veitchii*) is especially attractive. Its long, broad leaves are dark green all summer, then turn beige around the edge in fall. The leaves and shoots die when the temperature drops to 0°F, but the rhizomes are hardy to Zone 5 if protected by a thick mulch or some snow. Kuma bamboo spreads invasively in mild climates. Where it regularly freezes back, it spreads fast enough to fill a shady corner, but it won't take over your yard. The stems grow 2 to 4 feet tall.

Stalks

Herbaceous plants with large seedpods on stiff stalks make interesting accents in a winter garden. Honesty (*Lunaria biennis*) is a biennial often grown for everlasting bouquets. If you leave a few stalks in the garden, it will self-sow, but it isn't weedy. The flat round pods dangle from bushy stalks 2 to 3 feet tall. Zone 4.

Many garden perennials also have interesting pods and stalks that hold up well in winter. These are also useful in bouquets (see p. 125).

Maiden grass

Kuma bamboo

Honesty

Winter berries

Shiny ripe berries add bright high-lights to a winter garden. Like clusters of tiny Christmas ornaments, colored in bright shades of red, orange, or yellow, they sparkle against bare limbs or dark evergreen foliage.

Plants make berries to attract birds, who then disperse the seeds, but birds prefer some berries to others. They eat the most nourishing and palatable ones, such as blueberries or raspberries, immediately. They also eat elder (*Sambucus*), dogwood (*Cornus*), and honeysuckle (*Lonicera*) berries as soon as they ripen, in late summer or fall. Most winterberry holly (*Ilex verticillata*) and viburnum berries are gone by Christmas.

If you want berries to look at in winter, plant pyracanthas, crab apples, hawthornes (*Crataegus*), red chokeberry (*Aronia arbutifolia*), or evergreen hollies (*Ilex*). Their fruits hang uneaten for months, until they have been softened by repeated freezing and thawing, and until the birds run out of other food sources. In fact, if you keep a feeder stocked with sunflower seeds, the birds may never get around to eating these berries at all.

Pyracantha 'Gnome'

Pyracanthas

Most pyracanthas, or firethorns, are tender shrubs, but a few cultivars are hardy in Zone 6 and even in Zone 5 if planted against an east-facing wall, fence, or chimney. Try 'Gnome', 'Teton', 'Mohave', 'Yukon Belle', or 'Lalandei'. All have small semi-evergreen leaves, white flower in spring, and clusters of orange or orangish berries. Pyracanthas need well-drained soil and tolerate dry sites. Prune annually in early spring to control their size and shape.

Crab apples

Crab apples (*Malus*) have very showy white, pink, or rosy purple flowers in spring and small red, red-purple, or gold fruits that ripen in fall and provide winter and spring food for robins, bluebirds, waxwings, and many other songbirds. 'Donald Wyman' is a popular cultivar with white flowers and bright red fruits. It grows about 20 feet tall and wide, with a rounded crown. There are dozens of other fine crab apples. To choose one for your garden, consider its mature size and shape, as well as the colors of its flowers and fruits. Although all are small, these trees are varied—they can grow 8 to 25 feet tall, with rounded, oval, narrow, vase-shaped, horizontal, or weeping crowns. Make sure the foliage is disease-resistant, not subject to ugly leaf spots. Crab apples need full sun and fertile, well-drained soil. Most are hardy to Zone 5 or 4.

Crab apple 'Donald Wyman'

Vernal witch hazel

First flowers

Fresh flowers are the most remarkable feature in a winter garden. Their petals seem so tender and delicate, their colors so rich and intense, and their sweet scents so unexpected and delightful.

But plants that are called winter flowers in most gardening books may not bloom in your garden until spring, since bloom time depends on climate. The colder your winter, the longer you have to wait. Flowering quince blooms in January in Texas, February in Georgia, March in Maryland, April in New Jersey, and not until May in Vermont. Different plants that bloom in sequence over a season of several months in mild Seattle wait until the last minute and bloom all at once in chilly Detroit or Boston.

Sometimes you can encourage a tree or shrub to bloom earlier than usual by planting it on the east or south side of a building or against a brick or stone wall that absorbs solar heat. This strategy can backfire, if the buds start to swell then are hit by a hard frost, but it's worth taking a chance. Some years you'll lose, but often you'll gain a few weeks, or succeed with a plant that you otherwise couldn't grow at all.

Witch hazels

The vernal witch hazel (*Hamamelis vernalis*) is one of the first shrubs to bloom each year, starting by March even in New England and around the Great Lakes. It bears small clusters of yellow or reddish yellow flowers with four narrow petals that unfurl on warm days and curl up again on chilly nights. They have a delicious, penetrating aroma. This shrub grows slowly, reaching about 10 feet tall. Its leaves turn yellow or tan in fall but may not drop off until spring. This is the one of the hardiest witch hazels,

'Texas Scarlet' flowering quince

native to the Ozarks but hardy in Zone 4. The Chinese witch hazel (*H. mollis*) and hybrid witch hazels (*H. × intermedia*) have slightly larger flowers but are only hardy to Zones 6 or 5; even there, severe cold spells can freeze the buds and cancel that year's flowers.

Flowering quince

Another of the earliest shrubs is flowering quince (*Chaenomeles* hybrids, sometimes listed under *C. speciosa*). There are many cultivars, with flowers like apple blossoms in shades of pink, scarlet, orange, and white. 'Texas Scarlet' is watermelon-red. 'Cameo' has double flowers in apricot-pink. 'Snow' and 'Jet Trail' are white. 'Toyo Nishiki' has red, pink, and white flowers all at the same time. For some reason, flowering quinces often get mixed up at nurseries, so it's best to buy plants in bloom to be sure of the color you want.

The flowers last for several weeks, especially if the weather stays cool, and may still be there when the leaves come out. Flowering quinces are tough, adaptable shrubs with upright, rounded, or spreading shapes. They can be left unpruned, sheared for hedges, trained up a wall, or sculpted into bonsai-type specimens. The crooked, sometimes thorny twigs are popular with flower arrangers, who cut stems early and force them into bloom indoors. Zone 4.

More plants for cold-winter gardens

These are recommended for Zones 6, 5, and 4, where winters are so long and cold that it's especially important to grow something special you'll enjoy looking at while you wait for spring. Most are also adapted to Zones 7 and 8, and there are scores of other fine plants for winter gardens in those mild regions.

BROADLEAF EVERGREEN SHRUBS

Common **boxwood** (*Buxus sempervirens*) and most of its cultivars and hybrids are hardy to Zone 5. Some forms stay rich green all year, but others turn bronze in winter. Most boxwoods grow fairly slowly, so the plants are expensive, but once established, they are troublefree and long-lived.

Mountain laurel (*Kalmia latifolia*) has several erect trunks, 4 to 12 feet tall, topped with a crown of shiny yellow-green to rich green foliage and rounded clusters of white, pale pink, or rosy pink flowers in early summer. Zone 4.

Drooping leucothoe (*Leucothoe fontanesiana*) grows 3 to 6 feet tall and wide, with arching limbs, smooth leaves that are bright green in summer and purple-bronze in winter, and clusters of white flowers in spring. **Coast leucothoe** (*L. axillaris*) is similar but more compact. Both are Zone 5.

Japanese andromeda (*Pieris japonica*) has coppery red new leaves that later turn dark green and drooping clusters of fragrant white or pink flowers in early spring. It grows upright, 8 to 12 feet tall. There are dozens of cultivars. Zone 5. **Mountain andromeda** (*P. floribunda*) is a smaller shrub with erect clusters of white flowers. Zone 4.

Cherry laurel (*Prunus laurocerasus*) has glossy, dark green leaves and sweet-scented flowers in spring. 'For-est Green', 'Otto Luyken', and 'Schipkaensis' are fairly compact, usually under 4 feet tall, and hardy on sheltered sites in Zone 6.

Viburnum 'Conoy' (*Viburnum*) is one of the nicest hardy viburnums, with a dense spreading habit (3 to 4 feet tall) and neat, small, glossy leaves. Zone 5.

GOOD BARK OR TWIGS

Paperbark maple (*Acer griseum*) is a slow-growing small tree up to 30 feet tall. Its outer bark curls and peels, revealing glossy cinnamon-colored inner bark. Zone 5.

Kousa dogwood (*Cornus kousa*) bark flakes off the trunk and main limbs, exposing irregular patches of tan, gray, and brown. It grows 25 feet tall, spreads at least that wide, has white flowers in May or June and crimson fall foliage. Zone 5.

Harry Lauder's walking stick (*Corylus avellana* 'Contorta') is slow-growing shrub with gray twigs that twist like large corkscrews, and long dark catkins that dangle in late winter. Zone 3.

Oakleaf hydrangea (*Hydrangea quercifolia*) grows 4 to 8 feet tall, with reddish brown bark that cracks lenthwise and peels off the erect, broomstick-sized trunks. Zone 5.

Hardy orange (*Poncirus trifoliata*) is a large shrub that forms a dense mass of very thorny twigs with dark green bark. 'Flying Dragon' has twigs that twist and zigzag in a remarkable way. Zone 6.

Quaking aspen (*Populus tremuloides*) has smooth gray or beige trunks and gray-green twigs. The shimmering leaves turn warm gold in fall. It reaches 40 to 60 feet tall. Zone 2.

Amur chokecherry (*Prunus maackii*) has incredibly glossy, caramel-colored bark. It grows 25 feet tall, with bright white flowers in spring. Zone 2.

Corkscrew willows (*Salix matsudana* 'Scarlet Curls' and 'Golden Curls') are fast-growing small trees with spiraling twigs that turn bright-colored in winter. Some cultivars of *S. alba* have bright, straight twigs.All look best if pruned hard every few years in spring. Zone 4.

Mountain laurel

Saucer magnolia

Winterberry

February daphne (*Daphne mezereum*) has small but very fragrant magenta or white flowers all along its twigs, followed by red berries. It grows 2 to 3 feet tall. Zone 4.

Winter jasmine (*Jasminum nudiflorum*) is hardy only on protected sites in Zone 6, but there its bright yellow flowers appear sporadically all winter. It's a trailing shrub with small semievergreen leaves and green twigs.

Winter honeysuckle (*Lonicera fragrantissima*) is a nondescript shrub 6 to 8 feet tall and wide, but it has creamy white flowers with a delicious aroma. Zone 5.

Even young plants of saucer magnolia (*Magnolia × soulangeana*) and star magnolia (*Magnolia stellata*) bear large, white, pink, or purplish flowers on bare twigs in early spring. There are many fine cultivars of these small, carefree trees. Most grow 10 to 25 feet tall and are hardy to Zone 5.

Nanking, Manchu, or downy cherry (*Prunus tomentosa*) is a shrub 6 to 8 feet tall with fragrant white flowers, shiny cinnamon-colored bark, and small edible cherries. Zone 3. Cultivars of two early-flowering cherry trees, spring cherry (*P. subhirtella*) and Yoshino cherry (*P. × yedoensis*), are hardy to Zones 6 or 5 and grow about 20 feet tall. Some years they make a gorgeous show of pale flowers, but they're vulnerable to late frosts.

Rhododendron 'P.J.M.' (*Rhododendron*) is a compact, upright shrub 4 to 8 feet tall with fluorescent purple-pink flowers. R. 'Olga Mezitt' is a similar plant with clear pink flowers. Zone 4.

Golden currant (*Ribes aureum*) and clove currant (*R. odoratum*) have deliciously fragrant golden flowers and edible fruits. Both are small shrubs, 3 to 6 feet tall. Zone 4.

Pussy willows (*Salix caprea, S. discolor*) have fuzzy gray catkins on separate male and female plants; the males are more conspicuous, because their catkins are frosted with gold stamens. Pussy willows can grow tree-size, but are usually cut to the ground every few years to keep them bushy. Zone 4.

Japanese tree lilac (*Syringa reticulata*) is a small tree, to 30 feet, with glossy, tight, reddish brown bark and clusters of creamy white flowers in midsummer. Zone 3.

Lacebark elm (*Ulmus parvifolia*) is a neat, healthy elm up to 40 feet tall, with bark mottled like camouflage cloth in shades of green, gray, brown, and orange. Zone 5.

EARLY FLOWERS

Red, or swamp, maple (*Acer rubrum*) is a fast-growing tree, 40 feet or taller, with dangling clusters of scarlet flowers that last for weeks from late winter to early spring. It also has excellent fall color. Zone 4.

Serviceberries (*Amelanchier*) are small trees, usually multi-trunked, with delicate white or pale pink flowers in early spring, edible berries in summer, and glorious fall color. Zone 4.

Cornelian cherry dogwood (*Cornus mas*) is a multi-trunked shrub or small tree, usually under 25 feet tall, with clusters of tiny yellow flowers and cherry-like fruits in summer. Zone 4.

BRIGHT BERRIES

Cranberry cotoneaster (*Cotoneaster apiculatus*, Zone 3), rockspray cotoneaster (*C. horizontalis*, Zone 4), and bearberry cotoneaster (*C. dammeri*, Zone 5) are all low, spreading shrubs with arching stems and bright red berries. Many-flowered cotoneaster (*C. multiflorus*, Zone 3) is a large, fountain-like shrub, up to 10 feet tall and wide, with clusters of red berries.

Most hawthorns are small trees, usually under 25 feet tall, with bright red berries. Washington hawthorn (*Crataegus phaenopyrum*, Zone 3) has an oval crown and very thorny twigs. 'Winter King' green hawthorn (*C. viridis* 'Winter King', Zone 4) has a vase-shaped crown and fewer thorns.

Two deciduous hollies, possum haw (*Ilex decidua*, Zone 5) and winterberry (*I. verticillata*, Zone 3), are very showy in early winter, when they are covered with thousands of sparkling red berries. There are several cultivars. Most grow 6 to 15 feet tall.

Rugosa rose (*Rosa rugosa*) has cherry-sized red or orange "hips" on thorny twigs. Zone 3. Many other roses have showy hips, too.

INDEX

Page numbers in italics indicate illustrations or photos.